Autodesk

Acknowledgements

Art Direction:
Michiel Schriever

Sr. Graphic Designer:
Ian McFadyen

Cover Image:
© 2006 Sony Pictures Animation Inc.
All Rights Reserved.

Production Designer:
Mike Barker

Copy Editor:
Erica Fyvie

Technical Editor:
Cathy McGinnis

DVD Production:
Roark Andrade, Julio Lopez

Jr. Project Manager:
Skye Bjarnason

Project Manager:
Carla Sharkey

Product Manager, Learning Tools & Training:
Danielle Lamothe

Director, Packaged Services:
Michael Stamler

A special thanks goes out to:
Mariann Barsolo, Carmela Bourassa, Dan Brodnitz, Sylvana Chan, Ann Kemmer, Katriona Lord-Levins, Robert Lin, Peggy Miller, William Roberts, Lenni Rodrigues, Michael Stamler, Miriam Sterle, Christopher Vienneau

This book would not have been possible without the generous support of Sony Pictures Animation Inc.. We would like to extend a special thank you to Carlye Archibeque, Jerry Schmitz, and Sande Scoredos.

Primary Author

Marc-André Guindon, Realities Studios

Marc-André Guindon is the founder of Realities Studio (www.RealitiesStudio.com), a Montréal-based production facility. An advanced user of both Autodesk® Maya® and Autodesk® Alias MotionBuilder™ software products, Marc-André and Realities have allied with Autodesk (previously Alias) on several projects, including *The Art of Maya*, *Learning Maya 6 | MEL Fundamentals*, and the *Learning Maya 7* series. Realities Studio was also the driving force behind Pipeline Technique DVDs, such as *How to Integrate Quadrupeds into a Production Pipeline* and *Maya and MotionBuilder Pipeline*. Realities also created the *Maya Quick Reference Sheets* and contributed to *Creating Striking Graphics using Maya and Photoshop*.

Marc-André has established complex pipelines and developed numerous plug-ins and tools for a variety of projects in both the film and games industries. His latest projects include the integration of motion capture for the *Outlaw Game Series* (*Outlaw Volleyball*, *Outlaw Golf* 1 and 2, and *Outlaw Tennis*). He served as Technical Director on *XXX2*, *State of the Union* (Revolution Studios), *ScoobyDoo 2* (Warner Bros. Pictures), and *Dawn of the Dead* (Universal Pictures).

Marc-André was also an Autodesk MasterClass presenter. Marc-André continues to seek additional challenges for himself, Realities and his crew.

Contributing Author and Technical Editor:

Cathy McGinnis

Cathy McGinnis is an Autodesk Certified Instructor teaching at the Media Design School in Auckland, New Zealand. Prior to moving down under, Cathy was a technical product specialist for Autodesk, specializing in rendering in both Maya and mental ray® for Maya. Cathy has been a Maya trainer since the birth of the software and has been a contributor to several Autodesk publications including *Learning Maya 7 | Foundation*, *Learning Maya 7 | Modeling and Animation*, and *Learning Maya 7 | The Special Effects Handbook*.

Foreword

Danielle Lamothe Product Manager, Learning Tools & Training

Welcome to the exciting world of 3D animation and thank you for choosing Autodesk Maya. With Maya software, you've chosen a tool where the possibilities are limited only by your imagination. But you've probably already discovered that before you can unleash your creative vision, you'll need to learn some basic skills. Don't worry, though, this book is your solution to getting there.

Learning Autodesk Maya 8 | Foundation is an easy to follow, step-by-step project based book that will not only teach you solid 3D skills, but will instill an understanding of how the various stages of 3D production relate to one another in a typical pipeline. You'll explore modeling, animation, rendering and the creation of dynamic effects. You'll even get to take your creations into other environments with a bonus section on compositing in Autodesk Combustion. Unlike many other 3D books out there, *Learning Autodesk Maya 8 | Foundation* uses real world production images so that you can be inspired even as you learn. You'll benefit from working on characters and environments from the Sony Pictures Animation Inc. feature film *Open Season*.

This book provides you with everything you need to harness all of the power, technology, and innovation of Maya to make your dream a reality!

About *Open Season*

Open Season Sony Pictures Animation Inc.

With an all-star cast, and talented directors, Sony Pictures Animation Inc. debuts *Open Season* this fall in theaters around the world. Martin Lawrence voices the character of Boog, a nine hundred pound domesticated grizzly bear who shares the spotlight in the action-adventure comedy *Open Season* with a hapless, fast-talking mule deer named Elliot, voiced by Ashton Kutcher.

Directed by Roger Allers (*The Lion King*), Jill Culton (credits include *Monsters, Inc.,* and *Toy Story 2*), and Anthony Stacchi (credits include *Antz*), the 80-minute romp unwinds in the great northwest town of Timberline. When we meet Boog, he is living in a forest ranger's garage and stars in the ranger's amphitheatre shows. Every night, Ranger Beth, voiced by Emmy Award winning "Will & Grace" star Debra Messing, tucks Boog into bed with his teddy bear. Life is cushy until one day a hunter drives into town with Elliot, the mule deer, tied to his truck. Elliot is alive but unconscious, and when he wakes up, he begs Boog to untie him. Boog agrees and soon lives to regret it! "Elliot's a loser and he's desperate for friendship," says Allers. "He gloms onto Boog and makes Boog's life miserable. A series of events forces Ranger Beth to dart Boog and relocate him to the woods."

"When he wakes up," Culton continues, "Boog discovers that he is stuck with Elliot, who promises to help Boog find his way home – but *only* if Boog agrees to let him stay in Timberline!" The two embark on what turns out to be quite an adventure. They meet an over-zealous squirrel named McSquizzy (voiced by Billy Connolly) a pair of wise-talking skunks, crazy ducks, and Elliot's former herd. All in all, they are a very territorial group of animals, fiercely guarding their own grounds.

During their comical caper through the great outdoors, the unlikely pair form a friendship, but the forest has its dark side, too: Boog learns what hunting season really means. "He comes face to face with his inner animal," says Allers.

It's here that the story takes a wacky twist. "Every year, hunters have invaded the forest," says Culton. "But this year, the animals fight back."

How do they fight back? "We gave the villains guns, but we didn't want to have our heroes use guns, so we created this crazy battle with the animals using ridiculous human stuff like flaming marshmallows and toilet plungers," says Culton.

Ultimately, Boog must decide whether to live with Beth back in town or with his new friends in the woods. "It's a universal theme," Culton says, "about kids leaving home and parents watching their children grow up."

Work on *Open Season* began with a 10-page treatment from cartoonist Steve Moore ("In The Bleachers") and his producing partner John Carls (who both serve as executive producers for the film). "The story has evolved," says Culton, "but it was a buddy comedy with the twist that the animals were empowered to fight back against the hunters. That was enough to interest me."

Culton and Stacchi worked on the story during the first year, along the way adding a villain, Shaw the hunter (Gary Sinise). During filming, the actors delivered their lines individually, working from storyboards in a recording studio. "It's amazing when it's all cut together," producer Michelle Murdocca adds. "Usually, one director would read with the actor, and sometimes, the actors would riff on a line. Each actor brought something different to the film."

Once the story was underway, the directors began considering the visual style they wanted to use. "One of my favorite books is Eyvind Earle's book of Christmas cards," says Culton, referring to the legendary background painter at Disney. "Every card has this old graphic look with snow and trees and logs and little skewed churches. And, each card had a strong color palette."

Similarly, Main Street in Timberline is a bit skewed. "When you see non-organic shapes, like the buildings on Main Street, everything is a little bit off," says Doug Ikeler, visual effects supervisor at Sony Pictures Imageworks. "There are no parallel lines, the bricks aren't square. We call it the "wonky" factor. At first it was tough getting the modelers not to build everything perfectly."

The directors worked with the crew to develop a graphic shape language, color palettes, and an animation style for the film. "Our characters and backgrounds have strong shapes that were a challenge for 3D," Culton says. "We had to come up with special tools for the backgrounds and characters." New tools created at Imageworks made it possible for the directors to adopt the look and feel of traditional animation with 3D characters.

"Not only did the tools help us achieve the graphic look we wanted so that our characters have strong reading shapes," says Allers, "but they gave us greater stretch and squash. Older CG characters feel more like puppets because those animators didn't have flexible tools. In animation, you always need to exaggerate to make the characters feel real. I'm so happy to see the fun, the zip, the implausibility factor now in 3D."

Ikeler led the team at Imageworks charged with creating the innovative tools and finding the right balance between 3D reality and the stark graphic style of the 2D inspiration. "Our initial matte paintings could have been in a 2D movie," he says. "And simple profiles on geometry went against everything I knew. If you were to fill our geometry with a flat color, it would look almost 2D. So, we added the feeling of 3D that audiences like with texture, lights and shadows."

Thus, *Open Season*'s animals are furry, the water feels real, and, although the backgrounds are often in the kind of deep, raked shadows, the trees look three-dimensional, and pine needles blanket the ground.

"When you see Boog's fur, you want to go into the screen and hug him," says Allers. "It's amazing. The growth patterns, the swirls where it changes direction in the middle of his chest are brilliant." So that animators could shape the characters' fur into the readable, graphic silhouettes the directors wanted, Imageworks created special shaping tools.

"It was an exercise in negotiating and finding a happy medium," says Ikeler. "We had to find the place between what we're used to seeing and a stylized, cartoony world.".

The directors applied the same 'toonful mix of quirkiness and reality to the music, as well. "Songwriter Paul Westerberg contributed beautiful melodies for the film," says Allers. "And I think Ramin Djawadi's score really has its own identity. It's not orchestral. It's quirky and fun with bagpipes, tubas and banjoes and didgeridoos."

Open Season is scheduled for release in late September in the US and unspools through the rest of the world in October, November, and December.

Table of Contents

Project 1

Project 2

Project 3

Project 4

Project 5

How to use this book

How you use *Learning Autodesk Maya 8 | Foundation* will depend on your experience with computer graphics and 3D animation. This book moves at a fast pace and is designed to help you develop your 3D skills. If this is your first experience with 3D software, we suggest that you read through each lesson and watch the accompanying demo files on DVD which may help clarify the steps for you before you begin to work through the tutorial projects. If you are already familiar with Maya or another 3D package, you might choose to look through the book's index to focus on those areas you'd like to improve.

Updates to this book

In an effort to ensure your continued success through the lessons in this book, please visit our web site for the latest updates available: *www.autodesk.com/learningtools-updates/*.

Windows, and Macintosh

This book is written to cover Windows and Macintosh platforms. Graphics and text have been modified where applicable. You may notice that your screen varies slightly from the illustrations depending on the platform you are using.

Things to watch for:

Window focus may differ. For example, if you are on Windows, you have to click in the panels with your middle mouse button to make it active.

To select multiple attributes in Windows, use the **Ctrl** key. On Macintosh, use the **Command** key. To modify pivot position in Windows, use the **Insert** key. On Macintosh, use the **Home** key.

Autodesk packaging

This book can be used with either **Maya Complete 8**, **Maya Unlimited 8**, or the correspoinding version of **Maya Personal Learning Edition software, as the lessons included here** focus on functionality shared among all 3 software packages.

As a bonus feature, this hands-on book will also introduce you to compositing in Autodesk® Combustion®.

Learning Autodesk Maya DVD-ROM

The Learning Autodesk Maya DVD-ROM contains several resources to accelerate your learning experience including:

- Sketchbook Pro 1.1.1

- Learning Maya support files

- Instructor-led overviews to guide you through the projects in the book

- Excerpt from the Sony Pictures Animation Inc. feature film *Open Season*

- Interviews with Sony Pictures Animation Inc. artists Mike Ford and Max Bruce

- Link to trial version of Autodesk® Combustion®

Installing support files – before beginning the lessons in this book, you will need to install the lesson support files. Copy the project directories found in the *support_files* folder on the DVD disc to the Maya\projects directory on your computer. Launch Maya and set the project by going to **File → Project → Set...** and selecting the appropriate project.

Windows: *C:\Documents and Settings\username\My Documents\maya\projects*

Macintosh: *Macintosh HD:Users:username:Documents:maya:projects*

Understanding Maya

To understand Maya, it helps to understand how Maya works at a conceptual level. This introduction is designed to give you the *story* about Maya. In other words, the focus of this introduction will be on how different Maya concepts are woven together to create an integrated workspace.

While this book teaches you how to model, animate and render in Maya, these concepts are taught with a particular focus on how Maya's underlying architecture supports the creation of animated sequences.

You will soon learn how Maya's architecture can be explained by a single line – *nodes with attributes that are connected*. As you work through this book, the meaning of that statement becomes clearer and you will learn to appreciate how Maya's interface lets you focus on the act of creation, while giving you access to the power inherent in the underlying architecture.

The user interface (UI)

The Maya user interface (UI) includes a number of tools, editors and controls. You can access these using the main menus or special context-sensitive marking menus. You can also use *shelves* to store important icons or hotkeys to speed up workflow. Maya is designed to let you configure the UI as you see fit.

To work with objects, you can enter values using coordinate entry or you can use more interactive 3D manipulators. Manipulator handles let you edit your objects with a simple click+drag.

Maya's UI supports multiple levels of *undo* and *redo* and includes a drag-and-drop paradigm for accessing many parts of the workspace.

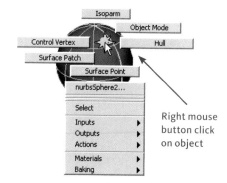

Marking menu

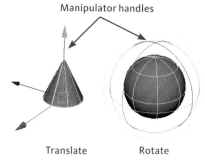

Maya manipulators

Working in 3D

In Maya, you will build and animate objects in three dimensions. These dimensions are defined by the cardinal axes that are labeled as X, Y and Z. These represent the length (X), height (Y) and depth (Z) of your scene. These axes are represented by colors – red for X, green for Y and blue for Z.

Maya has the Y-axis pointing up by default (also referred to as *Y-up*).

As you position, scale and rotate your objects, these three axes will serve as your main points of reference. The center of this coordinate system is called the *origin* and has a value of 0, 0, 0.

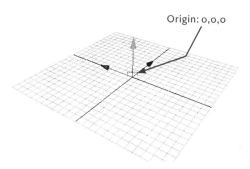

The cardinal axes

UV coordinate space

As you build surfaces in Maya, they are created with their own coordinate space that is defined by U in one direction and V in another. You can use these coordinates when you are working with *curve-on-surface* objects or when you are positioning textures on a surface.

One corner of the surface acts as the origin of the system and all coordinates lie directly on the surface.

You can make surfaces *live* in order to work directly in the UV coordinate space. You will also encounter U and V attributes when you place textures onto surfaces.

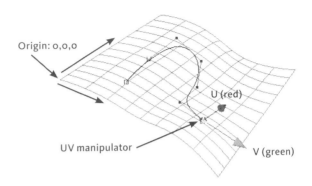

UV coordinates on a live surface

Views

In Maya, you visualize your scenes using view panels that let you see into the 3D world.

Perspective views let you see your scene as if you were looking at it with your own eyes or through the lens of a camera.

Orthographic views are parallel to the scene and offer a more objective view. They focus on two axes at a time and are referred to as the *top*, *side* and *front* views.

In many cases, you will require several views to help you define the proper location of your objects. An object's position that looks good in the top view may not make sense in a side view. Maya lets you view multiple views at one time to help coordinate what you see.

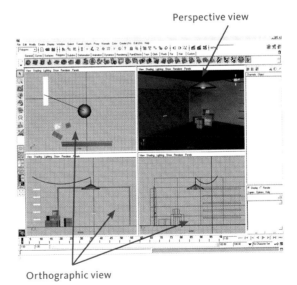

Orthographic and Perspective views

Cameras

To achieve a particular view, you look through a digital camera. An Orthographic camera defines the view using a parallel plane and a direction, while a Perspective camera uses an *eye point*, a *look at point* and a *focal length*.

Perspective and Orthographic cameras

Image planes

When you work with cameras, it is possible to place special backdrop objects called *image planes* onto the camera. An image plane can be placed onto the camera so that as the camera moves, the plane stays aligned.

The image plane has several attributes that allow you to track and scale the image. These attributes can be animated to give the appearance that the plane is moving.

Camera

Image plane

Image plane attached to a camera

Image plane seen looking through the camera

THE DEPENDENCY GRAPH

The system architecture in Maya uses a procedural paradigm that lets you integrate traditional keyframe animation, inverse kinematics, dynamics and scripting on top of a node-based architecture that is called the **Dependency Graph**. As mentioned on the first page of this introduction, the Dependency Graph could be described as *nodes with attributes that are connected*. This node-based architecture gives Maya its flexible procedural qualities.

To the right is a diagram showing a primitive sphere's Dependency Graph. A procedural input node defines the shape of the sphere by connecting attributes on each node.

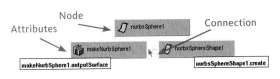

The Dependency Graph

Nodes

Every element, whether it is a curve, surface, deformer, light, texture, expression, modeling operation or animation curve, is described by either a single node or a series of connected nodes.

A *node* is a generic object type. Different nodes are designed with specific attributes so that the node can accomplish a specific task. Nodes define all object types including geometry, shading, and lighting.

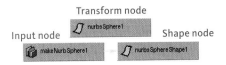

Node types on a sphere

Shown below are three typical node types as they appear on a primitive sphere:

Transform node - Transform nodes contain positioning information for your objects. When you move, rotate or scale, this is the node you are affecting.

Shape node - The shape node contains all the component information that represents the actual look of the sphere.

Input node - The input node represents options that drive the creation of your sphere's shape such as radius or endsweep.

Maya's UI presents these nodes to you in many ways. To the right is an image of the Channel Box where you can edit and animate node attributes.

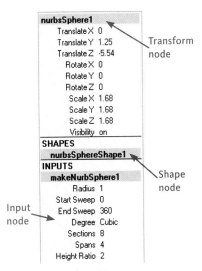

Channel Box

Understanding Maya

Attributes

Each node is defined by a series of attributes that relate to what the node is designed to accomplish. In the case of a transform node, *X Translate* is an attribute. In the case of a shader node, *Color Red* is an attribute. It is possible for you to assign values to the attributes. You can work with attributes in a number of UI windows including the *Attribute Editor*, the *Channel Box* and the *Spread Sheet Editor*.

One important feature is that you can animate virtually every attribute on any node. This helps give Maya its animation power. You should note that attributes are also referred to as *channels*.

Node tabs

Attribute Editor

Connections

Nodes don't exist in isolation. A finished animation results when you begin making connections between attributes on different nodes. These connections are also known as *dependencies*. In modeling, these connections are sometimes referred to as *construction history*.

Most of these connections are created automatically by the Maya UI as a result of using commands or tools. If you desire, you can also build and edit these connections explicitly using the *Connection Editor*, by entering *MEL*™ (Maya Embedded Language) commands, or by writing MEL-based expressions.

Pivots

Transform nodes are all built with a special component known as the *pivot point*. Just like your arm pivots around your elbow, the pivot helps you rotate a transform node. By changing the location of the pivot point, you get different results.

Pivots are basically the stationary point from which you rotate or scale objects. When animating, you sometimes need to build hierarchies where one transform node rotates the object and a second transform node scales. Each node can have its own pivot location to help you get the effect you want.

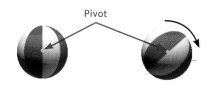

Rotation and scaling pivots

Hierarchies

When you are building scenes, you have learned that you can build dependency connections to link node attributes. When working with transform nodes or joint nodes, you can also build hierarchies, which create a different kind of relationship between your objects.

In a hierarchy, one transform node is *parented* to another. When Maya works with these nodes, it looks first at the top node, or *root* node, then down the hierarchy. Therefore, motion from the upper nodes is transferred down into the lower nodes. In the diagram below, if the *group1* node is rotated, then the two lower nodes will rotate with it. If the *nurbsCone* node is rotated, the upper nodes are not affected.

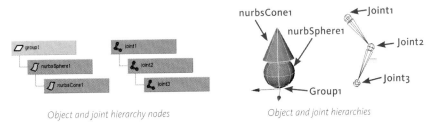

Object and joint hierarchy nodes   *Object and joint hierarchies*

Joint hierarchies are used when you are building characters. When you create joints, the joint pivots act as limb joints while bones are drawn between them to help visualize the joint chain. By default, these hierarchies work just like object hierarchies. Rotating one node rotates all of the lower nodes at the same time.

You will learn more about joint hierarchies later in this introduction (see "Skeletons and Joints"), where you will also learn how *inverse kinematics* can reverse the flow of the hierarchy.

MEL scripting

MEL stands for Maya Embedded Language. In Maya, every time you use a tool or open a window, you are using MEL. MEL can be used to execute simple commands, write expressions or build scripts that will extend Maya's existing functionality. The Script Editor displays commands and feedback generated by scripts and tools. Simple MEL commands can be typed in the Command Line, while more complex MEL scripts can be typed in the Script Editor.

```
File  Edit  Script  Help
move -r 0 10.178275 0 ;
move -r 4.350262 -2.048901 3.382116 ;
rotate -r -os 80.783877 0 0 ;
duplicate -rr;
// Result: nurbsCone2 //
move -r -0.132772 -3.884375 -1.402682 ;
rotate -r -os -71.334129 0 0 ;
select -r nurbsSphere1 ;
CreateNURBSSphere;
sphere -p 0 0 0 -ax 0 1 0 -ssw 0 -esw 360 -r 1 -d 3 -ut 0 -tol 0.01 -s
scale -r 3.837628 3.837628 3.837628 ;
move -r -2.213492 0.314328 -1.960627 ;
```

The Script Editor

MEL is the perfect tool for technical directors who are looking to customize Maya to suit the needs of a particular production environment. Animators can also use MEL to create simple macros that will help speed up more difficult or tedious workflows.

ANIMATION

When you animate, you bring objects to life. There are several different ways in which you can animate your scenes and the characters who inhabit them.

Animation is generally measured using frames that mimic the frames you would find on a film reel. You can play these frames at different speeds to achieve an animated effect. By default, Maya plays at 24 frames per second, or 24FPS.

Keyframe animation

The most familiar method of animating is called *keyframe animation*. Using this technique, you determine how you want the parts of your objects to look at a particular frame, then you save the important attributes as keys. After you set several keys, the animation can be played back with Maya filling motion in-between the keys.

When keys are set on a particular attribute, the keyed values are stored in special nodes called *animation curve* nodes.

These curves are defined by the keys that map the value of the attribute against time. The following is an example of several animation curve nodes connected to a transformation node. One node is created for every attribute that is animated.

Once you have a curve, you can begin to control the tangency at each key to tweak the motion in-between the main keys. You can make your objects speed up or slow down by editing the shape of these animation curves.

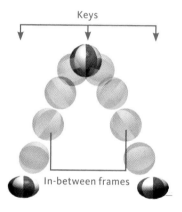

Keys and in-between frames

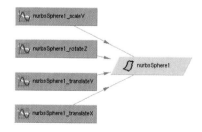

Dependency Graph showing curve nodes

Generally, the slope of the graph curve in the Graph Editors tells you the speed of the motion. A steep slope in the curve means fast motion, while a flat curve equals no motion. Think of a skier going down a hill. Steep slopes increase speed while flatter sections slow things down.

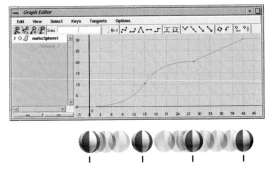

Graph Editor

Path animation

Path animation is already defined by its name. You can assign one or more objects so that they move along a path that has been drawn as a curve in 3D space. You can then use the shape of the curve and special path markers to edit and tweak the resulting motion.

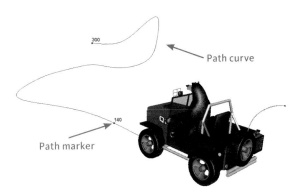

Path animation

Non-linear animation

Non-linear animation is a way to layer and mix character animation sequences non-linearly, i.e. independently of time. You can layer and blend any type of keyed animation, including motion capture and path animation. This is accomplished through the Trax Editor.

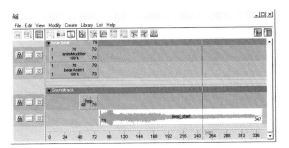

Trax Editor

Reactive animation

Reactive animation is a term used to describe animation in which one object's animation is based on the animation of another object.

An example of this technique would be moving gears when the rotation of one gear is linked to the rotation of other gears. You can set keys on the first gear and all the others will animate automatically. Later, when you want to edit or tweak the keys, only one object needs to be worked on and the others update reactively.

Diagram of animated gears

You can set-up reactive animation using a number of tools including those outlined below:

Set Driven Key

This tool lets you interactively set-up an attribute on one object to drive one or more attributes onto another.

Expressions

Expressions are scripts that let you connect different attributes on different nodes.

Constraints

Constraints let you set-up an object to *point at*, *orient to* or *look at* another object.

Connections

Attributes can be directly linked to another attribute using dependency node connections. You can create this kind of direct connection using the Connection Editor.

Dynamics

Another animation technique is *dynamics*. You can set-up objects in your scene that animate based on physical effects such as collisions, gravity and wind. Different variables are *bounciness*, *friction* or *initial velocity*. When you playback the scene, you run a simulation to see how all the parts react to the variables.

This technique gives you natural motion that would be difficult to keyframe. You can use dynamics with rigid body objects, particles or soft body objects.

Rigid body objects are objects that don't deform. You can further edit the rigid body by setting it as either *active* or *passive*. Active bodies react to the dynamics, whereas passive bodies don't.

To simulate effects such as wind or gravity, you add *fields* to your dynamic objects.

Particles are tiny points that can be used to create effects such as smoke, fire or explosions. These points are emitted into the scene where they are also affected by the dynamic fields.

Soft bodies are surfaces that you deform during a simulation. To create a soft body, create an object and turn its points into particles. The particles react to the dynamic forces, which in turn deform the surface.

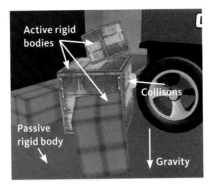

Rigid body simulation of truck and boxes colliding

Particles

Soft bodies

MODELING

The objects you want to animate are usually built using either NURBS surfaces or polygonal meshes. Complementary to these two basic geometry types, subdivision surfaces (SubDs), mix the best features of both NURBS and polygons. Maya offers you both of these geometry types so that you can choose the method best suited to your work.

NURBS curves

NURBS stands for *non-uniform rational b-spline* which is a technical term for a spline curve. By modeling with NURBS curves, you lay down control points and smooth geometry will be created using the points as guides.

Shown below is a typical NURBS curve with important parts labeled:

These key components define important aspects of how a curve works. The flexibility and power of NURBS geometry comes from your ability to edit the shape of the geometry using these controls.

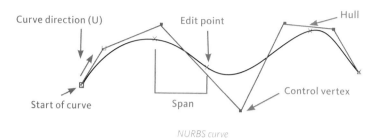

NURBS curve

As your geometry becomes more complex, you may need more of these controls. For this reason, it is usually better to start out with simpler geometry so that you can more easily control the shape. If you need more complex geometry, then controls can be inserted later.

NURBS surfaces

Surfaces are defined using the same mathematics as curves, except now they're in two dimensions – U and V. You learned about this earlier when you learned about UV coordinate space.

Below are some of the component elements of a typical NURBS surface:

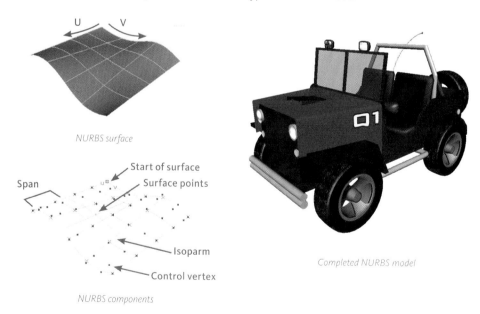

NURBS surface

NURBS components

Completed NURBS model

Complex shapes can be, in essence, sculpted using this surface type as you push and pull the controls to shape the surface.

Polygons

Polygons are the most basic geometry type available. Whereas NURBS surfaces interpolate the shape of the geometry interactively, polygonal meshes draw the geometry directly to the control vertices.

Below are some of the components found on a polygonal mesh:

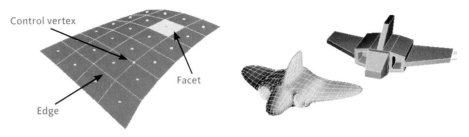

Polygon components

Polygonal model before and after smoothing

You can build up poly meshes by extruding, scaling and positioning polygonal facets to build shapes. You can then smooth the shape to get a more organic look for your model.

Subdivision surfaces

Subdivision surfaces exhibit characteristics of both polygon and NURBS surfaces, allowing you to model smooth forms using comparatively few control vertices. They enable you to create levels of detail exactly where you want.

Construction history

When you create models, the various steps are recorded as dependency nodes that remain connected to your surface.

In the example to the right, a curve has been used to create a revolved surface. Maya keeps the history by creating dependencies between the curve, a revolve node and the shape node. Edits made to the curve or the revolve node will update the final shape.

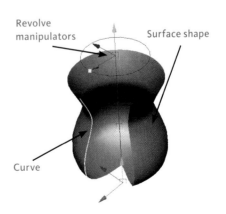

Revolve surface with dependencies

Understanding Maya

Many of these nodes come with special manipulators that make it easier to update the node attributes. In the case of the revolve, manipulators are available for the axis line and for the revolve's sweep angle.

It is possible to later delete history so that you are only working with the shape node. Don't forget though, that the dependency nodes have attributes that can be animated. Therefore, you lose some power if you delete history.

DEFORMATIONS

Deformers are special object types that can be used to reshape other objects. By using deformers, you can model different shapes, or give animations more of a squash and stretch quality.

Deformers are a powerful Maya feature; they can even be layered for more subtle effects. You can also bind deformers into skeletons or affect them with soft body dynamics.

The following lists some basic deformer types available:

Lattices

Lattices are external frames that can be applied to your objects. If you then reshape the frame, the object is deformed in response.

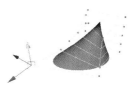

Lattice deformer

Sculpt objects

Sculpt objects lets you deform a surface by pushing it with the object. By animating the position of the sculpt object, you can achieve animated surface deformations.

Sculpt object deformer

Clusters

Clusters are groups of CVs or lattice points that are built into a single set. The cluster is given its own pivot point and can be used to manipulate the clustered points. You can weight the CVs in a cluster for more control over a deformation.

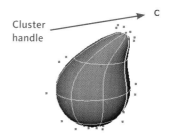

Cluster handle

Cluster deformer

CHARACTER ANIMATION

Character animation typically involves the animation of surfaces using skeleton joint chains and inverse kinematic handles to help drive the motion.

Skeletons and joints

As you have already learned, skeleton joint chains are actually hierarchies. A skeleton is made of joint nodes that are connected visually by bone icons. Binding geometry to these hierarchies lets you create surface deformations when the joints are rotated.

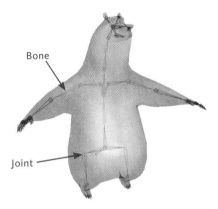

Joints and bones

Inverse kinematics

By default, joint hierarchies work like any other hierarchy - the rotation of one joint is transferred to the lower joint nodes. This is known as *forward kinematics*. While this method is powerful, it makes it hard to plant a character's feet or move a hand to control the arm.

Inverse kinematics lets you work with the hierarchy in the opposite direction. By placing an IK handle at the end of the joint chain, Maya will solve all rotations within that joint chain. This is a lot quicker than animating every single joint in the hierarchy. There are three kinds of inverse kinematic solvers – the *IK spline*, the *IK single chain* and the *IK rotate plane*.

Each of these solvers is designed to help you control the joint rotations with the use of an IK handle. As the IK handle is moved, the solver solves joint rotations that allow the end joint to properly move to the IK handle position.

The individual solvers have their own unique controls. Some of these are outlined on the following page:

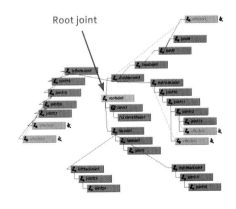

Character joint hierarchy

Single chain solver

The *single chain solver* provides a
straightforward mechanism for posing
and animating a chain.

Rotate plane solver

The *rotate plane solver* gives you more control.
With this solver, the plane that acts as the goal
for all the joints can be moved by rotating the
plane using a *twist attribute* or by moving the
pole vector handle.

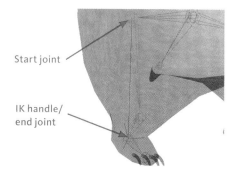

IK single chain solver

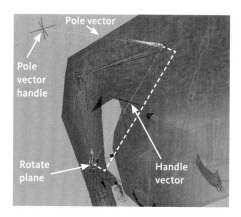

IK rotate plane solver

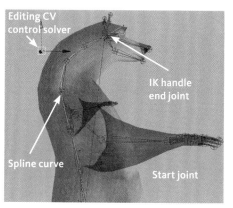

IK spline solver

IK spline solver

The IK spline solver lets you control the chain using
a spline curve. You can edit the CVs on the spline to
influence the rotation of the joints in the chain.

Skinning your characters

Once you have a skeleton built, you can bind skin
the surfaces of your character so that they deform
with the rotation of the joints. You can use either
soft skinning or hard skinning. Smooth skinning uses
weighted clusters while rigid skinning does not.

Surface deformations

Flexors

In some cases, skinning a character does not yield realistic deformations in the character's joint areas. You can use *flexors* to add this secondary level of deformations to help control the tucking and bulging of your character.

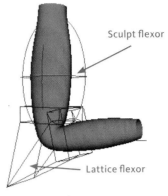

Flexors

RENDERING

Once your characters are set-up, you can apply color and texture, then render with realistic lighting.

Shading Networks

Adding texture maps and other rendering nodes create shading networks. At the end of every shading network is a shading group node. This node has specific attributes such as displacement maps and mental ray for Maya ports, but more importantly, it contains a list of objects that are to be shaded by that network at render time. Without this node at the end of the network, the shader won't render.

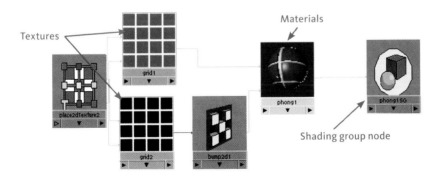

Shading group dependencies

You can think of a shading network as a bucket into which you place all the color, texture and material qualities that you want for your surface. Add a light or two and your effect is achieved.

Texture maps

To add detail to your shading groups, you can *texture map* different attributes. Some of these include bump, transparency and color.

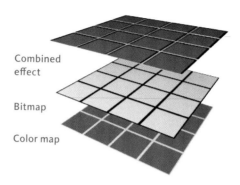

Texture map layers

Lighting

You can add light to your scenes using any number of lights. These lights let you add mood and atmosphere to a scene in much the same way as lighting is used by a photographer. You can preview your lights interactively as you model, or you can render to see the final effect.

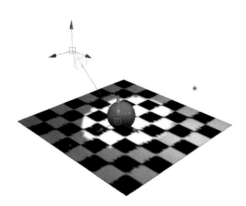

Light manipulator

Motion blur

When a real-life camera takes a shot of a moving object the final image is often blurred. This *motion blur* adds to the animated look of a scene and can be simulated in Maya. There are two types of motion blur – a 2 1/2 D solution and a 3D solution.

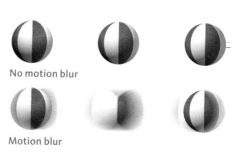

Motion blur

Hardware rendering

Hardware rendering uses the power of your graphics card to render an image. This is a quick way to render as the quality can be very good or it can be used to preview animations. You will need to use the hardware renderer to render most particle effects. These effects can be composited in later with software rendered images of your geometry.

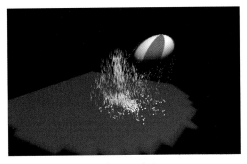

Hardware rendering

A-buffer rendering

The Maya rendering architecture is a hybrid renderer. It uses an EAS (Exact Area Sampling) or A-buffer algorithm for primary visibility from the eye (camera), and then raytraces any secondary rays.

A-buffer rendering

Raytrace rendering

Raytracing lets you include reflections, refractions and raytrace shadows into your scenes. Only objects that have their raytrace options turned on will use this renderer. Raytracing is slower than the A-buffer algorithm and should only be used when necessary.

Raytrace rendering

Note: Objects have raytracing turned On by default, but the renderer's raytracing is turned Off by default.

How the renderer works

The Maya renderer works by looking through the camera at the scene. It then takes a section or tile and analyzes whether or not it can render that section. If it can, it will combine the information found in the shading group (geometry, lights and shading network) with the Render Settings information, and the whole tile is rendered.

As the renderer moves on to the next section, it again analyzes the situation. If it hits a tile where there is more information than it wants to handle at one time, it breaks down the tile into a smaller tile and renders.

Rendering of A-buffer tiles in progress

When you use raytracing, each tile is first rendered with the A-buffer, then the renderer looks for items that require raytracing. If it finds any, it layers in the raytraced sections. When it finishes, you have your finished image, or if you are rendering an animation, a sequence of images.

IPR

The Interactive Photorealistic Renderer gives you fast feedback for texturing and lighting updates without needing to re-render.

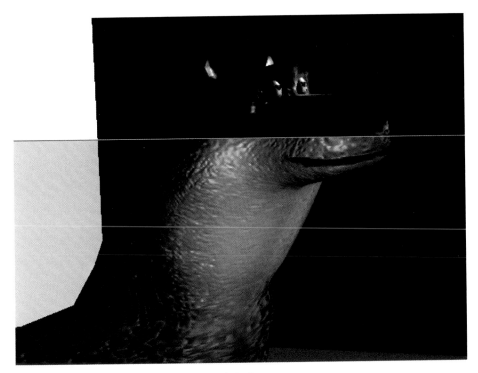

IPR rendering in progress

Conclusion

Now that you have a basic understanding of what Maya is designed to do, it is time for you to start working with the system directly. The concepts outlined in this introduction will be clearer when you experience them firsthand.

Project 01

In Project One, you are going to learn the basics of object creation, along with the fundamentals of animation, shaders and textures. This will give you the chance to explore the Maya workspace while building your scene.

You will start by creating a garage and filling it with objects in order to learn about building models. Then, you will explore the rudiments of hierarchies and animation by creating a garage door. After that, you will experiment with shaders and textures, which will allow you to render your scene.

These lessons offer you a good look at some of the key concepts and workflows that drive Maya. Once this project is finalized, you will have a better understanding of the Maya software user interface and its various modules.

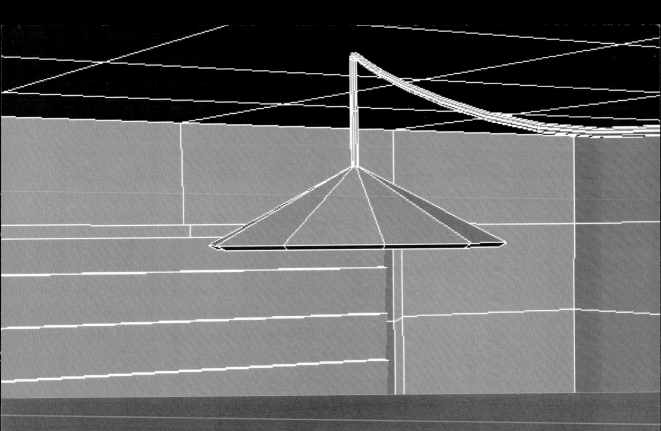

Lesson 01
Create a garage

This lesson teaches you how to build and transform primitives in 3D space in order to create a garage set in which you will set-up all animation in this book. You will explore the Maya user interface (UI) as you learn how to build and develop your scene.

In this lesson you will learn the following:

- How to set a new Maya project;
- How to create primitive objects;
- How to move objects in 3D space;
- How to duplicate objects;
- How to change the shape of objects;
- How to use the Maya View tools;
- How to change the display of your objects;
- How to name your objects;
- How to save your scene.

Setting up Maya

The first step is to install the Autodesk® Maya® software. Once that is done, you should copy the *Learning Maya* support files to your Maya *projects* directory. The support files are found in the *support_files* directory on the DVD-ROM included with this book.

In order to find your *projects* directory, you need to launch Maya at least once so that it creates your user directory structure. Here is typically where the *projects* directory is located on your machine:

Windows: *Drive:\Documents and Settings\[username]\My Documents\maya\projects*

Mac OS X: *Users/[username]/Library/Preferences/Autodesk/maya/projects*

> **Note:** To avoid the **Cannot Save Workspace** *error, ensure that the support files are not read-only after you copy them from the DVD-ROM.*

When Maya is launched for the first time and you have other Maya versions installed, you will be asked if you want to copy your preferences or create the default preferences. In order to follow the course, you should be using default preferences. If you have been working with Maya and changed any of your user interface settings, you may want to delete or back-up your preferences in order to start with the default Maya configuration.

Creating a new project

Maya uses a project directory to store and organize all of the files (scenes, images, materials, textures, etc.) related to a particular scene. When building a scene, you create and work with a variety of file types and formats. The project directory allows you to keep these different file types in their unique sub-directory locations within the project directory.

1   **Launch Maya**

2   **Set the project**

To manage your files, you can set a project directory that contains sub-directories for different types of files that relate to your project.

- Go to the **File** menu and select **Project → Set...**

  A window opens that directs you to the Maya projects directory.

- **Open** the *support_files* folder.

- Click on the folder named *project1* to select it.

- Click on the **OK** button.

- This sets *project1* of the *learningMaya* directory as your current project.

- Go to the **File** menu and select **Project → Edit Current...**

  Make sure that the project directories are set-up as shown below. This ensures that Maya is looking into the proper sub-directories when it opens up scene files.

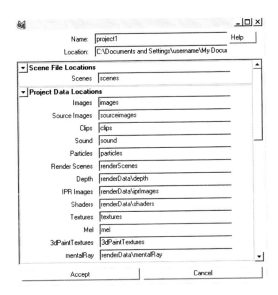

Edit Project window

3   **Make a new scene**

- Select **File → New Scene**.

  This will create a new scene in the current directory when you save it.

BUILDING OBJECTS

Every scene you create in Maya will most likely contain objects like surfaces, deformers, skeleton joints or particle emitters. For this scene, you will build a garage with several boxes and wires.

Creating the garage

To start, you will build a big cube, which will be the room itself with a floor, ceiling and walls. That first object will be a primitive polygonal cube. To view the finished scene, open the file called *01-garage_01.ma*.

1 Change menu sets

There are five main menu sets in Maya: *Animation*, *Polygons*, *Surfaces*, *Dynamics* and *Rendering*. These menu sets are used to access related tool sets.

- From the drop-down menu at the left edge of the Status Line (Toolbar), select **Polygons**.

  As you change menu sets, the first six menus along the top of the viewport remain the same while the remaining menus change to reflect the chosen menu set.

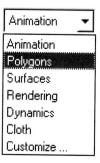

Menu set pop-up menu

2 Create a polygonal cube

A primitive cube will be used as a large surrounding room. It will be built using polygonal geometry. Throughout this lesson and in the next project, you will learn more about this geometry type.

- From the **Create** menu, select **Polygon Primitives → Cube**.

  A cube is placed at the origin.

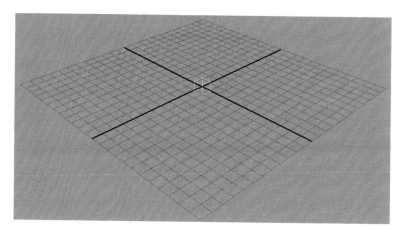

Perspective view of pCube1

4 Change the cube's dimensions

The cube is a *procedural model*. This means that it is broken down into parts called *nodes*. One node contains its positioning information, one contains its shape information and another contains input information that defines the cube's construction history using attributes such as width, height and depth. You can edit this input node's attributes in the **Channel Box** in order to edit the cube's shape.

The Channel Box is found at the right side of the screen and lets you make changes to key attributes very easily.

> **Note:** *If your Channel Box is not along the right side of the screen, you can access it by selecting* Display → UI Elements → Channel Box/Layer Editor.

- From the Channel Box's **Inputs** section, click on *polyCube1*.

  This will make several new attributes available for editing.

- Type **25** in the **Width** entry field and press the **Enter** key.

- Type **10** in the **Height** entry field and press the **Enter** key.

- Type **25** in the **Depth** entry field and press the **Enter** key.

  Now the cube is shaped like a room in the Perspective view.

pCube1	
TranslateX	0
TranslateY	0
TranslateZ	0
RotateX	0
RotateY	0
RotateZ	0
ScaleX	1
ScaleY	1
ScaleZ	1
Visibility	on
SHAPES	
pCubeShape1	
INPUTS	
polyCube1	
Width	25
Height	10
Depth	25
Subdivisions Width	1
Subdivisions Height	1
Subdivisions Depth	1
CreateU Vs	Normalize C

Channel Box

> **Note:** *Another method for increasing the size of the cube would be to scale it. In Maya, you can often achieve the same visual results using many different methods. Over time, you will begin to choose the techniques that best suit a particular situation.*

Lesson 01: Create a garage

5   **Rename the cube node**

You should rename the existing transform node to make it easier to find later.

- Click on the *pCube1* name at the top of the Channel Box to highlight it.

- Type the name *garage*, then press the **Enter** key.

Channels Object		
garage		
	TranslateX	0
	TranslateY	0
	TranslateZ	0

Renaming the node in the Channel Box

Moving the garage

You will now use the Move Tool to reposition the garage. This will involve the use of manipulator handles that let you control where you move your object.

1   **Four view panels**

By default, a single Perspective window is shown in the workspace. To see other views of the scene, you can change your panel layout.

- At the top of the Perspective view panel, go to the **Panels** menu and select **Saved Layouts → Four View**.

You can now see the cube using three Orthographic views – top, side and front – that show you the model from a projected view. You can also see it in a Perspective view that is more like the everyday 3D world. This multiple view set-up is very useful when positioning objects in 3D space.

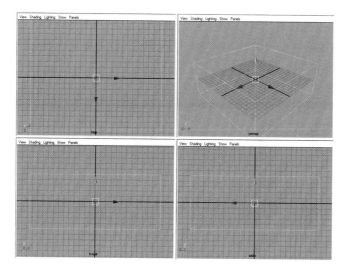

Four view panels

Tip: *Tapping the keyboard* **spacebar** *will switch from a single-view panel to a four-view panel.*

2 Position the garage

You can now use the **Move Tool** to reposition the cube's floor above the working grid.

- Select the **Move Tool** in the Toolbox on the left of the interface, or press **w**.

  A transform manipulator appears centered on the object.

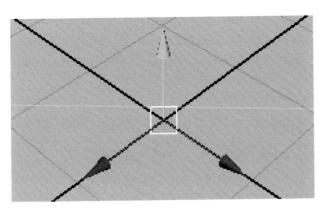

Manipulator handle

- **Click+drag** on the **green** manipulator handle to move the cube along the **Y-axis** until the bottom of the room is flush with the grid.

  You will notice that the manipulator handle turns **yellow** *to indicate that it is active.*

Tip: *The transform manipulator has three handles that let you constrain your motion along the X, Y and Z-axes. These are labeled using red for the X-axis, green for the Y-axis and blue for the Z-axis. The Y-axis points up by default. This means that Maya is "Y-up" by default.*

3 **Reposition the room**

When moving in an Orthographic view, you can work in two axes at once by dragging on the center of the manipulator or constraining the motion along a single axis using the handles.

- In the front view, **click+drag** on the square center of the manipulator to move the cube along both the **X** and **Y-axes**.

- Use the manipulator in the various view windows to position the cube's lower face on the ground plane, as shown.

  Be sure to refer to all four view windows to verify that the object is positioned properly.

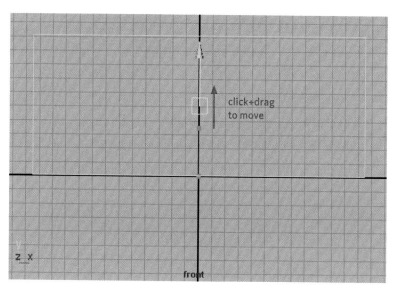

Appropriate position of the room

Note: *If you* **click+drag** *on the center of the manipulator in the Perspective view, you will notice that it doesn't move along any particular axis. It is actually moving along the camera's view plane.*

Viewing the scene

When you work in 3D space, it is important to see your work from different angles. The different view panels let you see your work from the front, top, side and Perspective angles.

You can also use the view tools to change the views in order to reposition how you see your scene. In some cases, a view change is like panning a camera around a room, while in other cases a view change might be like rotating an object around in your hand to see all the sides. These view tools can be accessed using the **Alt** key in combination with various mouse buttons.

1   **Edit the Perspective view**

You can use the **Alt** key with your mouse buttons to tumble, track and dolly in your Perspective view.

- Change your view using the following key combinations:

   - **Alt + LMB** to tumble;

   - **Alt + MMB** to track;

   - **Alt + LMB + MMB** or **Alt + RMB** to dolly.

   You can also combine these with the **Ctrl** *key to create a bounding box dolly where the view adjusts based on a bounding box. This is useful when you want to dolly on a precise section of the view or quickly dolly out to get a general look of the scene.*

   - **Ctrl + Alt + LMB** to box dolly;

   - **Click+drag** from left to right to dolly in and from right to left to dolly out.

   You can also undo and redo view changes using the following keys:

   - To undo views use **[**

   - To redo views use **]**.

- Alter your Perspective window until it appears as shown below:

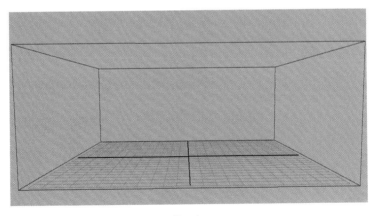

New view

2 Edit the view in the side view

Orthographic views use similar hotkeys – except that you cannot tumble by default in an Orthographic view.

- In the side view, change your view using the following key combinations:

    Alt + MMB to track;

    Alt + LMB + MMB or Alt + RMB to dolly.

- Keep working with the Orthographic views until they are set-up as shown:

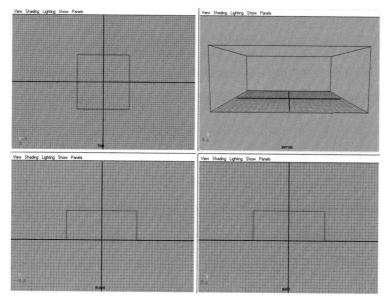

New Orthographic views

3 Frame Selected and Frame All

Another quick way to navigate in the different views is to use the *Frame Selected* or *Frame All* hotkeys for the active view.

- Select the *garage*.

- While in the *four view* panels, move your mouse over a view.

- Press the **f** hotkey to frame the selected geometry in the view under your mouse.

- Press the **a** hotkey to frame everything visible in the view under your mouse cursor.

- Press **Shift+a** hotkey to frame everything in all views at once.

Setting display options

The view panels let you interactively view your scene. By default, this means viewing your scene as a wireframe model. To better evaluate the form of your objects, you can activate hardware shading.

1 Turn on hardware shading

To help visualize your objects, you can use hardware shading to display a shaded view within any panel.

- From the Perspective view's **Shading** menu, select **Smooth Shade All**.

This setting affects all of the objects within the current view panel.

Smooth shaded view

> **Tip:** *You can also turn on Smooth Shading by moving your cursor over the desired panel, clicking with your middle mouse button and pressing the **5** key. The **4** key can be used to return the panel to a wireframe view.*

2   Hide the grid

You can hide the grid to simplify your view using one of two options:

- From the *Perspective* view panel's **Show** menu, select **Grid** to hide the grid for that view only.

OR

- From the **Display** menu, deselect **Grid** to hide the grid for all views.

Moving inside the garage

In order to have the feeling of being inside the garage in the Perspective view, you need to move the Perspective camera inside the cube geometry. You will soon realize that even if you can see inside the cube, sometimes one of its sides will appear in front of the camera while moving, thus hiding the interior. The following steps will prevent this from happening.

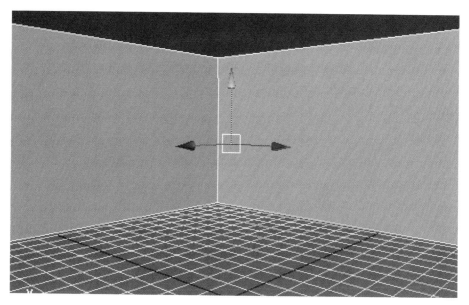

Perspective inside the cube

1   Change the garage's display

To simplify your scene interaction, there is a way of seeing inside the cube even when the camera is outside of it. To do so, you will have to change the way the cube is displayed. The following actions are somewhat more advanced than what you will undertake in this project, but they will allow you to see inside the room more easily.

- Select the *garage*.

- Select **Display** → **Polygons** → **Backface Culling**.

  This tells Maya to hide the sides of the cube facing away from the camera.

- With the cube still selected and in the **Polygons** menu set, select **Normals** → **Reverse**.

  This tells Maya that you want to turn the cube inside out.

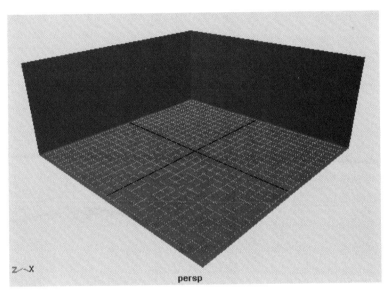

Seeing inside the room without backfaces

Create boxes

To create a box, follow the same steps as you did to create the primitive cube for the garage. You can use the hotbox as an alternative method for accessing tools.

1 **Create another polygonal cube**

- Press and hold the **spacebar** anywhere over the interface to display the hotbox.

- In the hotbox, select **Create** → **Polygon Primitives** → **Cube**.

  Another cube is placed at the origin.

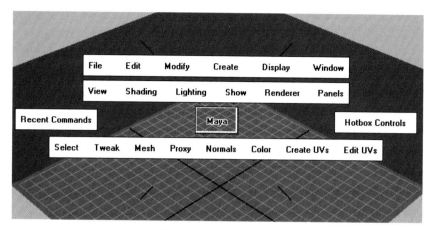

Hotbox access to menu items

Tip: *You can access all functions in Maya using either the main menus or the hotbox. As you become more familiar with the hotbox, you can use the UI options found in the* **Display** *menu to turn off the panel menus and therefore reduce screen clutter.*

2 Rename the cube node

It is a good idea to rename the existing transform node to make it easier to find later.

- Click on the *pCube1* node's name at the top of the Channel Box.

- Enter the name *box*.

3 Transform the cube

Instead of using the cube's input node to change its size, try using the scale manipulator. You can also experiment by translating and rotating the cube into a proper position on the floor surface.

- Select the **Scale Tool** in the Toolbox on the left side of the interface.

- Using the different axes of the **Scale Tool**, change the shape of the cube.

Toolbox

Tip: *Each cube on the scale manipulator represents a different axis except for the central one which controls all three axes at the same time. You can also hold down* **Ctrl** *and* **click+drag** *on an axis to proportionally scale the two other axes.*

- Switch to the **Translate Tool** by pressing the **w** hotkey and **move** the box above the floor.

- Switch to the **Rotate Tool** by pressing the **e** hotkey and **rotate** the box on its **Y-axis**.

- You can switch back to the **Scale Tool** by pressing the **r** hotkey.

4 Make more cubes

Instead of always creating a default primitive cube, you can duplicate an existing one, preserving its position and shape.

- Select your first *box* and select **Edit → Duplicate**.

  When using the duplicate function, the new box will be renamed to box1. Subsequent duplicates will be named box2, box3...

- Create a stack of boxes in a corner of the room.

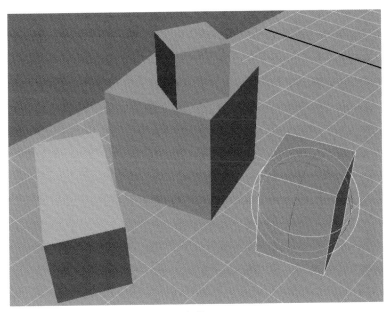

Stack of boxes

Tip: You can use the **Ctrl+d** hotkey to duplicate the selected geometry without going into the menu each time.

5 **Move the boxes**

- If your stack of boxes is not located at the correct position in the room, click on one cube, then hold down the **Shift** key and click all the remaining cubes to select them at once.

- **Translate** them all together in a corner of the garage.

Adding shelves, a lamp and a wire

Now that you know how to place objects and interact with the Perspective view, you will add some details to the garage. You will start by creating a bunch of shelves on one of the walls, then you will add a lamp hanging from the ceiling in the middle of the room, and finally, you will add a wire to hold the lamp.

1 **Making shelves**

The Duplicate Tool has options allowing you to duplicate multiple copies of the same object, separated by a fixed translation or rotation value. For example, if you make one shelf, you can make four other copies separated by five units, all in one easy step.

- **Create** a polygonal cube and place it against a wall.

- **Rename** the cube *shelf*.

- Select **Edit** → **Duplicate Special** → ❐.

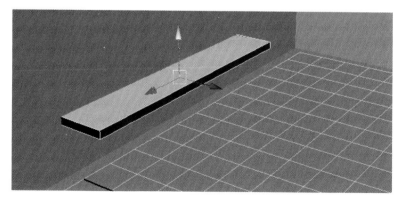

Placement of one shelf

- Set the **Number of Copies** to **4**.

In order to determine the proper translation axis, look at the view axis located at the bottom left corner of each view. If you want the copies to be created along the positive Y-axis, enter a positive value in the second field of the translation vector.

- Set the appropriate **Translate** value to **1.5** and leave the others to **0**.

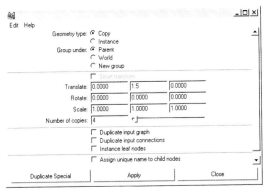

The Duplicate Special options

Axis letter points toward its positive values

- Click on the **Duplicate** button to execute the command.

- Select **Edit** → **Undo** or press **z** to undo the action and try again.

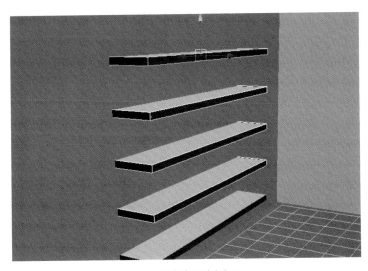

The duplicated shelves

2 **Lamp**

In this step, you will make a lamp from a polygonal cone.

- Select **Create** → **Polygon Primitives** → **Cone**.

- **Move** the *pCone1* near the ceiling.

- Highlight the cone's **INPUTS** in the Channel Box.

- Set the following:

  Radius to 2;

  Height to 1;

  Subdivisions Axis to 10;

  Subdivisions Cap to 2.

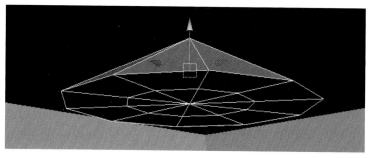

Modified cone primitive

- **RMB** on the *lamp* to display its contextual radial menu, and select **Vertex**.

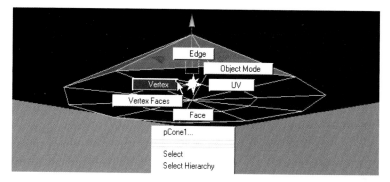

Polygon context menu

- Edit the cone vertices to get the following lampshade. Select each row of vertices and translate them up or down and scale them slightly where needed. For the inside of the lamp, select the central vertex in the middle of the base and move it up into the lamp. Make sure that it does not interpenetrate with the outside portion of the geometry.

Tip: *You might want to go into wireframe mode (hotkey 4), in order to select components more easily.*

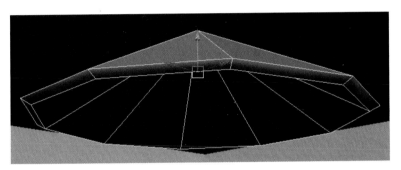

Lamp

- **Rename** the cone to *lamp.*

3 Electrical wire for the lamp

You now want to create another type of primitive geometry. In this step, you will create a NURBS cylinder. As you read in the Understanding Maya section at the beginning of this book, NURBS stands for *Non-uniform Rational B-spline*, which means that it is made out of curves instead of straight edges like polygons. NURBS geometry looks much smoother than polygons.

- Select **Create** → **NURBS Primitives** → **Cylinder**.

A cylinder will appear at the origin.

- Click on *makeNurbCylinder1* in the Channel Box to display the construction history of the cylinder.

Set **Radius** to 0.1;

Set **Spans** to 6;

Set **Height Ratio** to 50.

Project 01

- **Move** the cylinder closer to the ceiling so that the bottom edge of the wire touches the top portion of the lamp.

The base shape of an electrical wire

- If the radius of the cylinder is too wide, you can scale it down using the **Scale Tool**.

 Tip: *When scaling an object, you can hold down the control key and* **click+drag** *one of the axes to proportionally scale the other two axes.*

- Select the **Component** icon located in the Status Line at the top of the interface. Once clicked, make sure the **Vertices** button next to it is also enabled as follows:

Going into Component mode with Vertices enabled

Working in this mode will display the components of the currently selected geometry. You can then select and transform the points defining a surface's shape. A polygon point is called a **vertex/vertices** *and NURBS points are called* **control vertices** *or* **CVs**.

- Go to the side view and select all the CVs that are above the ceiling.

- **Rotate** the CVs of the wire so they are flat horizontally.

- **Scale** and **move** them so that it looks like the wire is going across the ceiling toward a wall.

- Select any row of CVs in the central area of the wire and move them down as if they were hanging from the ceiling.

- Continue moving the CVs until it looks like a proper lamp wire.

Tip: *When selecting components, hold down* **Shift** *to toggle the new selection, hold down* **Ctrl** *to deselect the new selection and hold down* **Ctrl+Shift** *to add the new selection to the currently selected group of components.*

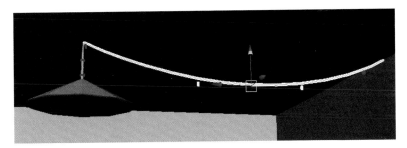

The final shape of the wire

- Get out of Component mode by clicking the Object mode button.

Going in Object mode

- **Rename** the cylinder *wire*.

4 Adjust NURBS smoothness

The display of NURBS surfaces in a viewport can be adjusted by increasing/decreasing its smoothness.

- Select the *wire*.

- From the main **Display** menu, select **NURBS**.

- Select any of the menu items between **Hull**, **Rough**, **Medium**, **Fine** or **Custom NURBS Smoothness**.

  These settings will affect how selected NURBS objects are displayed in all view panels.

Tip: *A NURBS object can have its smoothness set differently in each viewport using the following hotkeys:*

1 – rough   2 – medium   3 - fine

5 Save your work

- From the **File** menu, select **Save Scene As...**
- Enter the name *01-garage_01.ma*.

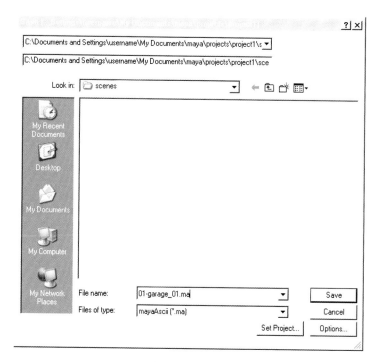

Windows Save As dialog box

- Click the **Save** button or press the **Enter** key.

  Make sure you save this file since you will be continuing with it in the next lesson.

Note: *Throughout this book, you will be using the final saved file from one lesson as the start file for the next, unless specified otherwise. Save your work at the end of each lesson to make sure that you have the start file ready. Otherwise, you can use the scene files from the support files.*

Conclusion

Congratulations! You have completed your first exercise using Maya. You should now be able to easily navigate the different views and change the basic hardware display settings. You should also be confident in creating, duplicating, transforming and renaming objects, along with using the translation, rotation, and scale manipulators. At this point you should also understand the difference between Component mode and Object mode. As well, be careful to save scene files.

In the next lesson, you will explore more in-depth how to model objects and details.

Lesson 02
Adding details

In this lesson you will change the shape of the garage to include a large door.
This is a good time to experiment with basic polygonal tools and concepts.

In this lesson you will learn the following:

- How to extrude polygonal faces;

- How to move polygonal faces;

- How to delete polygonal faces;

- How to combine polygonal objects;

- How to move the pivot of an object;

- About construction history;

- How to delete construction history.

Working with a good file

Use the scene that you saved in the previous lesson or use the one provided in your *scenes* directory, *01-garage_01.ma*.

1 Open a scene

There are several ways to open a scene in Maya software. Following are three easy options:

- From the **File** menu, select **Open Scene**.

OR

- Press **Ctrl+o**.

OR

File Open button

- Click on the **Open** button located in the top menu bar.

2 Find your scene

In the **File Open** dialog, if you cannot immediately locate *01-garage_01.ma*, it might be because your project is not set correctly or that Maya did not direct you into the scenes directory.

- At the top of the dialog, if the path is not pointing into the project created in the last lesson, click the **Set Project...** button at the bottom of the window and browse to find the correct project directory. When you find it, click **OK**.

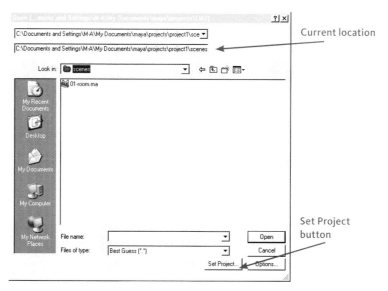

File Open dialog

When you open a scene, it should now automatically take you to your current project's scenes directory. If it doesn't, open the combo box located at the top of the dialog and select **Current scenes**.

• Select *01-garage_01.ma* and click **Open**.

3 Save Scene As

Since you will be modifying this scene, it is a good idea to save this file under a new name right away. Doing so will allow you to keep a copy of the previous lesson in case you would like to start this lesson over.

• Select **File** → **Save Scene As...**.

• Type *02-garage_01* in the **File name** field.

• Select *MayaASCII (*.ma)* in the **Files of type** field.

Maya can save its files in two different types of formats:

Maya ASCII (.ma) *saves your scene into a text file which is editable in a Text Editor. Though this format takes more space on your drive, it is possible to review and modify its content without opening it in Maya. Experienced users find this very useful.*

Maya Binary (.mb) *saves your scene into a binary file which is compiled into computer language. This format is faster to save and load, and takes less space on your drive.*

Garage opening

In order to create a garage door, you will need to change the room's geometry and create an opening.

4 Change the garage geometry

Since the polygonal cube still has construction history and was not yet modified, you can change its number of subdivisions.

• Select the *garage* object.

• In the **Inputs** section of the Channel Box, click on *polyCube1*.

• Select all three **Subdivisions** attributes by **click+dragging** on their names.

• In any viewport, **MMB+drag** to the right to increase the attributes' value to **5**.

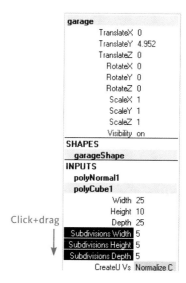

Select the attribute names

Tip: *When attributes are highlighted in the Channel Box, middle mouse dragging in a viewport invokes a virtual slider that changes the attributes' values.*

5   **Extrude polygon faces**

Extruding polygons is a very common action. To do an extrusion, you first need to pick polygonal face components, and then execute the tool that will display a useful all-in-one manipulator to move around the new polygons.

- With the *garage* still selected, press the **F11** hotkey to go into Component mode with the polygonal faces enabled.

Tip: *There are several hotkeys for going into Component and Object modes. The more you use Maya, the better you will know the difference between those modes. The polygon related hotkeys are listed below.*

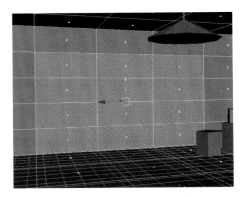

F8 – *Toggle between Object mode and the last Component mode*

F9 – *Display vertices*

F10 – *Display edges*

F11 – *Display faces*

F12 – *Display UVs*

- **Click+drag** with your **LMB** to select a face of the wall that will be used to create the door opening.

   The faces will be highlighted in orange to show that they are currently selected.

Pick the center of the faces to select them

Tip: *You can also click on face centers to highlight faces. Combine this action with the Shift key to toggle, the Control key to deselect or the Shift and Control keys to add faces to the current selection.*

- Select **Edit Mesh → Extrude**.

  A manipulator is displayed at the selection. This manipulator has all translation, rotation and scale manipulators integrated.

  LMB *on an arrow to display the translation manipulator.*

  LMB *on the outer circle to display the rotation manipulator.*

  LMB *on a square to display the scale manipulator.*

  Toggle between local and global transformation by clicking on the round icon.

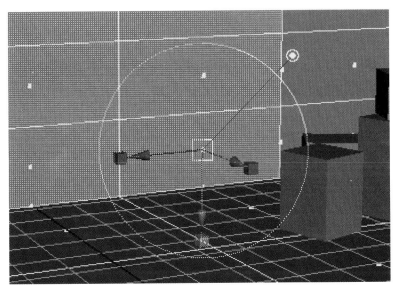

The all-in-one manipulator

- **Click+drag** the blue arrow manipulator to translate the faces slightly inward to create a small border.

- Select **Edit Mesh → Extrude** again.

- **LMB** on a square of the manipulator to enable its scale function.

- **LMB+drag** on the squares to scale the extruded faces.

- **LMB** on an arrow of the manipulator to use the translate function.

- **LMB** translate the faces down so the bottom border is almost even with the garage floor.

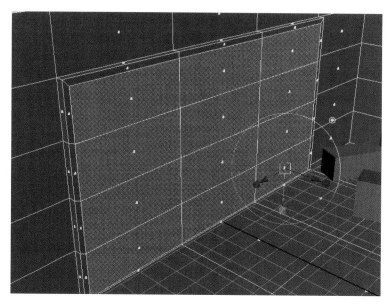

Manipulate the faces to make a border

- Select **Edit Mesh** → **Extrude** again.

- **LMB** translate the new faces toward the outside of the garage to create the inside of the door frame.

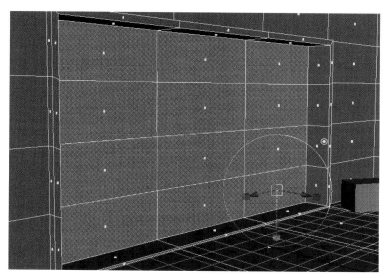

Final shape of the door frame

6 **Delete polygon faces**

- With the door faces still selected, press the **Delete** key on your keyboard to delete them.

  Doing so will create the door opening.

- Press **F8** to return to Object mode.

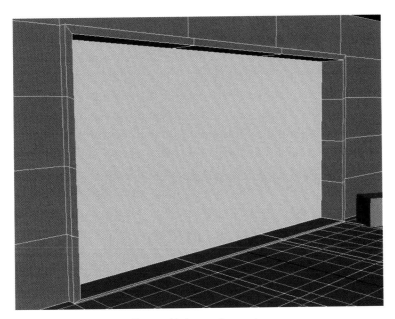

The completed garage door opening

Note: *Since most of the scenes in this book are located inside the garage, you will not bother modeling the exterior of the building.*

Garage door

Now you can model a garage door to fit the opening. You will do so by modeling a single plank of the door, then duplicating it to create the complete door. Once that is done, you will combine all the pieces together.

1 **Door plank**

- Select **Create** → **Polygon Primitives** → **Cube.**

- **Move** the new cube at the bottom of the door opening.

- **Scale** the cube to look like a plank and have it fit the door in width.

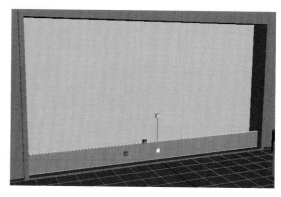

The first plank of the garage door

2 Full door

- With the cube selected, press **Ctrl+d** to duplicate it.

- **Move** the plank up above the other one, making sure they are touching each other.

- **Repeat** the last steps to duplicate the plank and complete the door.

- **Shift-select** all the planks.

- Press **e** to invoke the **Rotate Tool**.

- From a side Orthographic view, **rotate** the planks all together to create relief to the door.

- **Scale** the planks if needed in order to fully close any gaps between the planks.

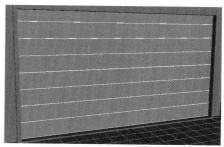

Closed garage door

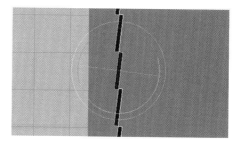

Rotating the planks all at once

3 Combine the door

In order to simplify the door manipulation, you can combine all of its polygonal parts together.

- With the planks still selected, select **Mesh → Combine**.

Maya now considers the pieces of the door one piece of geometry.

- **Rename** the model to *door*.

Note: *Construction history is always kept when doing such operations. This history is sometimes not wanted as it increases file size and loading time. Later in this lesson, you will learn how to delete construction history.*

4 Center pivot

Notice that when objects are combined together, the pivot of the new object is placed at the center of the world. There are different ways of placing the object's pivot at a better location.

- With the *door* selected, press the **Insert** key on your keyboard (**Home** on Macintosh).

  Doing so changes the current manipulator to the **Move Pivot Tool**.

- Using the different axes on the manipulator, place the pivot at the desired location.

- Press the **Insert** key again to recover the default manipulator.

OR

- Select **Modify → Center Pivot**.

  Using this command automatically places the object's pivot at its center.

5 Test the door

You can now test the door's behavior by dragging it on its Y-axis. If something is not working correctly, you can undo your actions and redo the appropriate steps.

- **Undo** by either selecting **Edit → Undo** or by pressing **z** on your keyboard.

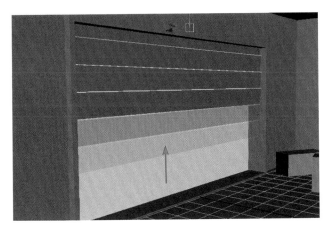

Moving the door up

Note: *Make sure to place the door outside the room geometry so that when you move it up, you don't see it interpenetrating with the door's border.*

6   Doorknob

You will now create a small doorknob for the garage door.

- **Move** the garage door to its default position by setting its **TranslateY** to **o**.

Note: *When combining objects together, the transformation values of the new object are set to its default. Manipulating the object's pivot does not affect translation values.*

- **Create** a polygonal cube and **rename** it to *knob*.

- **Transform** the door knob and set its **Subdivisions** attributes as indicated to the right:

- **RMB** on the *knob* object and select **Face**.

- Select the two faces on either side of the knob to use for extrusion.

- Select **Edit Mesh** → **Extrude**.

- Using the extrude manipulator, translate the faces out on the Z-axis.

  Since the extrude manipulator extrudes based on the face's direction, the faces are moved in different directions.

- Continue extruding, moving and scaling the same two faces to get the following shape:

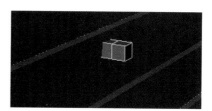

The door knob starting point

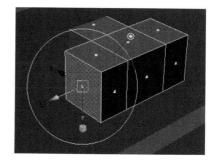

Extruding opposing faces

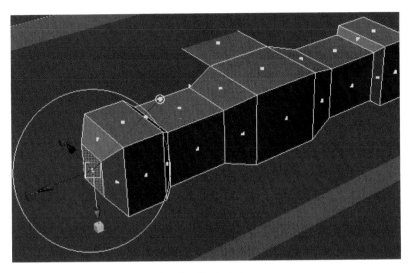

The refined doorknob shape

Tip: *You can invoke the last command (Extrude) by pressing the **g** key rather than always going back into the menus.*

7 **Smooth doorknob**

The look of the doorknob is quite rough and boxy at this time. This can be changed using the polygon smooth command.

- **RMB** on the *knob* and select **Object Mode**.

- Click on the *knob* to select it.

- Select **Mesh** → **Smooth.**

  Doing so will smooth out the geometry.

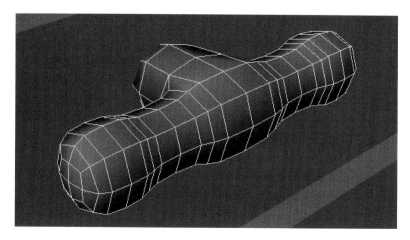

The smoothed door knob

8 Construction history

All the different tools used on the doorknob thus far are still accessible through the Inputs section of the Channel Box. Highlighting them will allow you to tweak action taken without undoing and losing all of your work.

- With the *knob* selected, highlight any of the *polyExtrudeFace* nodes in the Inputs section of the Channel Box.

  The extrude manipulator is automatically displayed.

- Try translating the manipulator to see its effect on the geometry.

- Try to change attributes for the orginal *polyCube* node or the *polySmooth* node to see their effect.

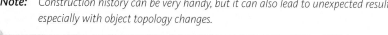

> **Note:**   *Construction history can be very handy, but it can also lead to unexpected results, especially with object topology changes.*

- Once the shape of the doorknob is correct, with the knob still selected, select **Edit → Delete by type → History.**

  The construction history is now gone from the Inputs section of the Channel Box.

- To delete all the history in the scene, select **Edit → Delete All by type → History.**

Tip: *Be careful when deleting an entire scene's history since history is sometimes required. For instance, character deformations are done via history. To delete only construction history, use* **Edit** → **Delete All by type** → **Non-Deformer History**.

9 Save your work

- Select **File** → **Save Scene As...**

- Save the scene as *02-garage_01.ma*.

Conclusion

You have begun to develop skills that you will use throughout your work with Maya. Polygonal modeling is an entire subject on its own, especially when it comes to character modeling. You will get to do more in-depth modeling in the second project, but for now, you will continue experiencing different general Maya topics.

In the next lesson, you will bring colors into your scene by assigning shaders and textures to your objects.

Lesson 03
Shaders and textures

Now that you have created an environment, you are ready to add colors and render your scene. The rendering process involves the preparation of materials and textures for objects.

In this lesson you will learn the following:

- How to work with a menu-less UI;
- How to work with the Hypershade;
- How to create shading groups;
- How to texture map an object;
- How to unitize a texture on polygons;
- How to render a single frame.

Hiding the general UI

In the last two lessons, you used menus, numeric input fields and other UI elements to work with your scene. In this lesson, you will hide most of the user interface and rely more on the hotbox and other hotkeys to access the UI without actually seeing it onscreen. Feel free to continue using the file you created from the last lesson or open *02-garage_01.ma* from the *support_files/scenes* directory.

1 Turn off all menus

- Position your cursor over the Perspective view panel, then press the spacebar quickly to pop this panel to full screen.

- Press and hold on the spacebar to evoke the hotbox.

Tip: *Tapping and holding down the spacebar, respectively, can be used to toggle between window panes and bring up the hotbox.*

- Click on **Hotbox Controls**.

- From the Marking Menu, go down to **Window Options** and set the following:

    Show Main Menubar to **Off** (Windows only);

    Show Pane Menubars to **Off**.

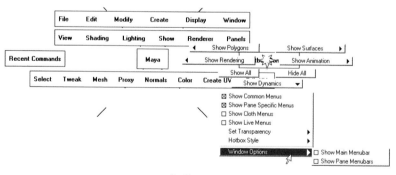

Marking menu

Now the various menus are hidden and you must rely on the hotbox to access tools.

2 Turn off all the workspace options

- From the hotbox, select **Display** → **UI Elements** → **Hide UI Elements**.

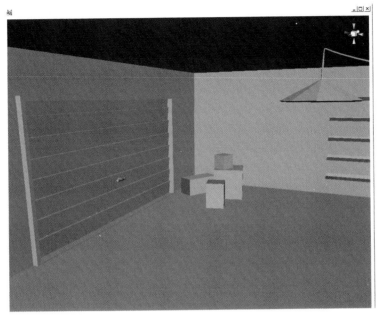

Simplified UI

You now have a much larger working area that will let you focus more on your work.

3   Change the panel organization

- Press and hold on the spacebar to evoke the hotbox.

- Click in the area above all the menus to apply the north Marking Menu.

- Select **Hypershade/Render/Persp** from this Marking Menu.

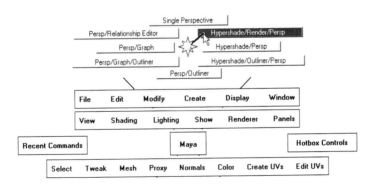

Hypershade/Render/Persp layout

Tip: *Each of the four quadrants surrounding the hotbox and the hotbox's center all contain their own Marking Menu sets. You can edit the contents of these menus using* **Window** → **Settings/Preferences** → **Marking Menus...**

This saved layout puts a Hypershade panel above a Perspective panel and a Render View panel.

The Hypershade is where you will build shading networks and the Render View is where you will test the results in your scene.

Tip: **Click+drag** *the pane divisions to change the width/height of the different windows in the layout.*

4 Open the Attribute Editor

- From the hotbox, select **Display** → **UI Elements** → **Attribute Editor**.

Now you also have an Attribute Editor panel on the right side of the workspace. This will make it easy to update shading network attributes.

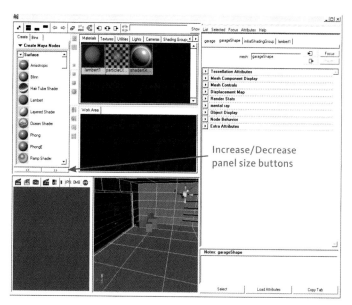

New UI layout

Hotkeys

When working with a minimal UI, you will rely on the hotbox and hotkeys for your work. The following is a list of relevant hotkeys that you may need to use as you work:

spacebar	Hotbox/window popping
Ctrl + a	Show/hide Attribute Editor
f	Frame selected
a	Frame all
q	Pick Tool
w	Move Tool
e	Rotate Tool
r	Scale Tool
t	Show Manipulator Tool
y	Invoke last tool
g	Repeat last command
Alt + v	Start/stop playback
Alt + Shift + v	Go to first frame

Note: *For a complete list of available hotkeys, go to* **Window** → **Settings/Preferences** → **Hotkeys...**

Shading networks

To prepare the garage and objects for rendering, you need to add color and texture. This is accomplished using *shading networks* that bring together material qualities, textures, lights and geometry to define the desired look.

The Hypershade

The Hypershade panel is made up of three sections: the Create bar, the Hypershade tabs and the work area. The Create bar allows you to create any rendering nodes required for your scene. The Hypershade tabs list all nodes that make up the current scene, while the work area allows you to look more closely and alter any part of the shading network's graph.

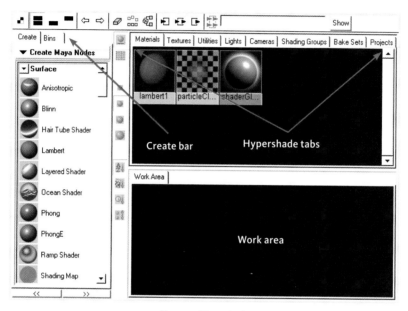

Close-up of Hypershade

 Tip: Note that all the same mouse and key combinations that you use in the viewports can be used for maneuvering in the Hypershade work area.

Creating shading networks

A shading network consists of a series of nodes that input into a *shading group*. A shading group is a node that defines the various rendering attributes of its related objects, such as surface shading, volumetric shading, displacement shading, etc.

In the following examples, you will create several nodes that define the material qualities of the garage, boxes, shelves, lamp and door.

1   **Lamp material**

To build a material for the lamp, you will use the Hypershade and Attribute Editor.

- At the top of the Create bar section, click on the tab **Create**.

- Click on the **down arrow** just below the **Create** tab, and make sure **Create Maya Nodes** is selected from the pop-up.

This offers you a series of icons that represent new Maya nodes, such as surface materials.

- Click on **Blinn**.

This adds a new Blinn material under the materials' Hypershade tab and in the work area. You will also see the Attribute Editor update to show the new node information.

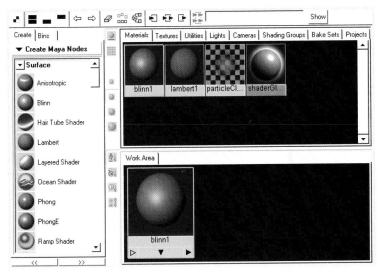

New node in Hypershade

> **Note:**   Blinn is a particular type of shading model that defines how the material will look. The Blinn model gives you control over the look of the materials' highlights using special attributes.

2   **Rename the material node**

- In the Attribute Editor, change the name of the material node to *lampM*.

The M designation is to remind you that this node is a material node.

Tip: You can also hold down the Ctrl key and double-click on the node in the Hypershade to rename it.

3 Edit the material's color

To define how the material will render, you will need to set several key material attributes, such as color.

- In the Attribute Editor, click on the color swatch next to the **Color** attribute.

  This opens the Color Chooser. This window lets you set color by clicking in a color wheel and editing HSV (Hue, Saturation, Value) or RGB (Red, Green, Blue) values.

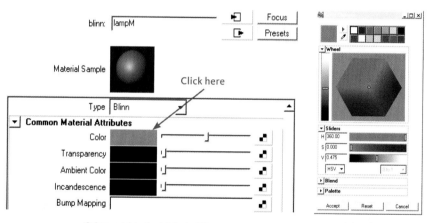

Color swatch in the Attribute Editor   *Color Chooser*

- Choose any color you want and click the **Accept** button.

4 Assign the material

- With your **MMB**, **click+drag** on the *lampM* node, drag it from the Hypershade panel into the Perspective view and drop it on the *lamp* object.

  This assigns the material to the object.

 Tip: It is a good idea to be in Hardware Shading mode to ensure that the assignment is correct. The hotkey is **5** on your keyboard.

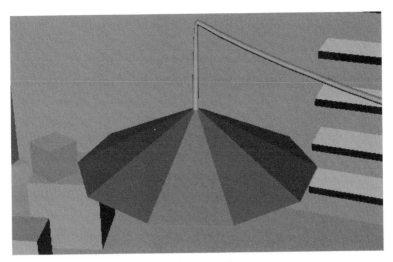

Assigned shader

5 Polygon normals

In the above image, notice how the material seems to be flat, perfectly following the polygonal edges. This is because the edges on the lamp are said to be *hard*. In order to have the lamp's polygons look more round, you need to set its edges to *soft*.

- With the *lamp* selected, select **Normals** → **Soften Edges** from the hotbox.

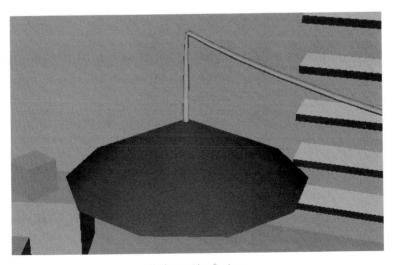

The lamp with soft edges

6   More materials

- Click with your **RMB** in the work area and select **Graph** → **Clear Graph**.

  This clears the workspace so that you can begin working on a new shading network.

- From the Create bar section, create a **Phong** material with a black color.

  Phongs have an intense specular that looks more like plastic.

- In the Attribute Editor, change the name of the material node to *wireM*.

- Select the *wire*, then **RMB** on your material *wireM* and select **Assign Material to Selection**.

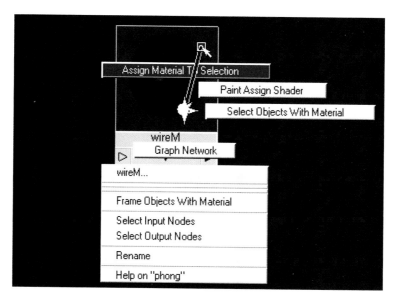

Assign to selection

Tip: *This method of assigning materials works better than the click+drag method when you want to assign a material to multiple objects.*

- Create a **Lambert** material with a *bright yellow* color and **rename** it *bulbM*.

- Change the **incandescence** color to *dark yellow*.

Lambert does not have any specular component and is matte compared to the other material you have just created. Adding incandescence tends to flatten the material out, as well as giving the illusion that it is illuminating light.

- **Create** a NURBS sphere, **rename** it to *bulb* and place it in the *lamp*.

- **RMB** on the *bulb*, then select **Assign Existing Material** → **bulbM**.

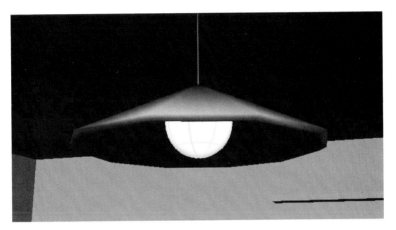

The latest materials on the lamp

Creating a procedural texture map

To give one of the boxes a pattern, a grid procedural texture will be added to the *box's* material color. A *procedural texture* means the look of the texture is driven by attributes and drawn by mathematical functions. You will also experiment with the drag and drop capabilities of the Hypershade.

1   **Create a material for the boxes**

To build a textured material for the box, you will use the Hypershade panel to build up the material using a grid texture.

- In the Hypershade, clear the work area by holding down the right mouse button and selecting **Graph** → **Clear Graph** or press the **Clear Graph** button at the top of the Hypershade.

The Clear Graph button

- Create a **Lambert** material and name it *boxM*.

2 Create a grid texture

- In the Create bar section, scroll down to the **2D Textures** section.

  This section allows you to create new textures.

- **MMB+drag** a **Grid** from the menu anywhere into the work area.

- In the work area of the Hypershade, click with your **MMB** on the **Grid** icon and drag it onto the *boxM* material node.

  When you release the mouse button, a pop-up menu appears offering you a number of attributes that can be mapped by the grid texture.

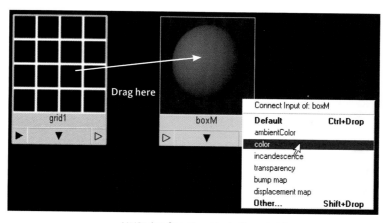

MMB+drag from the grid onto the material

- Select **color** from the menu to map the *grid* to the material node's *color* attribute.

- Click on the **Rearrange Graph** button at the top of the Hypergraph panel.

The Rearrange Graph button

Tip: *Rearranging the work area will organize the view so connections appear from left to right. This is very useful for following the flow of connections.*

3 Assigning the material

You will assign the texture map to one of the boxes and then use hardware shading to preview it.

- With your **MMB**, click on the *boxM* material node and drag it onto one of the box surfaces in the Perspective view.

- Over the Perspective window, click with your **MMB** to make it the active window.

- Evoke the hotbox and select **Shading** → **Hardware Texturing**.

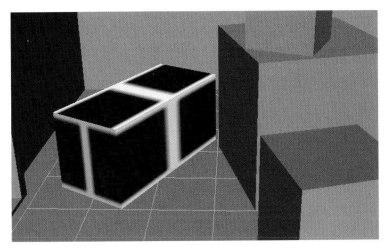

Hardware texturing

> **Tip:**   *You can also turn on hardware texturing by making the desired panel active and pressing the **6** key.*

4 Edit the grid attributes

- In the Hypershade, click on the *grid* node.

- In the Attribute Editor (**Ctrl+a** to show it, if hidden), click on the color swatch next to the **Line Color** attribute.

- Choose any color you want and click the **Accept** button.

- Click on the color swatch next to the **Filler Color** attribute.

- Choose any color you want and click the **Accept** button.

- At the top of the Attribute Editor, select the *place2dTexture* tab.

  This tab shows different placement options for the grid texture.

Lesson 03: Shaders and textures

- Change the grid's placement attributes as shown below:

  Repeat U to **8**;

  Repeat V to **8**.

  The Attribute Editor allows you to easily update the look of a procedural texture.

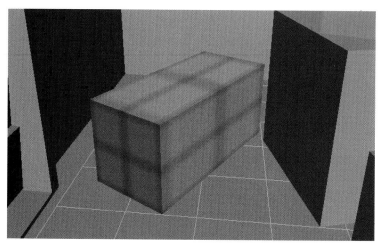

New grid

Note: *The viewport texture shading is a representation of what your textures look like, but it might not reflect perfectly how your scene will render.*

---

5 Display the whole shading group

- With the *grid* texture selected in the Hypershade, click on **Input and Output Connections.**

Input and Output Connections button

  This displays some other nodes that help define this shading group.

- Press the **Alt** key and **click+drag** with your left and middle mouse buttons to zoom out.

- Press the **a** hotkey to frame everything in the view.

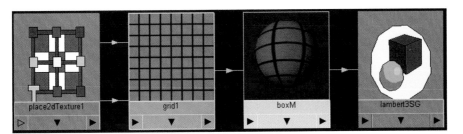

Complete shading network

Creating a texture map

You will create a material for one of the boxes that uses a file texture instead of a procedural texture. Many digital artists like to create textures in a 2D paint package. For the box, you will use a crate texture.

Crate texture

1 **Create a material for the box**

- From the Hypershade panel's work area **RMB+click** and select **Graph → Clear Graph**.

- Scroll to the **Surface** section in the Create bar and select **Phong**.

- **Rename** this node *crateM*.

2 **Create a file texture node**

To load an external texture, you need to start with a file texture node.

- **Double-click** on the *crateM* material to display its Attribute Editor (if hidden).

- In the Attribute Editor, click on the **Map** button next to **Color**. The map button is shown with a small checker icon.

This opens the Create Render Node window.

- Click on the **Textures** tab.

- In the **2D Textures** section, click on **File**.

A file node is added to the Phong material. The appropriate connections have already been made.

Map button

New file texture node

3 Import the file texture

- In the Attribute Editor for the file node, click on the **File folder** icon next to **Image name**.

- Select the file named *crate.tif* from your project *sourceimages* directory, then click on the **Open** button.

  The file texture is now loaded into the shading network.

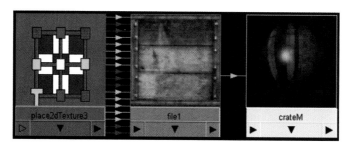

File texture node

Note: *This file will be available only if you set-up your project correctly from the support_files and if it is set to current.*

Note: *The file texture does not import the image in Maya. Instead, it keeps a path to the specified file and loads it on request from your drive.*

4 Apply the textured material to the boxes

- Select some of the boxes in the Perspective view.

- In the Hypershade, click on the *crateM* node with your **RMB** and choose **Assign Material to Selection** from the pop-up menu.

  The texture is assigned to the boxes, but notice that the crate texture is not mapped properly.

- With the same boxes still selected, select **Edit UVs → Unitize**.

  Doing so forces the textures to be mapped entirely to each box face.

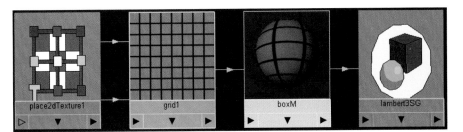

Complete shading network

Creating a texture map

You will create a material for one of the boxes that uses a file texture instead of a procedural texture. Many digital artists like to create textures in a 2D paint package. For the box, you will use a crate texture.

Crate texture

1 Create a material for the box

- From the Hypershade panel's work area **RMB+click** and select **Graph → Clear Graph**.

- Scroll to the **Surface** section in the Create bar and select **Phong**.

- **Rename** this node *crateM*.

2 Create a file texture node

To load an external texture, you need to start with a file texture node.

- **Double-click** on the *crateM* material to display its Attribute Editor (if hidden).

- In the Attribute Editor, click on the **Map** button next to **Color**. The map button is shown with a small checker icon.

Map button

This opens the Create Render Node window.

- Click on the **Textures** tab.

- In the **2D Textures** section, click on **File**.

A file node is added to the Phong material. The appropriate connections have already been made.

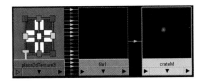

New file texture node

3   Import the file texture

- In the Attribute Editor for the file node, click on the **File folder** icon next to **Image name**.

- Select the file named *crate.tif* from your project *sourceimages* directory, then click on the **Open** button.

  The file texture is now loaded into the shading network.

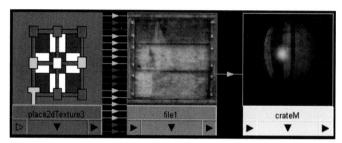

File texture node

Note: *This file will be available only if you set-up your project correctly from the support_files and if it is set to current.*

Note: *The file texture does not import the image in Maya. Instead, it keeps a path to the specified file and loads it on request from your drive.*

4   Apply the textured material to the boxes

- Select some of the boxes in the Perspective view.

- In the Hypershade, click on the *crateM* node with your **RMB** and choose **Assign Material to Selection** from the pop-up menu.

  The texture is assigned to the boxes, but notice that the crate texture is not mapped properly.

- With the same boxes still selected, select **Edit UVs → Unitize**.

  Doing so forces the textures to be mapped entirely to each box face.

Note: This last step actually changed the UVs of the geometry. You will learn more about polygonal UVs in the next project.

Boxes with texture not applied correctly

Boxes with good texture mapping

5 Complete the scene

Before continuing with the next lesson, it is a good idea to assign materials to the remaining objects in your scene. Experiment with fractal, ramp and cloth procedural texture nodes. Following is an example of the completed room:

Completed room

Note: *A wood texture can be found in the support_files sourceimages directory.*

Tip: *You can assign textures to polygonal faces by first selecting the faces and then assigning a shader to them.*

Test render

Now that you have materials and textures assigned, it is a good time to do a test render.

1 Display Resolution Gate

Your current view panel may not be displaying the actual proportions that will be rendered.

You can display the camera's resolution gate to see how the scene will actually render.

- Make the Perspective view the active panel.

- Use the hotbox to select **View** → **Camera Settings** → **Resolution Gate**.

The view is adjusted to show a bounding box that defines how the default render resolution of **640x480** *pixels relates to the current view.*

- Dolly into the view so that it is well composed within the resolution gate. Try to set-up a view where you see every object, looking toward the boxes in the other corner of the room.

Keep in mind that only objects within the green surrounding line will be rendered.

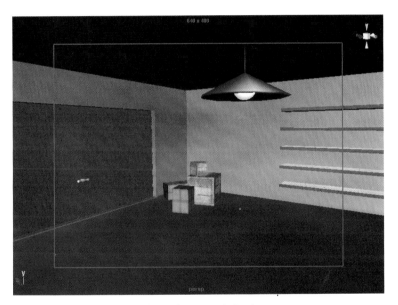

The resolution gate displayed

2 Your first render

- In the Render view panel, click with your **RMB** and select **Render** → **Render** → **persp** from the pop-up menu.

You can now see a rendered image of your scene. However, because you have not created any lights, the image renders using a default light.

- Try adding lighting to your scene by creating lights from the **Create** → **Lights** menu.

Lesson 03: Shaders and textures

size: 640 480 zoom: 1.000   (Maya Software)
Frame: 5   Render Time: 0:03   Camera: persp

Render view panel

Note: *Lights are going to be covered later in this book.*

• **Render** your scene again.

Note: *If your render is grey, it is most likely because your camera is outside the room.*
            Remember, in the viewport you specified to see through back facing polygons,
            but the renderer will still render the entire room. To correct the problem, make
            sure to move the camera inside the garage.

3   Zoom into the rendering

You can zoom in and out of the rendered image using the **Alt** key and the dolly and track hotkeys.

- Use the **Alt** key and the **LMB** and **RMB** to zoom in and out of the view.

  Now you can evaluate in more detail how your rendering looks at the pixel level.

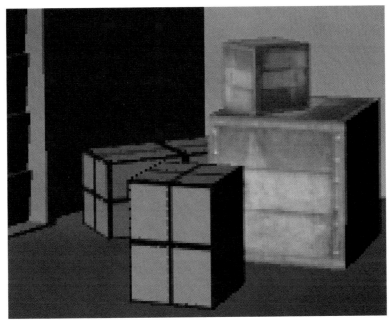

Close-up of rendering

- In the Render view panel, click with your **RMB** and choose **View** → **Real Size**.

4 Save your work

- Through the hotbox, select **Save Scene As** from the **File** menu.
- Enter the name *03-textures_01.ma*, then press the **Save** button.

Conclusion

You have now been introduced to some of the basic concepts for texturing and rendering a 3D scene. The Maya shading networks offer a lot of depth for creating the look of your objects. You have learned how to create materials, procedural textures and file textures, and rendered a single frame to preview the look of your shaders with default lighting.

In the next lesson, you will add light and shader effects that will only be visible at render time.

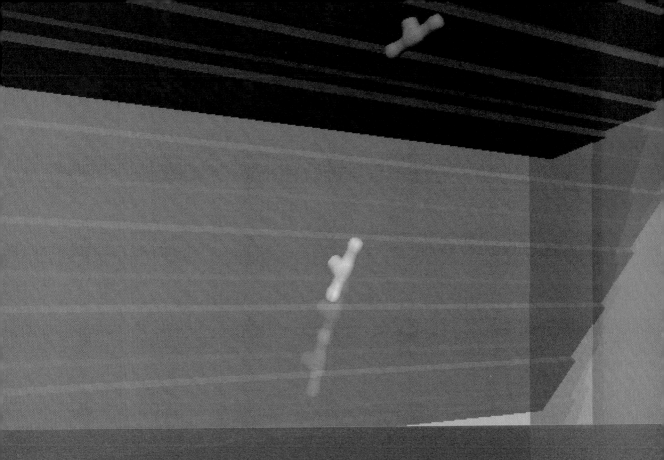

Lesson 04
Animation basics

You have built a garage using various primitive objects and then textured them. You will now learn about the basics of hierarchies and animate the door so that it opens.

In this lesson you will learn the following:

- How to change and save preferences;

- How to group and parent objects;

- How to understand parent inheritance;

- How to set keyframes;

- How to use the Time Slider;

- How to use the Graph Editor;

- How to traverse a hierarchy.

Preferences

You can now reset the interface to its default settings. You can also make sure here to set your preferences to have an infinite undo queue.

1 Turn on all menus

- From the hotbox, click on **Hotbox Controls**.

- From the Marking Menu, go down to **Window Options** and set the following:

  Show Main Menubar to **On**;

  Show Pane Menubars to **On**.

  The menu bars are back to normal.

2 Turn on all of the workspace options

- Select **Display** → **UI Elements** → **Show UI Elements**.

  You are now back to the default Maya interface.

3 Change the Attribute Editor settings

You might want the Attribute Editor to open in its own window rather than in the Maya interface. The following will show you how to set your preference accordingly.

- Select **Window** → **Settings/Preferences** → **Preferences**.

- In the left **Categories** list, make sure **Interface** is highlighted.

- Set **Open Attribute Editor:** to **In separate window**.

- You can do the same for **Open tool settings** and the **Open Layer Editor** if desired.

  The different editors will now open in their own separate windows.

4 Infinite undo option

By default, Maya has a limited amount of undo options. You must specify here if you want Maya to keep an undo queue larger than the default setting.

- In the **Categories** list, highlight **Undo**.

- Make sure **Undo** is set to **On**.

- Set the **Queue size** to what you think is an appropriate value, such as **50**.

OR

- Set the **Queue** to **Infinite**.

  The amount of undo is now defined to your liking.

5 Save your preferences

- In order to save those preferences with Maya, you must click the **Save** button.

  The next time you open Maya, those settings will be used.

Organize your scene

Before animating objects, you need to make sure that the task will be as simple as possible. You will need to easily find the objects in your scene and animate them as intended. Placing objects logically into hierarchy is going to do just that. To do so, you will learn how to group and parent objects together as well as learn how to use the Outliner.

You can think of scene organization as having groups and sub-groups. For instance, you can have a *garage* group that contains everything that is part of the garage. Then you can have a *shelves* group, followed by a *shelfObject* group.

Thus far you have modeled a bunch of objects, but you haven't looked at how they were organized behind what you saw in the viewports.

1 Hierarchy

It is very important to understand the concept of a **hierarchy**. A *hierarchy* consists of the grouping of child nodes under parent nodes. When transforming a parent node, all of its children will inherit its transformation. The following steps explain how to create a hierarchy of objects.

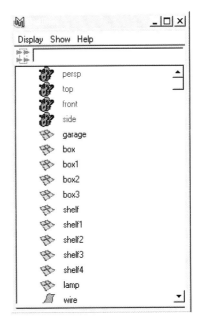

- To better visualize what you are about to do, open the Outliner by selecting **Window → Outliner....**

  The Outliner lists all the nodes in your scene along with their hierarchies. Currently, in your scene, you can see the default Maya cameras, all of the prior lesson objects, every component of your solar system and, at the very bottom, two default sets.

The Outliner

- Scroll in the Outliner to see the current organization of the scene.

  The first four nodes in the Outliner are always the default cameras. Following that are your scene contents, and then the different default object sets.

2 Groups

- Using the **Ctrl** and **Shift** keys, **select** all your scene's content starting from the *garage* down to *bulb*.

  Doing so selects the geometry just like when selecting in a viewport.

- Select **Edit → Group**.

  The selected geometry is now all grouped under group1.

- **Expand** the newly created group to see its content by clicking on the **plus** (+) sign next to *group1*.

- **Double-click** on *group1* to enable the rename function directly in the Outliner.

- **Enter** the name *garageGroup*, then hit **Enter** to confirm the name change.

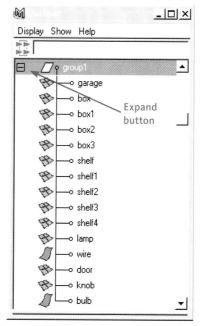

Expand button

Hierarchy expanded

> **Note:** A new default group has its pivot at the origin and all of its attributes are set to their default values.

3 Organizing the hierarchy

You will now create a group for the shelves within the garage group.

- Select the object called *shelf* on its own.

- Press **Ctrl+g** to group it.

  A new group1 is created with only the shelf object within it.

- **Rename** *group1* to *shelvesGroup*.

- **Select** all the remaining *shelves* that are not already in *shelvesGroup*.

- **Press and hold** the **MMB** over the selection and drag them over the *shelvesGroup*.

  As you can see in the following images, dragging nodes onto another one will set them as the child of the object it was dragged onto.

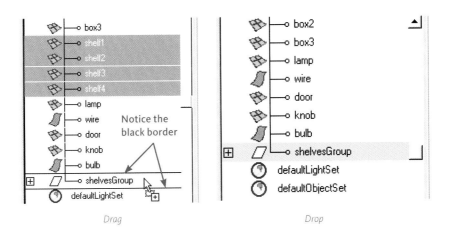

Drag   Drop

Note: Notice the green highlight on the shelvesGroup, which shows one or more of its children is currently selected.

- **Select** *shelvesGroup*.

- **MMB+drag** it in the Outliner just under the *garage* geometry.

  Doing so reorders the scene hierarchy.

Tip: Notice that when dragging objects in the Outliner, one black line shows that it will be placed in-between two nodes, while two black lines show that the objects will be parented.

4 Completing the hierarchy

- In the Outliner or in a viewport, select the light *bulb*.

- Hold **Ctrl**, then select the *lamp*.

- From the **Edit** menu, select **Parent**.

OR

- Press **p** on your keyboard.

  Doing so will parent the bulb object to the lamp object.

- Organize the hierarchy so that it looks like the completed hierarchy on the right:

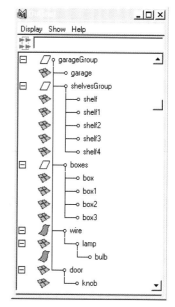

The completed hierarchy

Tip: To expand a hierarchy along with all the children, hold down the **Shift** key before clicking the Expand button in the Outliner.

Understanding inheritance

Hierarchies are useful for organizing your scene, but they also play a role with animation. For instance, if you transform a parent object, all of its children and grandchildren will follow that transformation. It is thus essential to freeze transformations of objects to reset the transformation attributes to their default without moving the object. You must also make sure that all objects' pivots are appropriately placed for your needs.

1 Freezing transformations

At this time, most of your objects have some values in their translate, rotate and scale attributes. When you animate your objects, those values will come into play and make your task more difficult. You can thus freeze an object's transformations without moving it in space.

- Select the *garageGroup.*

- Select **Edit** → **Select Hierarchy.**

- Select **Modify** → **Freeze Transformations.**

  Doing so resets all the selected objects' attributes to their default values.

Tip: *If you do not want to freeze all the attributes of an object, you can open the command's option box to specify which attributes need freezing.*

2 Child values

When you transform a parent object, none of its children's values change.

- Select the *wire.*

- **Rotate** and **translate** it in to modify its positioning.

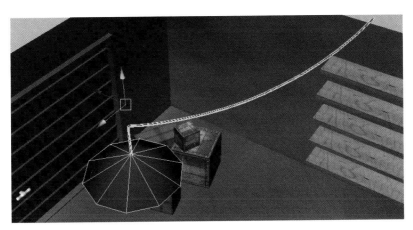

Rotate and translate the wire

- Select any of its children (*lamp* or *bulb*), and notice that all of their values are still zero.

- Select *lamp* and **rotate** it.

- Notice the *bulb*'s rotation values did not change.

- Select the *wire* and **scale** it.

  All of its children follow the parent scaling, but none of their values are changing.

Animating the door

Your scene is now ready for simple animation. Once you have keyframed the garage door, you will have a greater understanding of how to use inheritance to your advantage.

1 The timeline

The first step with animation is to determine how long you would like your animation to be. By default, Maya plays animation at a rate of **24** frames per seconds (FPS), which is a standard rate used for film. So if you want your animation to last one second, you need to animate 24 frames.

- In the Time Slider and Range Slider portion of the interface, change **Playback End Time** to **100**.

The frames in the Time Slider now go from 1 to 100. One hundred frames is just above four seconds of animation in 24 FPS.

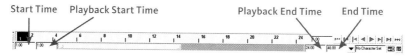

Time Slider and Range Slider

2 Setting keyframes

Luckily, you do not need to animate every single frame in your animation. When you set keyframes, Maya will interpolate the values between the keyframes, giving you animation.

- Press the **First Frame** button from the playback controls to make the current frame **1**.

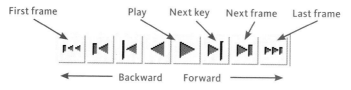

Playback controls

- Select the *door*.

- Make sure all of its rotation and translation values are set to **0**.

- At the top of the interface, change the current menu sets for **Animation**.

Tip: *The menu sets can be changed using the following hotkeys:*
      F2 - *Animation* **F4** - *Surfaces*   **F6** - *Rendering*
      F3 - *Polygons*   **F5** - *Dynamics*

- With the *door* still selected, select **Animate** → **Set Key**.

Tip: *Set Key can also be executed by pressing the* **s** *hotkey.*

- In the current frame field on the left of the rewind button, type **100** and hit **Enter**.

  Notice the position of the current frame mark in the Time Slider.

- Type **5.0** in the **Translate Y** field of the *door* and hit **Enter**.

- Press the **Alt** key over the viewport in order to remove focus from the Y-axis field, then hit the **s** hotkey to **Set Key** at frame **100**.

Current frame mark   Current frame field

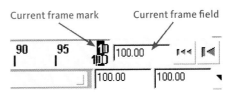

The current frame mark

3 Playback

Before you play your animation, you need to set the Maya playback properly.

- Click the **Animation Preferences** button found at the far right side of the Range Slider.

  This opens the preferences window directly on the animation and playback options.

The animation preferences button

- In the **Timeline** category, under the **Playback** section, make sure that **Playback Speed** is set to **Real-time (24 fps)**.

- Click the **Save** button.

- Press the **Play** button in the playback controls area to see your animation.

- To stop the playback of the animation, press the **Play** button again or hit **Esc**.
- You can also drag the current frame by **click+dragging** in the Time Slider area.

Click+drag in the Time Slider

Notice the red ticks at frame 1 and frame 100, specifying keyframes on the currently selected objects.

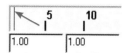

A keyframe tick in the Time Slider

4 Tweak the animation

You now have a partially animated door, but it is still missing refinement. The doorknob should first be rotated, and then the door should go up and pivot into the garage. In order to do that, more animation is required.

- With the *door* still selected, hold down the **Shift** key, then click on frame **1** in the Time Slider.

  Doing so highlights frame 1 with a red zone. This zone is actually a manipulator that allows you to translate keyframes in the Time Slider.

- **Click+drag** the red zone to frame **20**.

  The door animation now starts only at frame 20, leaving you time to animate the doorknob from frame 1 to 20.

The tick manipulator

- Select the *door knob*.

- Make sure you are at frame **1**, then press **Shift+e**.

  This hotkey sets a keyframe on the rotation attributes.

- Drag the Time Slider to frame **20**.

- **Rotate** the *doorknob* on its appropriate axis; in this case, the **Z-axis**.

- Click on the **RotateZ** attribute name in the Channel Box.

- Click and hold the **RMB** over that same attribute.

  This will pop the attribute context menu.

- Select **Key Selected**.

  Doing so will set a keyframe on that attribute for every selected object.

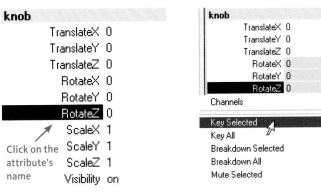

Select only the Rotate Z attribute   *Select Key Selected from the attribute menu*

- Tweak the keyframe of the *door* at frame **100** to look as follows:

The door's last position keyframe

- **Playback** your animation to see what it looks like.

Note: Notice how the doorknob follows the door animation because of inheritance, even though it is animated on its own.

5 Graph Editor

The *Graph Editor* is the place where you can look at all the keyframes on an object and see their interpolations as curves (*function curves* or *fcurves*).

- Select the animated *doorknob*.

- Select **Window → Animation Editors → Graph Editor**.

- Select **View → Frame All** to frame the entire curve, or press the **a** hotkey.

- Press the **Alt** key and **click+drag** with the **LMB** and **MMB** to dolly in and out of the graph.

- Press the **Shift+Alt** keys and **click+drag** up and down with the **RMB** to dolly only along the Y-axis.

- Press the **Shift+Alt** keys and **click+drag** up and down with the **RMB** to track along the Y-axis.

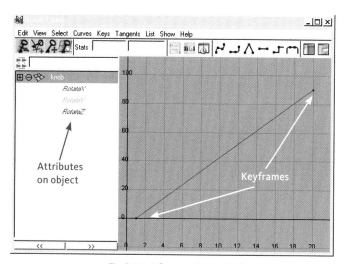

The Rotate Z fcurve on the doorknob

The two keyframes you have set on the Z-axis are represented by black dots. The animation curve linking the two keys is blue because animation curves are always color coded red, green and blue for X, Y and Z axes.

- Experiment selecting curves and keyframes in the Graph Editor.

- With the **Move Tool** selected, **MMB+drag** keys around.

Tip: Use **Shift+MMB** *dragging to constrain the axis of translation of the keyframe.*

- Select the entire animation curve.

- Select **Tangents** → **Flat.**

  This sets the keyframes to be flat, which causes a gradual acceleration and deceleration of the animation.

- Test your animation.

- Once you like your animation, **close** the Graph Editor.

6 Traversing a hierarchy

You can traverse hierarchies using the arrows on your keyboard. Traversing a hierarchy is useful for selecting objects without manually picking the object in the viewport or through the Outliner.

- Select the door *knob*.

- Press the **Up arrow** to change the selection to the parent of the current selection.

- Press the **Up arrow** again to select the *garageGroup*.

Tip:	You can use the following hotkeys to traverse a hierarchy:	
	Up arrow - *Parent*	**Down arrow** - *First child*
	Right arrow - *Next child*	**Left arrow** – *Previous child*

7 Save your work

- From the **File** menu, select **Save.**

Conclusion

You have now touched upon some of the basic concepts of hierarchies and animation. Maya utilizes more powerful tools than described here to help you bring your scenes to life, but these basic principles represent a great step forward. As well as learning how to group and parent objects together, you also learned about inheritance of transformation and animation and worked with two of the most useful editors: the Outliner and the Graph Editor.

The next lesson is a more in-depth look at most of the tools that you have been using since the beginning of this project. Once you have read this lesson, you will be able to make your own decisions about how to reach the different windows, menu items and hotkeys.

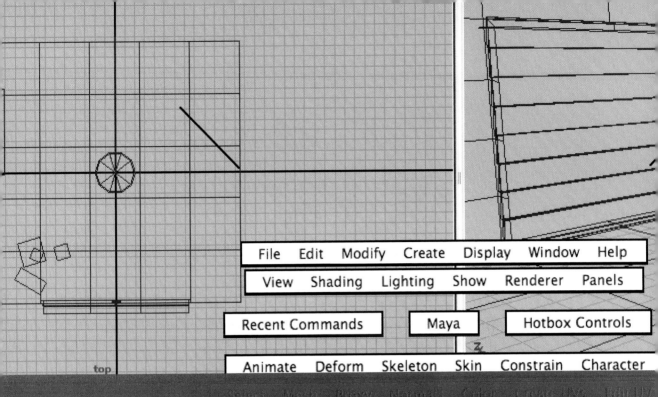

Lesson 05
Working with Maya

If you completed the first four lessons, you have worked with Maya software from modeling and animation to shading and rendering. Now is a good time to review some of the UI concepts that you worked with and introduce new concepts in order to provide a more complete overview of how Maya works.

It is recommended that you work through this lesson before proceeding with the subsequent lessons in the book. This lesson explores the basic UI actions that you will use in your day-to-day work.

In this lesson you will learn the following:

- About the Maya interface;
- About the different UI parts;
- About the view tools;
- About the different hardware displays;
- About menus and hotkeys;
- About the manipulators and the Channel Box;
- About selection and selection masks;
- About the difference between tools and actions.

The workspace

You have learned how to build and animate scenes using different view panels and UI tools. The panels offer various points of view for evaluating your work – such as Perspective views, Orthographic views, graphs and Outliners – while the tools offer you different methods for interacting with the objects in your scene.

Shown below is the workspace and its key elements:

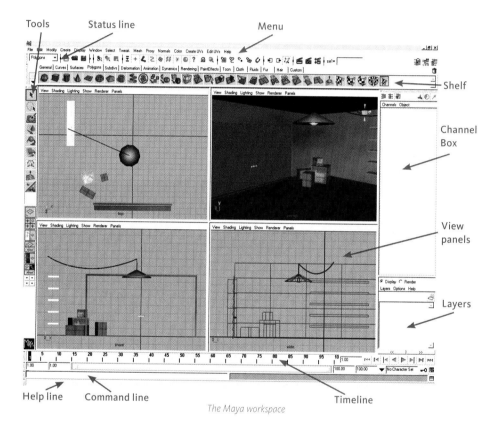

The Maya workspace

Layouts

When Maya is first launched, you are presented with a single Perspective view panel. As you work, you may want to change to other view layouts.

To change your view layouts:

- Go to the view panel's **Panels** menu and select a new layout option from the **Layouts** pop-up.

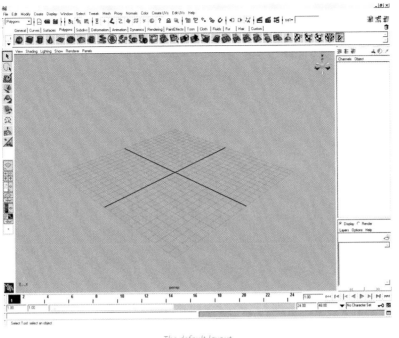

The default layout

You can set-up various
types of layouts ranging
from two to four panels.

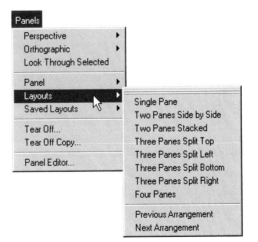

The Layouts pop-up menu

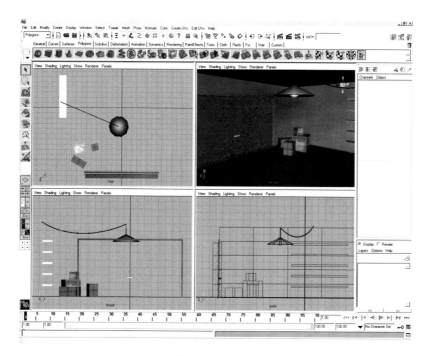

A four-view layout

Tip: *If you are looking at several view panels simultaneously and want to focus on one of them, put your cursor in that view and tap the spacebar. The view will become full-screen. Tap the spacebar again and the panels will return to the previous layout.*

View panels

As you begin to build and animate objects, you will want to view the results from various points of view. It is possible to place either Perspective or Orthographic views in each panel.

To change the content of a view panel:

- Go to the view panel's **Panels** menu and select a view type from either the **Perspective** or **Orthographic** pop-ups.

View tools

When you are working with Perspective and Orthographic views, you can change your viewpoint by using hotkey view tools. The following view tools allow you to quickly work in 3D space using simple hotkeys:

To tumble in a Perspective view:

- Press the **Alt** key and **click+drag** with the **LMB**.

> **Tip:** *The ability to tumble an Orthographic view is locked by default. To unlock this feature, you need to select the desired Orthographic view and under* **View***, go to* **Camera Tools** *and unlock it by going to the* **Tumble Tool** → ❑*.*

To track in any view panel:

- Press the **Alt** key and **click+drag** with the **MMB**.

To dolly in or out of any view panel:

- Press the **Alt** key and **click+drag** with both the **LMB** and **MMB** or with the **RMB** alone.

> **Tip:** *You can also track and dolly in other view panels, such as the Hypergraph, the Graph Editor, Visor, Hypershade and even the Render View window. The same view tools work for most panel types.*

View Compass

The View Compass appears in the top right corner of the scene's Perspective view and shows your current camera view: Perspective, top, bottom, left, right, front, or back.

You can move between views by clicking parts of the View Compass. Clicking any of the six cones rotates the current camera view to an Orthographic view. Clicking the central cube moves the camera back to Perspective view.

The View Compass

To turn the View Compass on and off per camera:

- Select **View** → **Camera Settings** → **View Compass**.

Other panel types

As well, you can change the content of
the view panel to display other types
of information, such as the Hypershade
or Graph Editor.

To change the content of a view panel:

• Go to the view panel's **Panels** menu
and select a panel type from the
Panels pop-up.

In the workspace below, you can see
a Hypergraph panel for helping select
nodes, a Graph Editor for working with
animation curves and a Perspective
view to see the results.

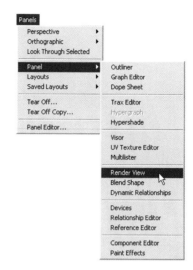

The Panels pop-up menu

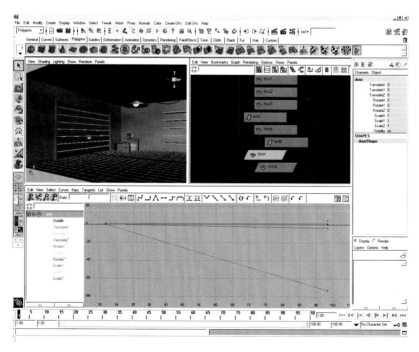

The workspace with various panel types

Saved layouts

As you become more familiar with Maya, you may want to set-up an arrangement of panels to suit a particular workflow. For example, you may want a Dope Sheet, a Perspective view, a top view and a Hypergraph view all set-up in a particular manner.

To add a new layout of your own:

- Go to the view panel's **Panels** menu and select **Saved Layouts** → **Edit Layouts...**

    In the Edit window, you can add a new saved layout and edit the various aspects of the layout.

To add a new layout to the list:

- Select the **Layouts** tab and click on **New Layout**.

- Select and edit the layout's name.

- Press the **Enter** key.

To edit the configuration of a saved layout:

- Press the **Edit Layouts** tab.

- Choose a configuration, then **click+drag** on the separator bars to edit the layout's composition.

- Press the **Contents** tab.

- Choose a panel type for each of the panels set-up in the configuration section.

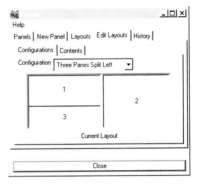

Layout Editor

Layout toolbox

Tip: *There is quick access to preset layouts, panel types and layout configuration through the toolbox on the left side of the Maya UI.*

Display options

Using the Shading menu on each view panel, you can choose which kind of display you want for your geometry.

To change your panel display:

- Go to the panel's **Shading** menu and select one of the options.

  OR

- **Click** in a panel to set it as the active panel and use one of the following hotkeys to switch display types:

  4 for wireframe;

  5 for smooth shaded.

Smooth shaded with wireframe on shaded   Smooth shaded

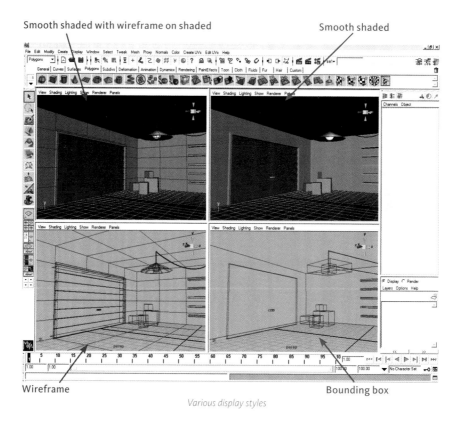

Wireframe   Bounding box

Various display styles

Texturing and lighting

Another important option found on this menu is hardware texturing. This option allows you to visualize textures and lighting interactively in the view panels.

To use hardware texturing:

- Build a shader that uses textures.

- Go to the panel's **Shading** menu and select **Hardware Texturing**.

  OR

- Press the **6** hotkey.

To display different textures:

It is possible to display different texture maps on your surface during hardware texturing. For example, you could display the color map or the bump map if those channels are mapped with a texture.

- Select the material that is assigned to your objects.

- In the Attribute Editor, scroll down to the **Hardware Texturing** section and set the **Textured channel** to the desired channel.

- You can also set the **Texture quality** in the Attribute Editor for each material node so that you can see the texture more clearly in your viewport.

To add hardware lighting to your scene:

- Add a light into your scene.

- Go to the panel's **Lighting** menu and select one of the options.

  OR

- Press the **7** hotkey
  for all lighting.

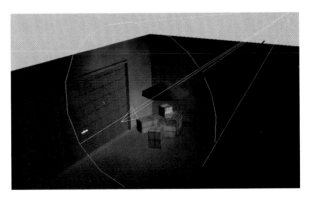

Hardware lighting and texturing

High quality rendering

When high quality interactive shading is turned on, the scene views are drawn in high quality by the hardware renderer. This lets you see a very good representation of the final render without having to software render the scene.

To turn on high quality rendering:

- Go to the panel's **Renderer** menu and enable **High Quality Rendering**.

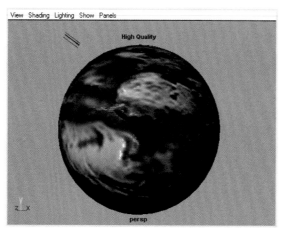

High Quality Rendering

Display smoothness

By default, NURBS surfaces are displayed using a fine smoothness setting. If you want to enhance playback and interactivity, you can have the surfaces drawn in a lower quality.

To change NURBS smoothness:

- Go to the **Display** menu and under **NURBS** choose one of the smoothness options.

  OR

- Use one of the following hotkeys to switch display types:

    1 - for rough;

    2 - for medium;

    3 - for fine.

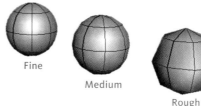

NURBS smoothness

> **Tip:** To speed up camera movement in a scene with heavy NURBS geometry, go to the **Window** → **Settings/Preferences** → **Preferences...** in the **Display** section to enable the **Fast Interaction** option. This option shows the rough NURBS smoothness any time a camera is moving.

Show menu

The **Show** menu is an important tool found on each view panel's menu. This menu lets you restrict or filter what each panel can show on a panel-by-panel basis.

Restricting what each panel shows lets you display curves in one window and surfaces in another to help edit construction history. Or, you can hide curves when playing back a motion path animation while editing the same curve in another panel.

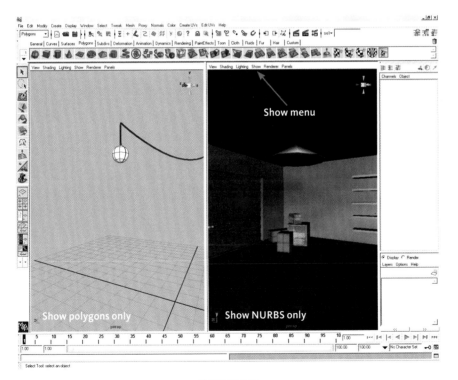

The Show menu

UI preferences

The Maya workspace is made up of various UI elements that assist you in your day-to-day work. The default workspace shows all of them on screen for easy access.

To reduce the UI to only view panels and menus:

* Go to the **Display** menu and select **UI Elements** → **Hide UI Elements**.

With less UI clutter, you can rely more on hotkeys and other UI methods for accessing tools while conserving screen real estate.

To return to a full UI:

* Go to the **Display** menu and select **UI Elements** → **Restore UI Elements**.

Menus

Most of the tools and actions you will use in Maya are found in the main menus. The first six menus are always visible, while the next few menus change depending on which UI mode you are in.

Menus and menu pop-ups that display a double line at the top can be torn off for easier access.

To tear off a menu:

* Open the desired menu, then select the double line at the top of the menu.

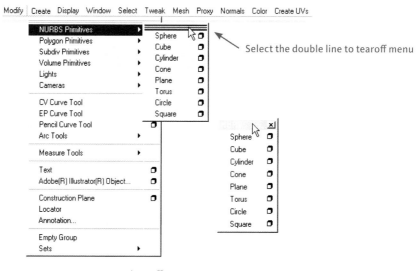

A tearoff menu

Menu sets

There are five menu sets in Maya Complete: *Animation, Polygons, Surfaces, Dynamics and Rendering*. Each menu set allows you to focus on tools appropriate to a particular workflow.

To choose a menu set:
- Select the menu set from the pop-up menu found at the left of the Status Line bar.

To choose a menu set using hotkeys:
- Press the **h** key and choose the desired UI mode from the radial Marking Menu.

To choose a menu set using function keys:

Press **F1** - to invoke **Help**;

Press **F2** - for **Animation**;

Press **F3** - for **Polygons**;

Press **F4** - for **Surfaces**;

Press **F5** - for **Dynamics**;

Press **F6** - for **Rendering**.

Shelves

Another way of accessing tools and actions is using the shelves. You can move items from a menu to a shelf to begin combining tools into groups based on your personal workflow needs.

To add a menu item to a shelf:
- Press **Ctrl+Shift** and select the menu item. It will appear on the active shelf.

To edit the shelf contents and tabs:
- Go to the **Window** menu and select **Settings/Preferences** → **Shelves...**

  OR

- Select the **Shelf Editor** from the arrow menu located to the left of the shelves.

To remove a menu item from a shelf:
- **MMB+drag** the shelf icon to the trash icon located at the far right of the shelves.

Status Line

The Status Line, located just under the Maya main menu, provides feedback on settings that affect the way the tools behave. The display information consists of:

- The current menu set;
- Icons that allow you to create a new scene, open a saved one, or save the current one;
- The selection mode and selectable items;
- The snap modes;
- The history of the selected lead object (visible by pressing the input and output buttons);
- The construction history flag;
- The render into a new window and IPR buttons;
- The Quick Selection field and Numeric Input field.

To collapse part of the shelf buttons:
- Press the small handle bar next to a button set.

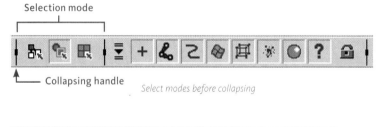

Selection mode

Collapsing handle

Select modes before collapsing

Select modes button collapsed

Hotbox

As you learned, tapping the spacebar quickly pops a pane between full-screen and its regular size, but if you press and hold the spacebar, you gain access to the hotbox.

The hotbox is a UI tool that gives you access to as much or as little of the Maya UI as you want. It appears where your cursor is located and offers the fastest access to tools and actions.

To access the hotbox:

* Press and hold the spacebar.

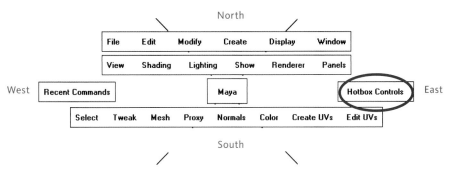

The hotbox with four quadrants marked

The hotbox offers a fully customizable UI element that provides you with access to all of the main menus as well as your own set of Marking Menus. Use the hotbox controls to display as many or as few menus as you need.

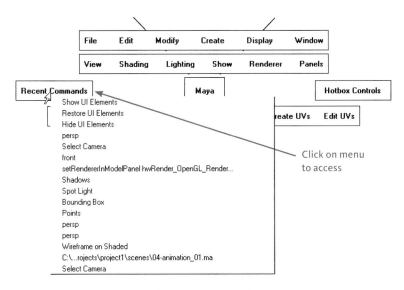

Accessing the recent commands menu

Hotbox Marking Menus

You can access Marking Menus in five areas of the hotbox. Since each of these areas can have a Marking Menu for each mouse button, it is possible to have fifteen menus in total. You can edit the content of the Marking Menus by going to the **Window** menu and selecting **Settings/ Preferences** → **Marking Menus...**

To access the center Marking Menu:

• Press the **spacebar**.

• **Click+drag** in the center area to access the desired menu.

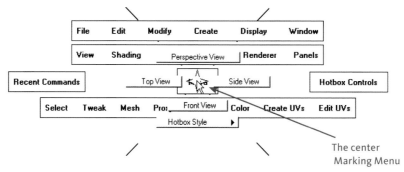

The center Marking Menu

To access the edge Marking Menus:

• Press the **spacebar**.

• **Click+drag** in either one of the north, south, east, or west quadrants to access the desired Marking Menu.

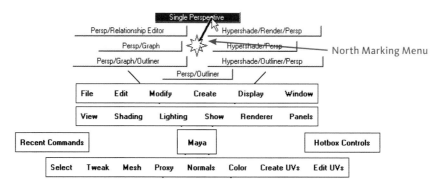

A quadrant-based Marking Menu

Customizing the hotbox

You can customize the hotbox to make it as simple or complex as you need. You can choose which menus are available and which are not.

If you want, you can reduce the hotbox to its essentials and focus on its Marking Menu capabilities.

A reduced hotbox layout

Alternatively, you could hide the other UI elements, such as panel menus, and use the hotbox to access everything. You get to choose which method works best for you.

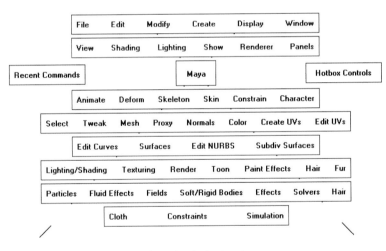

A complete hotbox layout

To customize the hotbox:

- Use the **Hotbox Controls**.

  OR

- Use the center Marking Menu.

- Choose an option from the **Hotbox Styles** menu.

Tool manipulators

To the left of the workspace you have access to important tools. These include the **Select, Move, Rotate, Scale and Show Manipulator** tools. Each of these is designed to correspond to a related hotkey that can be easily remembered using the **QWERTY** keys on your keyboard.

These tools will be used for your most common tool-based actions, like selecting and transforming.

QWERTY tool layout

Note: The Y key drives the last spot on the QWERTY palette, which is for the last tool used. The advantages of this will be discussed later in this lesson under the heading Tools and Actions.

Universal Manipulator

The **Universal Manipulator** lets you transform geometry in translation, rotation or scaling, both manually and numerically. A single click on any of the manipulators will display a numeric field allowing you to type in a specific value.

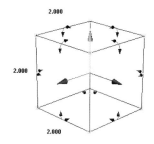

Universal manipulator

Soft Modification Tool

The **Soft Modification Tool** lets you push and pull geometry as a sculptor would on a sculpture. The amount of deformation is greatest at the center of the push/pull, and gradually falls off further away from the center. The corresponding action is **Deform → Soft Modification**.

Transform manipulators

One of the most basic node types in Maya is the *transform node*. This node contains attributes focused on the position, orientation and scale of an object. To help you interactively manipulate these nodes, there are three transform manipulators that make it easy to constrain along the main axes.

Each of the manipulators uses a color to indicate their axes. RGB is used to correspond to X, Y, Z. Therefore, red is for X, green for Y and blue for Z. Selected handles are displayed in yellow.

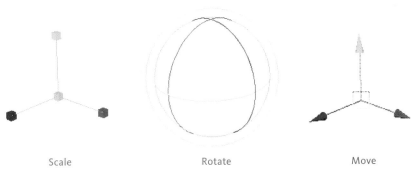

Scale   Rotate   Move

Transform manipulators

To explore some of the options available with manipulators, you will use the transform manipulator.

To use a transform manipulator in view plane:

- **Click+drag** on the center of the manipulator to move freely along all axes.

To constrain a manipulator along one axis:

- **Click+drag** on one of the manipulator handles.

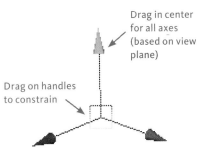

Drag in center for all axes (based on view plane)

Drag on handles to constrain

The move manipulator

To constrain a manipulator along two axes:

- Hold the **Ctrl** key and **click+drag** on the axis that is aligned with the desired plane of motion.

  This now fixes the center on the desired plane, thereby letting you **click+drag** *on the center so that you can move along the two axes. The icon at the center of the manipulator changes to reflect the new state.*

To go back to the default view plane center:

- Press the **Ctrl** key and click on the center of the transform manipulator.

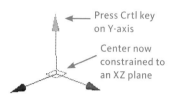

Press Crtl key on Y-axis

Center now constrained to an XZ plane

Working along two axes

> **Note:** *The ability to constrain in two axes at one time is available for the move and scale manipulators.*

Using the mouse buttons

You can interact directly with manipulators by using the left mouse button (**LMB**) to select objects.

The **MMB** is for the active manipulator and lets you **click+drag** without direct manipulation.

To select objects:

- Set up selection masks.
- Click with the **LMB**.

To select multiple objects:

- Use the **LMB** and **click+drag** a bounding box around objects.

To add objects to the selection:

- Press **Ctrl+Shift** while you select one or multiple objects.

To manipulate objects directly:

- **Click+drag** on a manipulator handle.

To manipulate objects indirectly:

- Activate a manipulator handle;

- **Click+drag** with the **MMB**.

Shift gesture

The manipulators allow you to work effectively in a Perspective view panel when transforming objects.

If you want to work more quickly when changing axes for your manipulators, there are several solutions available.

To change axis focus using hotkeys:

- Press and hold on the transform keys:

  w - for move;

  e - for rotate;

  r - for scale.

- Choose an axis handle for constraining from the Marking Menu.

To change axis focus using Shift key:

- Press the **Shift** key.

- **Click+drag** with the **MMB** in the direction of the desired axis.

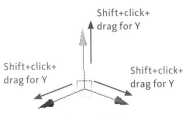

Transform manipulators

Set pivot

The ability to change the pivot location on a transform node is very important for certain types of animation.

Setting pivot using Insert / Home key

To change your pivot point:

- Select one of the manipulator tools;

- Press the **Insert** key
  (**Home** on Macintosh);

- **Click+drag** on the manipulator
  to move its pivot;

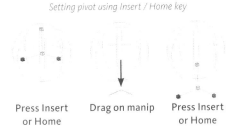

Press Insert   Drag on manip   Press Insert
or Home   or Home

- Press **Insert** to return to the manipulator tool (**Home** on Macintosh).

Channel Box

Another way of entering accurate values is through the *Channel Box*. This powerful panel gives you access to an object's transform node and any associated input nodes.

If you have multiple objects selected, then your changes to a channel will affect every node sharing that attribute.

To put one of the selected objects at the top of the Channel Box so that it is visible, choose the desired node from the Channel Box's **Object** menu.

If you want to work with a particular channel, you can use the **Channels** menu to set keys, add expressions and complete other useful tasks. You can also change the display of Channel Box names to short MEL-based names.

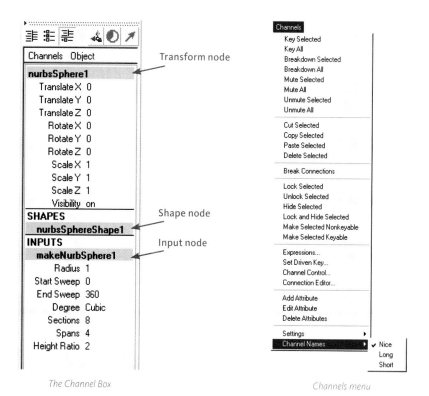

The Channel Box   Channels menu

Note: *To control what channels are shown in the Channel Box, go to the **Window** menu, and choose **General Editors** → **Channel Control**...*

Channel Box and manipulators

One of the features of the Channel Box is the way in which you can use it to access manipulators at the transform level.

By default, the Channel Box is set to show manipulators every time you tab into a new Channel Box field. You will notice that as you select the channel names such as Translate Z or Rotate X, the manipulator switches from translate to rotate.

One fast way to edit an attribute is to invoke the virtual slider by selecting the name of the desired channel in the Channel Box, then using the **MMB+drag** in a view panel to change its value.

There are three options for the Channel Box manipulator setting:

Default manipulator setting

This setting lets you activate the appropriate field in the Channel Box, and then modify the values with either the left or middle mouse button.

To use the default method, complete the following steps:

- Click on the desired channel name or input field, then **click+drag** directly on the active manipulator with the **LMB**.

  OR

- Click on the desired channel name or input field, then **click+drag** in open space with the **MMB**.

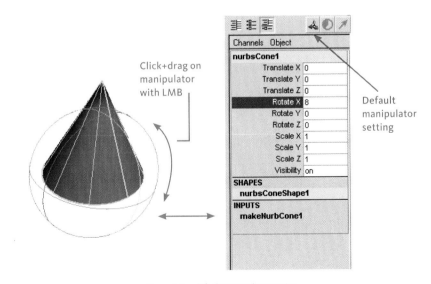

Channel Box default manipulator setting

No-manipulator setting

You can click on the manipulator icon over the Channel Box to turn manipulation off, which leaves the Channel Box focused on coordinate input. With this setting, you cannot use the middle or left mouse button for manipulation. To manipulate objects in this mode, you must do one of the following:

- Click in the channel's entry field and type the exact value.

  OR

- Use one of the normal transform tools such as **Move**, **Rotate** or **Scale**.

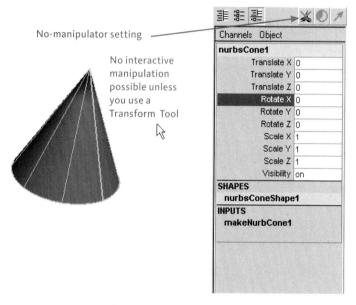

Channel Box no-manipulator setting

No-visual manipulator setting

A third option found on this manipulator button returns manipulator capability to the Channel Box – but now you will not see the manipulator on the screen.

- Click on the desired channel name or within the channel's input field.

- **Click+drag** in open space with the **MMB**.

  You can now use the two new buttons that let you edit the speed and dropoff of the manipulations.

No-visual manip setting

Click+drag in
open space with
mouse button

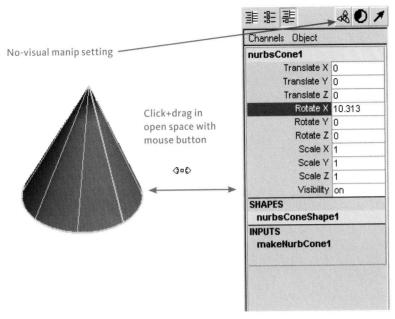

Channel Box no-visual manipulator setting

The first button that becomes available with
the No-visual setting is the **speed** button
which lets you **click+drag** with your **MMB**
either slow, medium or fast.

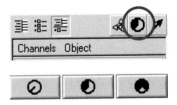

Channel speed controls

The second button is the **drop-off** button
which lets you choose between a linear
motion as you **click+drag** with the **MMB**, or
a **click+drag** that is slow at first and faster as
you drag further.

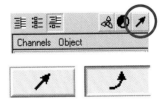

Channel drop-off options

Attribute Editor

If the Channel Box lets you focus on attributes that are keyable using **Set Key**, then the Attribute Editor gives you access to all the other attributes/channels.

The Attribute Editor is used for all nodes in Maya. This means that shaders, textures, surfaces, lattices, Render Globals, etc. can all be displayed in this one type of window.

To open the Attribute Editor window:

- Select a node.

- Go to the **Window** menu and select **Attribute Editor**.

To open the Attribute Editor panel:

- Select a node.

- Go to the **Display** menu and select **UI Elements → Attribute Editor**. The Channel Box is now replaced by an Attribute Editor panel.

When you open up the Attribute Editor, you get not only the active node, but also related nodes based on dependency relationships. In the example to the right, a sphere's transform, shape and *makeNurbsSphere* nodes are all present. These are the same input and shape nodes shown in the Channel Box.

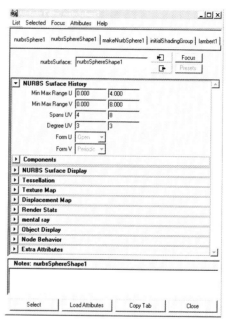

A typical Attribute Editor

Tip: You can also press the **Ctrl + a** *hotkey to open the Attribute Editor. You can set your preference for having the Attribute Editor in a panel or in its own window through* **Window → Settings/Preferences → Preferences...** *and click on the* **Interface** *section to modify the* **Open Attribute Editor** *option.*

Numeric Input

To add accurate values to your transformations, you can use the numeric input box. This allows you to apply exact values to the attributes associated with the current manipulator. You can use the Help Line to confirm your results.

To display the Help Line:

- From the **Display** menu, select
  UI Elements → **Help Line**.

Numeric input field

To change all values at once:

- Enter three values in a row, with spaces in-between.

> **Note:**   Beside the coordinate box is a button to toggle between absolute and relative values. Depending on which mode you are in, your transformation will happen either relative to your current object or as an absolute value.

To enter a value for the active manipulator:

- Click on the desired handle. (e.g. – Translate Z arrow).

- Enter a single value.

Inputting active manipulator value

> **Note:**   If no manipulator handle is active, then the single value will be applied to X.

To enter a value while preserving others:

- Type in periods [.] for channels that you want to stay the same. Remember to add spaces in-between.

- Enter a numeric value for the channels that will change.

Entering periods to keep values constant

The example below would keep the X and Y values constant and change only the Z information.

SELECTING

One of the most important tasks when working in Maya software is your ability to select different types of nodes and their key components.

For instance, you need to be able to select a sphere and move it, or you need to select the sphere's control vertices and move them. You also need to distinguish between different types of objects so that you can select only surfaces or only deformers.

Selection masks

To make selecting work, you have a series of selection masks available to you. This allows you to have one Select Tool that is then masked so that it can only select certain kinds of objects and components.

The selection mask concept is very powerful because it allows you to create whatever combination of selecting types that you desire. Sometimes, you only want to select joints and selection handles, or maybe you want to select anything but joints. With selection masks, you get to set-up and choose the select options.

The selection UI

The UI for selecting offers several types of access to the selection masks. You can learn all of them now and then choose which best suits your way of working down the line.

Grouping and parenting

When working with transform nodes, you can create more complex structures by building hierarchies of these node types.

To build these structures, you can choose to group the nodes under a new transform node, or you can parent one of the nodes under the other so that the lower node inherits the motion of the top node.

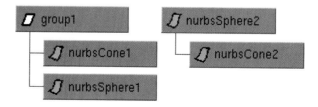

Grouped and parented nodes

Selection modes

At the top of the workspace, you have several selection mask tools available. These are all organized under three main types of select modes. Each type gives you access to either the hierarchy, object type, or components.

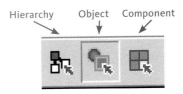

The select modes

Scene hierarchy mode

Hierarchy mode gives you access to different parts of the scene hierarchy structure. In the example shown below, the leaf node and the root node are highlighted. This mode lets you access each of these parts of the hierarchy. You can select root nodes, leaf nodes and template nodes using the selection masks.

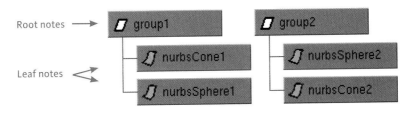

Hierarchy types

Object mode

Object mode lets you perform selections based on the object type. Selection masks are available as icons which encompass related types of objects.

With your **RMB**, you can access more detailed options that are listed under each mask group. If you create a partial list, the mask icon is highlighted in orange.

Object mode with selection masks

> **Tip:** *Once you choose selection masks, Maya gives priority to different object types. For instance, joints are selected before surfaces. You will need to use the* **Shift** *key to select these two object types together. To reset the priorities, select* **Window** → **Settings/Preferences** → **Preferences...** *and click on the* **Selection** *section to modify the* **Priority**.

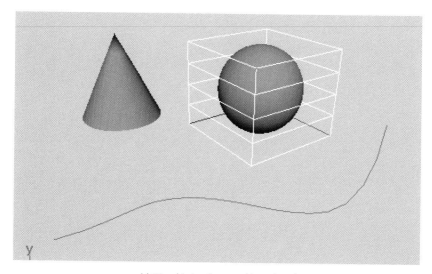

A lattice object and a curve object selected

Pop-up menu selection

When objects overlap in a view, the pop-up menu selection lets you display a pop-up list of the objects to select. **LMB** click the overlap area to display the menu. Your selection is highlighted in the scene viewports as you select an item in the list.

*   This option is disabled by default. To turn it on, select **Window** → **Settings/Preferences** → **Preferences...** and click on the **Selection** section to enable **Pick chooser**.

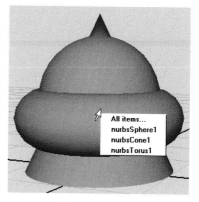

Selection pop-up menu

Component mode

The shape nodes of an object contain various components such as control vertices or isoparms. To access these, you need to be in Component mode.

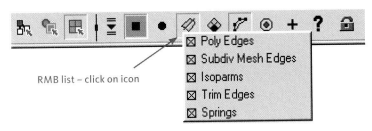

Component selection masks

When you select an object in this mode, it first highlights the object and shows you the chosen component type; you can then select the actual component.

Once you go back to Object mode, the object is selected and you can work with it. Toggling between Object and Component modes allows you to reshape and position objects quickly and easily.

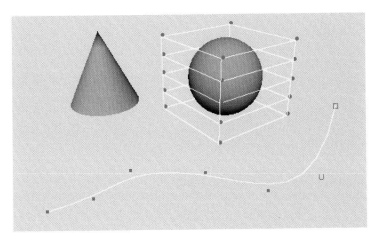

CV components and lattice point components

> **Tip:**   To toggle between Object and Component modes, press the **F8** key.

RMB select

Another way of accessing the components of an object is to select an object, then press the **RMB**. This brings up a Marking Menu that lets you choose from the various components available for that object.

If you select another object, you return to your previous select mask selection. This is a very fast way of selecting components when in hierarchy mode, or for components that are not in the current selection mask.

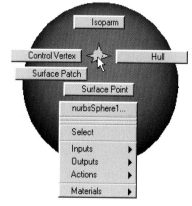

The RMB select menu

Combined select modes

In front of the selection mask mode icons is a pop-up menu that gives you different preset mask options. These presets let you combine different object and component level select options.

An example would be the NURBS option. This allows you to select various NURBS-based mask types such as surfaces, curves, CVs, curve control points and isoparms.

> **Note:** *In this mode, if you want to select CVs that are not visible by default, you must make them visible by going to the* **Display** *menu and selecting* **NURBS → CVs**.

When using a combined select mode, objects and components are selected differently. Objects are selected by **click+dragging** a select box around a part of the object while components can be selected with direct clicking.

> **Note:** *If you have CVs shown on an object and the select box touches any of them, you will select these components instead of the object. To select the object, you must drag the select box over part of the surface where there are no CVs.*

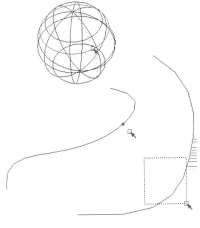

NURBS select options

TOOLS AND ACTIONS

In Maya, a large group of menu items let you act on your scenes in a number of ways. These menu items can be broken down into two types of commands: tools and actions, each working in their own particular manner. Almost every function can be set as a tool or action.

Tools

Tools are designed to remain active until you have finished using them. You select a tool, use it to complete a series of steps, then select another tool. In most cases, the Help line at the bottom of the workspace can be used to prompt your actions when using the tool.

Earlier you were introduced to the **y** key on the **QWERTY** toolbox. By default, this button is blank because it represents the last tool used. When you pick a tool from the menus, its icon inserts itself into the **QWERTY** menu.

As tool option:

- Pick a menu item and go to the options.

- Under the **Edit** menu, select **As Tool**.

  By default you will remain in this tool until you pick another tool. There is also an option that will deselect the tool after completion.

To return to the last tool used:

- Press the **y** key.

Actions

Actions follow a selection-action paradigm. This means that you first have to pick something and then act on it. This allows you to choose an action, return to editing your work and refine the results immediately.

Actions require that you have something selected before acting on it. This means that you must first find out what is required to complete the action.

To find out selection requirements of an action:

- Move your cursor over a menu item.

- Look at the Help line at the bottom-left of the interface.

  *If you have the Help Line UI element visible, the selection requirements are displayed. For instance, a **Loft** requires curves, isoparms or curves on surfaces while Insert Isoparm requires isoparms to be picked.*

To complete the action:

- If the tool is not already set as an action, select **Edit** → **As Action** from the menu item's options.

- Use either pick modes or the **RMB** pick menu to make the required selections.

- Choose the action using the hotbox, shelf or menus.

  The action is complete and the focus returns to your last transform tool.

Tip: *If a menu item contains the word "Tool" such as "Align Curves Tool" it uses tool interaction. If the word "Tool" is not mentioned, the menu item is set as an action. This dynamically updates according to your preferences.*

2D fillet as an action

A good example of a typical action is a 2D fillet. As with all actions, you must start with an understanding of what the tool needs before beginning to execute the action.

1 **Draw two curves**

- Select **Create** → **CV Curve Tool**.

- Place several points for one curve.

- Press **Enter** to complete.

- Press the **y** key to refocus on the Curve Tool.

- Draw the second curve so that it crosses the first.

- Press the **Enter** key to complete.

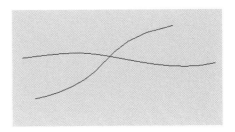

Two curves for filleting

2 **Find out 2D fillet requirements**

- In the **Surfaces** menu set, move your cursor over the **Edit Curves** → **Curve Fillet** menu item.

- Look in the Help line to determine what kind of pick is required.

  The Help line says: "Select curve parameter points".

3 **Pick the first curve point**

- Click on the first curve with the **RMB**.

- Pick **Curve Point** from the selection Marking Menu.

- Click on the curve to place the point on the side you want to keep.

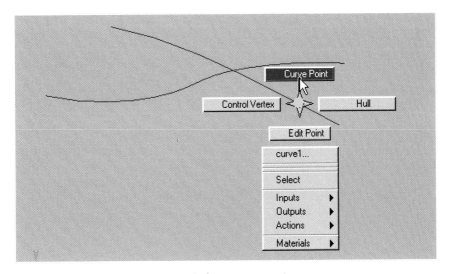

RMB pick of curve parameter point

4 Pick the second curve point

- Click on the second curve with the **RMB**.

- Pick **Curve Point** from the selection Marking Menu.

- Press the **Shift** key and click on the curve to place the point on the side of the curve you want to keep.

  The **Shift** *key lets you add a second point to the selection list without losing the first curve point.*

Note: *You must first use the Marking Menu and then the* **Shift** *key to add a second point to the selection list, otherwise the selection menu will not appear.*

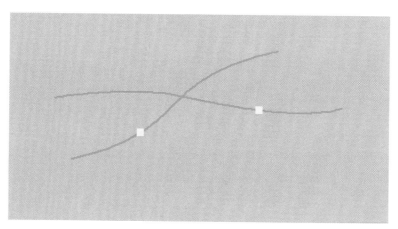

Two curve points in place

5 Fillet the curves

- Select **Edit Curves → Curve Fillet → ❑** to open the tool options.

- Turn the **Trim** option **On**.

- Click on the **Fillet** button.

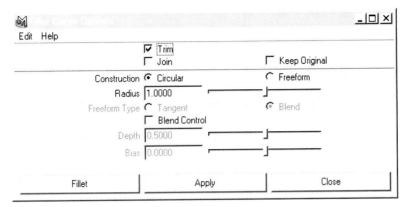

Fillet Tool options window

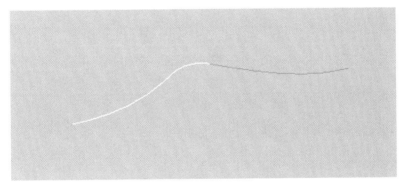

Final filleted curves

2D fillet as a tool

With this example you will use the menu item as a tool rather than an action.

1 **Draw two curves**

- In a new scene, draw two curves as in the last example.

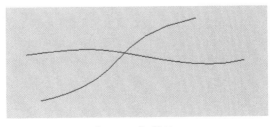

Two curves for filleting

2 **Change curve fillet to tool**

- Select **Edit Curves** → **Curve Fillet** → ❑.

- Select **Edit** → **As Tool** from the Options window.

- Set **Trim** to **On**.

- Press the **Fillet Tool** button.

Note: *Notice the menu item now says "Curve Fillet Tool".*

3 **Pick the first curve**

- Click with the **LMB** on the first curve.

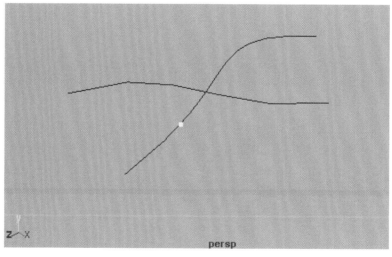

First curve selected

4 **Pick the second curve**

- Click with the **LMB** on the second curve.

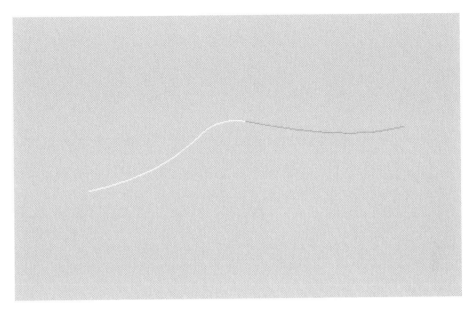

Final filleted curves

Conclusion

You now know how to navigate the Maya UI and how tools and actions work. The skills you learned here will be applied throughout the rest of this book and with your career. You have the knowledge now to determine how you want to use the interface. Experiment with the different techniques taught here as you work through the Learning Maya projects.

The instructions for the following projects will not specify whether or not you should use the hotbox or menus to complete an action. The choice will be yours.

In the next lesson, you will explore the Dependency Graph. You will learn about the different nodes and how to build them into hierarchies and procedural animations.

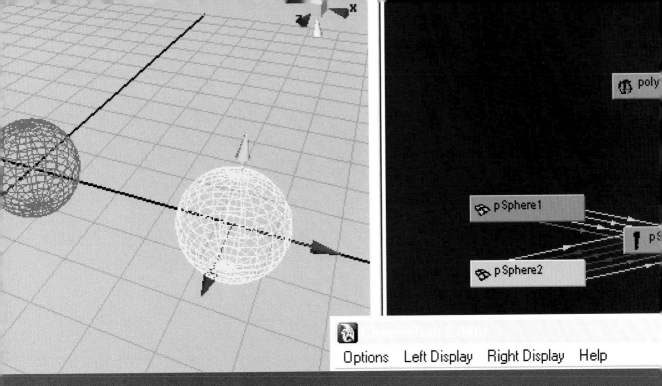

Lesson 06
The Dependency Graph

In the first five lessons of this book, you encountered many nodes that helped you animate and render your scene. You were introduced to input nodes, hierarchy nodes, shading networks and texture nodes. These nodes, among others, represent key elements within Maya – each node contains important attributes that help you define and animate your scenes.

In this lesson, you are going to explore nodes, attributes and connections by animating objects at various levels. You will explore how attributes are connected by Maya and how you can connect them yourself. You will also learn how to distinguish scene hierarchies from object dependencies.

This lesson might seem a bit abstract at first, but in the end you will see how the various nodes contribute to an animated scene that will help you in later lessons.

In this lesson you will learn the following:

- About hierarchies and dependencies;
- About connections;
- About construction history.

Maya architecture

The Maya architecture is defined by a node-based system, known as the Dependency Graph. Each node contains attributes that can be connected to other nodes. If you wanted to reduce Maya to its bare essentials, you could describe it as *nodes with attributes that are connected*. This node-based approach gives Maya its open and flexible procedural characteristics.

Hierarchies and dependencies

If you understand the idea of *nodes with attributes that are connected*, you will understand the Dependency Graph. Building a primitive sphere is a simple example involving the Dependency Graph.

1 Set-up your view panels

To view nodes and connections in a diagrammatic format, the Hypergraph panel is required along with a Perspective view.

- Select **Panels → Layouts → 2 Panes Side by Side**.

- Set-up a Perspective view in the first panel and a Hypergraph in the second panel.

- Dolly into the Perspective view to get closer to the grid.

2 Create a primitive sphere

- Select **Create → NURBS Primitives → Sphere**.

- Press **5** to turn on smooth shading.

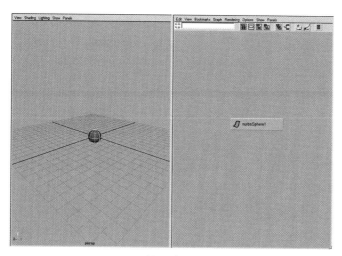

New sphere

3 View the shape node

In the Hypergraph panel, you are currently looking at the scene view. The scene view is focused on *transform nodes*. This type of node lets you set the position and orientation of your objects.

Right now, only a lone *nurbsSphere* node is visible. In actual fact, there are two nodes in this hierarchy, but the second is hidden by default. This hidden node is a *shape node* which contains information about the object itself.

- In the Hypergraph, select **Options** → **Display** → **Shape nodes**.

  You can now see the transform node which is, in effect, the positioning node, and the shape node which contains information about the actual surface of the sphere. The transform node defines the position of the shape below:

- In the Hypergraph panel, select **Options** → **Display** → **Shape nodes** to turn these **Off**.

  Notice that when these nodes are expanded, the Shape node and the Transform node have different icons.

  When collapsed, the Transform node takes on the Shape node's icon to help you understand what is going on underneath.

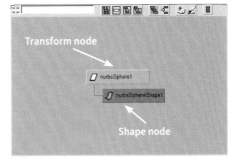

Transform and Shape nodes

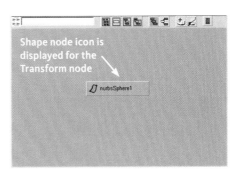

Transform node on its own

4 View the dependencies

To view the dependencies that exist with a primitive sphere, you need to take a look at the up and downstream connections.

- In the Hypergraph panel, click on the **Input and Output Connections** button.

  The original transform node is now separated from the shape node. While the transform node has a hierarchical relationship to the shape node, their attributes are not dependent on each other.

Lesson 06: The Dependency Graph

The input node called makeNurbsSphere is a result of the original creation of the sphere. The options set in the sphere's tool option window have been placed into a node that feeds into the shape node. The shape node is dependent on the input node. Changing values for the input node will affect the shape of the sphere.

You will also see the initial shading group connected to the sphere. This is the default grey lambert that is applied to all new objects.

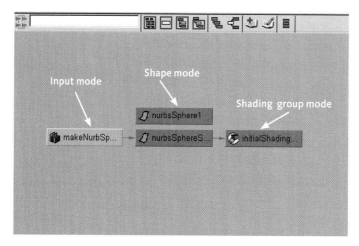

Sphere dependencies

5 Edit attributes in the Channel Box

In the Channel Box, you can edit attributes belonging to the various nodes. Every node type can be found in the Channel Box. This lets you affect both hierarchical relationships and dependencies.

If you edit an attribute belonging to the *makeNurbsSphere* node, then the shape of the sphere will be affected. If you change an attribute belonging to the *nurbsSphere* transform node, then the positioning will be altered. Use the Channel Box to help you work with the nodes.

- For the transform node, change the **Rotate Y** value to 45.

- For the *makeNurbsSphere* input node, change the **Radius** to 3.

Note: *You can set attribute values to affect either the scene hierarchy or the Dependency Graph.*

Shading group nodes

In earlier lessons, the word *node* was used a great deal when working with shading groups. In fact, shading group nodes create dependency networks that work the same way as Shape nodes.

1 Create a shading network

When you create a material, it automatically has a shading group connected to it.

- Select **Window** → **Rendering Editors** → **Hypershade...**

- In the Hypershade window, select **Create** → **Materials** → **Phong**.

- **Assign** this material to the sphere.

- Select the sphere in the Perspective panel and click on the **Input and Output Connections** button.

In the Hypergraph view, you will notice how the input node is connected to the Shape node which relates to the phong shading group.

A line is now drawn between the sphere's Shape node and shading group node. This is because the shading group is dependent on the surface in order to render.

Every time you assign a shading network to an object, you make a Dependency Graph connection.

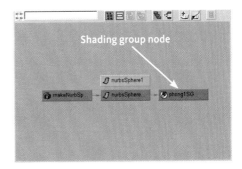

Shading group dependencies

- Select the *nurbsSphere1* node and the *phong1SG* node in the Hypergraph.

- Again, click on the **Input and Output Connections** button.

You can now see how the phong material node and the sphere's Shape node both feed the shading group. You can move your cursor over any of the connecting lines to see the attributes that are being connected.

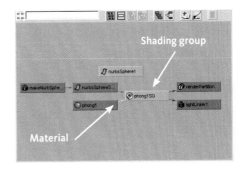

Assigned shading group

2 Open the Attribute Editor

You have seen how the nodes in the Hypergraph and Channel Box have been used to view and edit attributes on connected nodes. Now you will see how the Attribute Editor displays nodes, attributes and connections.

- Click on the **Scene Hierarchy** button in the Hypergraph panel to go back to a scene view.

- Select the *sphere*'s Transform node.

- Press **Ctrl+a** to open the Attribute Editor.

In this integral window, you will see several tabs, each containing groups of attributes. Each tab represents a different node. All the tabs displayed represent parts of the selected node's Dependency Graph that are related to the chosen node. By bringing up several connected nodes, you have easier access to particular parts of the graph.

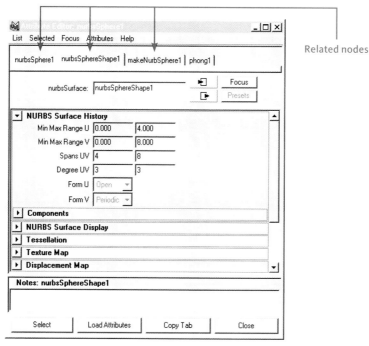

Nodes and attributes in Attribute Editor

> **Note:** *The Attribute Editor lets you focus on one part of the Dependency Graph at a time.*

Making connections

To help you understand exactly what a Dependency Graph connection is, you are going to make your own connection and see how it affects the graph.

1 Open the Connection Editor

- Select the *sphere*.

- Select **Window** → **General Editors** → **Connection Editor...**

- Click on the **Reload Left** button.

  The selected Transform node is loaded into the left column. All of the attributes belonging to this node are listed.

Note: *There are more attributes here than you see in the Channel Box. The Channel Box only shows attributes that have been set as keyable. Other attributes can be found in the Attribute Editor.*

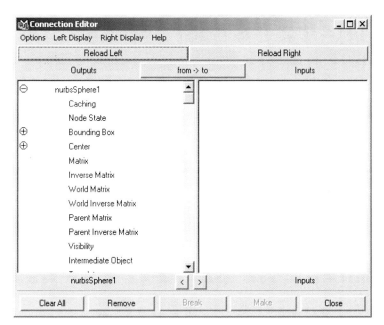

Transform node in Connection Editor

2 Add phong as the output node

- In the Hypergraph, select **Rendering** → **Show Materials**.

- Select the *phong1* material node.

- In the Connection Editor, click on the **Reload Right** button.

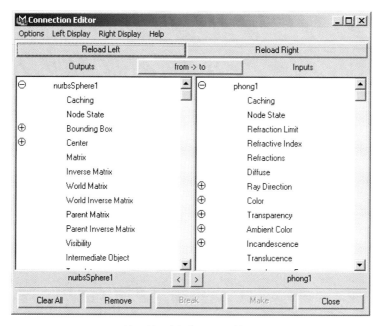

Material node in Connection Editor

3 Make connections

You will now connect some attributes in from the Transform node to the Material node.

- In the left column, scroll down until you find the *Translate* attributes.

- Click on the **plus (+)** sign to expand this multiple attribute and see the *Translate X, Y* and *Z* attributes.

- In the right column, scroll down until you find the *Color* attribute.

- Click on the **plus (+)** sign to expand this multiple attribute and see the *Color R, G* and *B* attributes.

- Click on the **Translate X** attribute in the left column.

- Click on the **Color R** in the right column.

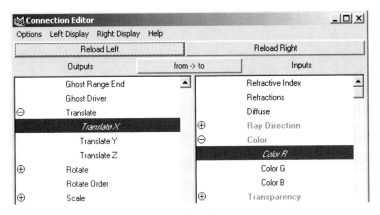

Connected attributes

- Use the same method to connect the following attributes:

  Translate Y to **Color G**;

  Translate Z to **Color B**.

4 **View the connections**

- In the Hypergraph panel, select the *phong1* node and click on the **Input and Output Connections** button.

- Move your cursor over one of the arrow connections between the Transform node and Material node.

The connection arrow is highlighted and the connected attributes are displayed. You now see the diagrammatic results of your action.

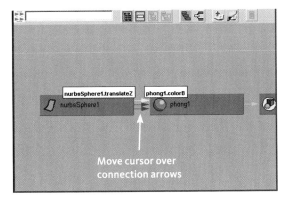

Viewing attribute connections

5 Move the sphere

You should see the effect of your connections when moving the sphere in the Perspective view.

- In the Perspective view, select the *sphere*.

- **Move** the sphere along the **X-axis**.

  The color of the sphere changes to red. By increasing the value of the translation along X, you add red to the color.

- Try moving the sphere along each of the three main axes to see the colors change.

Adding a texture node

While it is a fun and educational exercise to see the material node's color dependent on the position of the ball, it may not be very realistic. You will now break the existing connections and map a texture node in their place.

1 Delete connections

You can delete the connections in the Hypergraph view.

- In the Hypergraph view panel, select one of the three connection arrows between the Transform node and the Material node.

- Press the **Backspace** or **Delete** key to delete the connection.

- **Repeat** for the other two connections between these nodes.

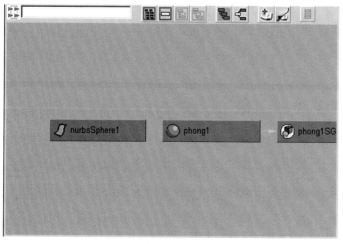

Broken connections

2 Add a checker texture map

You will now use the Attribute Editor to help add a texture to the existing shading group.

- Click on the *phong1* material node.

- Press **Ctrl+a** to open the Attribute Editor.

- Click on the **Map** button next to **Color**.

- Choose a **Checker** texture from the **Create Render Node** window.

- **MMB** in the Perspective view to make it active and press **6**.

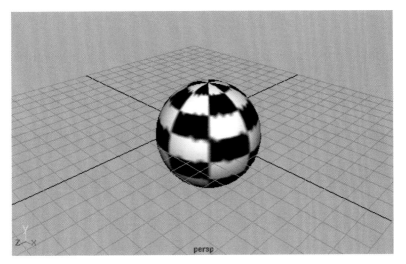

Textured sphere

In the Hypergraph, you can see the dependencies building up for the shading group. The texture is built using two nodes: the checker node, which contains procedural texture attributes, and the placement node, which contains attributes that define the placement of the texture on the assigned surfaces.

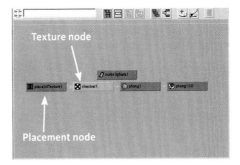

Shading group network

Animating the sphere

When you animate, you are changing the value of an attribute over time. You use keys to set these values at important points in time, then tangent properties to determine how the attribute value changes in-between the keys.

The key and tangent information is placed in a separate animation curve node that is then connected to the animated attribute.

1 Select the sphere

- In the Hypergraph panel, click on the **Scene Hierarchy** button.

- Select the *nurbsSphere* Transform node.

2 Return the sphere to the origin

Since you moved the sphere along the three axes earlier, it's a good time to set it back to the origin.

- Select the sphere's **Translate** attributes through the Channel Box by clicking on the **Translate X** value and dragging to the **Translate Z** value.

  Doing so will highlight all three translate values, allowing you to enter a single value to change all of them at once.

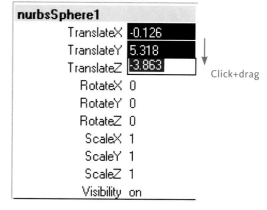

Click+drag on the translation values

- In the Channel Box, type **o** and hit **Enter**.

  Make sure all three translation values changed simultaneously.

- Make sure to also set all **Rotate** values to **o** and all **Scale** values to **1**.

3 Animate the sphere's rotation

- In the Time Slider, set the playback range to **120** frames.

- Go to frame **1**.

- Click on the **Rotate Y** attribute name in the Channel Box.

- Click with your **RMB** and select **Key Selected** from the pop-up menu.

  This sets a key at the chosen time.

- Go to frame **120**.

- In the Channel Box, change the **Rotate Y** attribute to **720**.

- Click with your **RMB** and select **Key selected** from the pop-up menu.

- **Playback** the results.

  The sphere is now spinning.

4 View the dependencies

- In the Hypergraph panel, click on the **Input and Output Connections** button.

  You see that an animation curve node has been created and then connected to the Transform node. The Transform node is shown as a trapezoid to indicate that it is now connected to the animation curve node. If you move the mouse cursor over the connection arrow, you will see that the connection is to Rotate Y.

  If you select the animation curve node and open the Attribute Editor, you will see that each key has been recorded along with value, time and tangent information. You can actually edit this information here, or use the Graph Editor where you get more visual feedback.

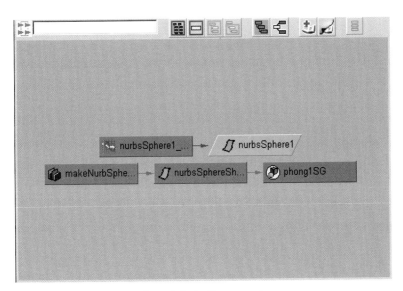

Connected animation curve node

Procedural animation

If the Maya procedural nature is defined as *nodes with attributes that are connected*, then a procedural animation would be set-up by animating attributes at various levels of a Dependency Graph network.

You will now build a series of animated events that build on each other to create the final result.

1 Create an edit point curve

- Hide everything in your scene by selecting **Display** → **Hide** → **All**.

- Select **Create** → **EP Curve Tool**.

- Press and hold the **x** hotkey to turn on grid snap.

- Draw a curve as shown below:

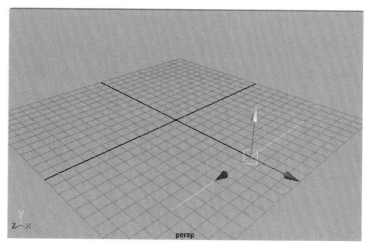

New curve

- When you are finished, press **Enter** to finalize the curve.

- Select **Modify** → **Center Pivot**.

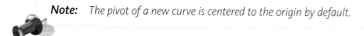

Note: *The pivot of a new curve is centered to the origin by default.*

2 **Duplicate the curve**

- Select **Edit → Duplicate**.

- **Move** the new curve to the opposite side of the grid.

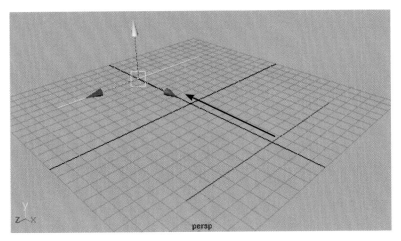

Moved curve

3 **Create a lofted surface**

A lofted surface can be created using two or more profile curves.

- **Click+drag** a selection box around both of the curves.

- Select **Surfaces → Loft**.

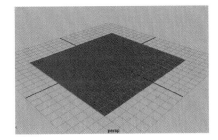

Lofted surface

4 **Change your panel display**

- In the Hypergraph panel, select **Panels → Perspective → persp**.

- In the Perspective panel, select **Show → None** and then **Show → NURBS Curves**.

Now you have two Perspective views. One shows the surface in Shaded mode and the second shows only the curves. This makes it easier to pick and edit the curves in isolation from the surface itself.

5 Edit CVs on the original curves

- Select the first curve.

- Click with your **RMB** to bring up the selection Marking Menu and select **Control Vertex**.

- **Click+drag** a selection box over one of the CVs and **Move** it down.

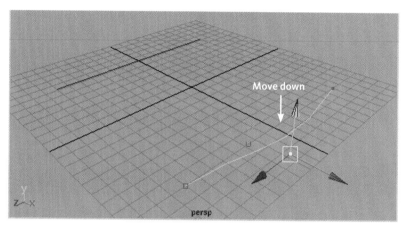

Edited profile curve

In the original Perspective view, you can see the effect on the lofted surface. Since the surface was dependent on the shape of the curve, you again took advantage of the Dependency Graph.

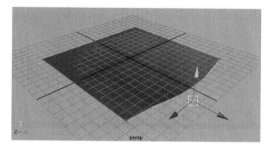

Resulting surface update

Note: The dependencies associated with models are sometimes referred to as construction history. By updating the input shape, you have, in effect, updated the history of the lofted surface.

Curve on surface

You will now build a curve directly onto the surface. This curve will become dependent on the shape of the surface for its own shape.

The surface was built as a grid of surface lines called *isoparms*. These lines help define a separate coordinate system specific to each surface. Whereas world space coordinates are defined by X, Y and Z, surface coordinates are defined by U and V.

1   Make the surface live

So far, you have drawn curves into the world space coordinate system. You can also make any surface into a *live* surface and draw into the UV space of the surface.

- Select the lofted surface.

  The CVs on the curve disappear and you are able to focus on the surface.

- Select **Modify → Make Live**.

  Live surface display changes to a green wireframe.

- Select **Display → Grid** to turn off the ground grid.

2   Draw a curve on the surface

- Select **Create → EP Curve Tool**.

- **Draw** a curve on the live surface.

3   Move the Curve on Surface

- Press the **Enter** key to complete the curve.

New Curve on Surface

- Select the **Move Tool**.

  The move manipulator looks a little different this time. Rather than three manipulator handles, there are only two. One is for the U direction of the surface and the other is for the V direction.

- **Click+drag** on the manipulator handles to move the curve around the surface space.

Moving the Curve on Surface

Tip: *This UV space is the same one used by texture maps when using 2D placement nodes.*

4 Revert live surface

- Click in empty space to clear the selection.

- Select **Modify** → **Make Not Live**.

  With nothing selected, any live surfaces are reverted back to normal surfaces.

Tip: *You can also use the **Make Live** button on the right of the snap icons in the Status bar.*

Group hierarchy

You are now going to build a hierarchy by grouping two primitives, then animating the group along the Curve on Surface using path animation.

1 Create a primitive cone

- Select **Create** → **NURBS Primitives** → **Cone**.

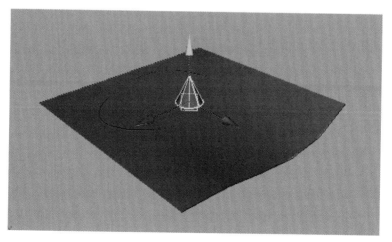

New primitive cone

2 Create a primitive sphere

- Select **Create** → **NURBS Primitives** → **Sphere**.

- **Move** the sphere above the cone.

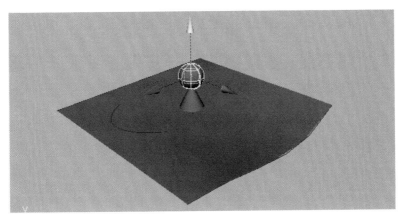

Second primitive object

3 Group the two objects

- Select the cone and the sphere.

- Select **Edit** → **Group** or use the **Ctrl + g** hotkey.

- Select **Display** → **Transform Display** → **Selection Handles**.

  The selection handle is a special marker that will make it easier to pick the group in Object selection mode.

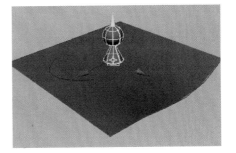

Grouped objects with selection handle

Note: *Selection handles have higher selection priority than curves and surfaces.*

Path animation

To animate the new group, you will attach it to the Curve on Surface. You can use the Curve on Surface to define the group's position over time.

1 **Attach to the Curve on Surface**

- With the group still selected, press the **Shift** key and select the Curve on Surface.

- Go to the **Animation** menu set.

- Select **Animate** → **Motion Paths** → **Attach to Motion Path** → **❐**.

- In the Option window, make sure that the **Follow** option is turned **Off**.

- Click **Attach**.

- **Playback** the results.

  As the group moves along the path curve, you will notice that it is always standing straight up.

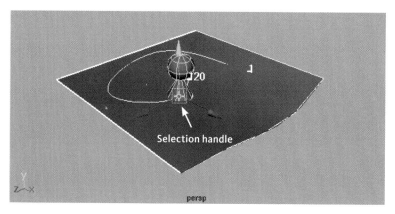

Path animation

2 **Constrain to the surface normal**

You will now constrain the orientation of the group to the normal direction of the lofted surface. The normal is like the third dimension of the surface's UV space.

- Click on the loft surface to select it on its own.

- Press the **Shift** key and select the grouped primitives using the selection handle.

- Select **Constrain** → **Normal** → **❐**.

- In the Option window, set the following:

  Aim Vector to 0, 1, 0;

  Up Vector to 1, 0, 0.

- Click **Add** to create the constraint.

- **Playback** the results.

Note: *If your group is upside down, it could be because the surface normals are reversed. To fix this, select your plane and select* **Edit NURBS → Reverse Surface Direction***.*

Now the group is orienting itself based on the normal direction of the surface. The group is dependent on the surface in two ways. Firstly, its position is dependent on the path curve, which is dependent on the surface for its shape. Secondly, its orientation is directly dependent on the surface's shape.

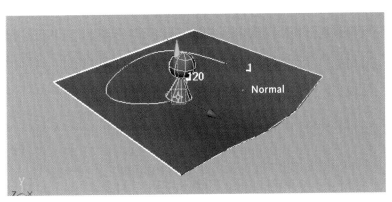

Constrained orientation

Layer the animation

The various parts of the Dependency Graph can all be animated to create exciting results. To see the Dependency Graph in motion, you will animate different nodes within the network to see how the dependencies react.

1 Edit the loft curve shape

Since the shape of the surface is dependent on the original loft curves, you will start by animating the shape of the second curve.

• Select the second loft curve.

Tip: *You may want to use the second Perspective panel, which is only displaying curves.*

• Click with your **RMB** to bring up the selection Marking Menu and select **Control Vertex**.

Control vertices define the shape of the curve. By editing these, you are editing the curve's shape node.

• **Click+drag** a selection box over one of the CVs and **Move** it up to a new position.

As you move the CV, the surface updates its shape, which in turn redefines the Curve on Surface and the orientation of the group. All the dependencies are being updated.

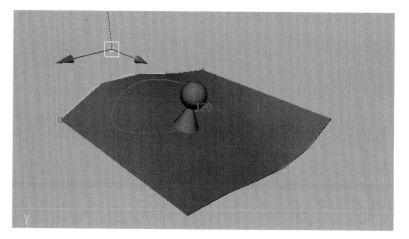

Updating the dependencies

2 Set keys on the CV position

• Go to frame **1**.

• Press **s** to set key.

- Go to frame **120**.

- Press **s** to set key.

- Go to frame **60**.

- **Move** the CV to a new position.

- Press **s** to set key.

- **Playback** the results.

  You can see how the dependency updates are maintained as the CV is animated. You are animating the construction history of the lofted surface and the connected path animation.

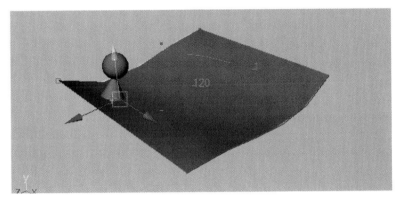

Animated history

3 Animate the Curve on Surface

To add another layer of animation, you will key the position of the Curve on Surface.

- Select the Curve on Surface.

- Go to frame **1**.

- Press **s** to set key.

- Go to frame **120**.

- **Move** the Curve on Surface to another position on the lofted surface.

- Press **s** to set key.

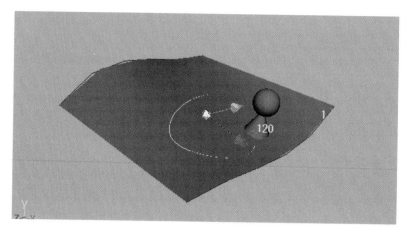

Animated Curve on Surface

4 Assign the phong shading group

To make it easier to see the animating objects, apply the checker shading group created earlier to the primitive group.

- Select the primitive group using its selection handle.

- Go to the **Rendering** menu set.

- Select **Lighting/Shading** → **Assign Existing Material** → **phong1**.

- **Playback** the scene.

5 View the dependencies

Of course, you can view the dependency network that results from all these connections in the Hypergraph view, which will probably be a bit more complex than anything you have seen so far.

- Select the primitive group that is attached to the motion path.

- Open the Hypergraph panel and click on the **Input and Output Connections** button.

  The resulting network contains the various dependencies that you built during this example.

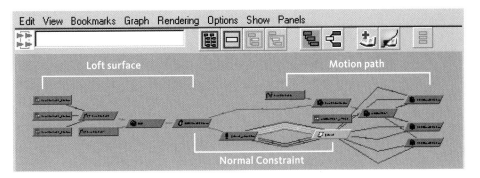

The dependency network

Conclusion

The procedural qualities of Maya are tied to how the Dependency Graph uses nodes, attributes and connections. You can see how deep these connections can go and how they are maintained throughout the animation process. Similar techniques can be used on other node types throughout Maya.

Obviously, you don't have to use the Hypergraph and the Connection Editor to build, animate and texture map your objects. But, in most cases, you will be thinking more about the motion of your character's walk or the color of their cheeks. In this way, it is a good idea to know that the Dependency Graph supports everything you do and can always be used to your advantage.

In the next project, you will model, texture, set-up and animate a bear character.

Project o2

The model is duplicated as a mirrored instance. An instanced object uses the exact same geometry as the original object, except that it can have a different position, rotation and scaling in space. Any adjustments done on one side will simultaneously be done on the other side.

The model with instance

7 **Save your work**

• Save your scene as *07-boog_02.ma*.

Refine the head

Perhaps the most important part of the character is the face. This exercise will go through some steps in order to refine the head, but most of the work will have to be done by yourself, since this is an artistic task.

Several new tools will be explained here with some key examples that will require experimentation. If you would like to use the final scene of this exercise as a reference, look for the scene *07-boog_03.ma* in the support files.

1 Delete the construction history

After all the operations done thus far on the model, the construction history list is starting to look impressive, but also useless. Now is a good time to delete the history on your model. This also deletes history from the entire scene.

- Select **Edit → Delete All by Type → History**.

2 Offset Edge Loop Tool

The head is now very simplistic and the first step is to add more geometry to play with. You will add several edge loops for the neck and head.

- With the *body* geometry selected, select **Edit Mesh → Offset Edge Loop Tool**.

  This tool allows you to simply add two edge loops on either side of an existing edge loop.

- **Click+drag** on any horizontal edge at the top of the neck.

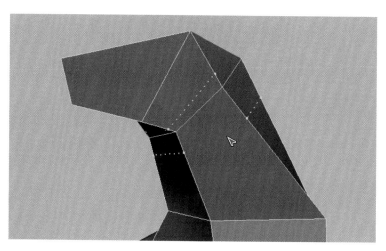

Offset edge loop

- **Release** the mouse button to execute the tool and insert the new edges.

3 Delete edges

If you need to delete edges, it is possible to simply select them and press the delete key on your keyboard. However, working this way leaves vertices on the perpendicular edges that are not wanted. In order to compensate for this, there is a specialized command that can be used to correctly delete edges and vertices.

- Select **Select → Select Edge Loop Tool**.

This tool requires you to double-click on an edge in order to select its related edge loop.

- **Deselect** any edges by clicking in an empty space in the viewport.

- **Double-click** on one of the edges from which you used the offset command in the last step.

  The entire edge loop is selected.

- Select **Edit Mesh → Delete Edge/Vertex**.

The entire edge loop is properly deleted.

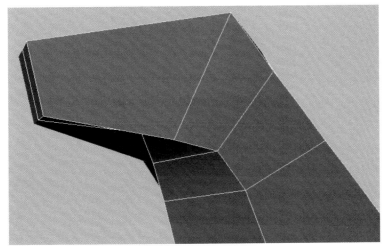

The deleted edge loop

4 Insert an edge loop

There are several ways to access the different modeling commands other than with the menus. If you like working with the menus, keep doing so, but following is an alternative that involves a hotkey and a Marking Menu.

- **Deselect** any edges from the *body* geometry.

- **Choose** one of the vertical edges from the lower part of the neck.

- Hold down the **Ctrl** key and then **RMB** on the geometry.

  This brings up a polygonal modeling Marking Menu.

- From the Marking Menu, select **Edge Ring Utilities**.

  Doing so automatically pops a second Marking Menu related to edge rings.

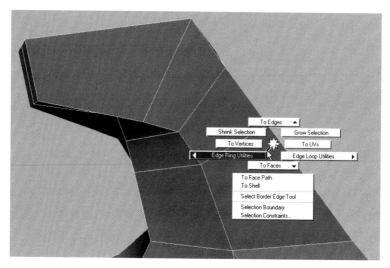

The modeling Marking Menu

- Select **To Edge Ring and Split**.

  The command automatically selects the related edge ring about the chosen edge, and then does a split on those edges.

5 Insert more edge loops

- **Insert** two more vertical **edge loops** on the nose of the character.

6 Split polygons

Notice that when you use the Insert Edge Loop Tool, the tool keeps splitting polygonal faces with four sides. If it encounters polygonal faces with more or less than 4 sides, the tool stops splitting more edges. This can be very useful, but it can also go through your entire character before it stops splitting edges. In order for you to control how many edges are split, the tool has an option that allows you to choose the start and end edge to split. Following is an example of such an application:

- Select **Edit Mesh** → **Insert Edge Loop Tool**.

- **Click** on one of the vertical edges on the side of the character's head.

- **Undo** the last operation.

- **Double-click** on the **Insert Edge Loop Tool** in the bottom portion of the Toolbox or select **Edit Mesh** → **Insert Edge Loop Tool** → ❒.

The Split Tool splits the entire character

- In the shown window, turn **Off** the **Auto Complete** option.
- Click the **Close** button.
- **Click** the central vertical edge on the tip of the nose.

  The tool now requires you to choose subsequent edges in order to define an edge loop.

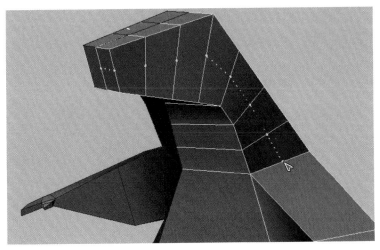

The solved edge loop

- **Choose** the edge at the base of the neck.

  The tool displays the solved edge loop.

> **Note:** *You can keep selecting other edges to define a longer edge loop. The edges do not need to be part of the same edge ring.*

- Hit the **Enter** key when you are ready to insert the proposed edge loop.

7 Tweak the head vertices

There is now much more geometry to refine in the head area. This is where the artistic work comes in, and where you must use your own judgment to define the head to your liking. In the following, you will use different options in the Subdiv Proxy command.

- **Delete** the instanced geometry.

- Select the *body* geometry.

- Select **Proxy → Subdiv Proxy → □**.

- Set the following in the option window:

  Mirror Behavior to **Full**;

  Mirror Direction to **–X**;

  Merge Vertex Tolerance to **0.1**.

  Since your geometry has been split in half, setting this option will automatically make a mirrored and merged geometry.

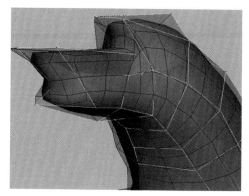

- Click the **Smooth** button.

- Select the proxy geometry.

- Go in Component mode with vertices enabled.

- **Tweak** the head vertices as follows:

8 Save your work

- Save your scene as *07-boog_03.ma*.

The refined head

Keep on modeling

You now have a good understanding of polygonal modeling basics. By continuing to refine the bear character, you will see that the time spent experimenting will provide invaluable experience. Throughout the modeling process, you can get into trial and error processes that will eventually achieve great solutions. At some point, you will be able to visualize the different steps to take without ever touching the model.

Following are some general directions to finish modeling the head of the character. To see the final scene of this exercise, look for the scene *07-boog_04.ma* in the support files.

1   Removing the proxy

The proxy geometry is a great way to create a general shape for your character, but at some point, you will need to refine the smoothed version. Proxy geometry will need to be deleted when refining the higher resolution model.

The high resolution model

- Select **Edit** → **Delete All by Type** → **History.**

  Doing so removes any history between the proxy and smooth geometry.

- Select the *body* proxy geometry and its mirrored instance, and then hit the **Delete** key.

- **Rename** the high resolution geometry to *body.*

2   Tweak the vertices

Now that you have more vertices defining your character, you can play with the shape of the bear.

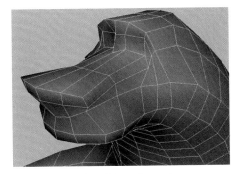

High resolution refinements

Tip: *Don't be afraid of moving vertices one by one. You will most likely end up moving each vertex by hand for the entire model anyway.*

While you are tweaking the vertices around the eyes, nose, mouth and ears, try to delimiter the different facial areas with edges. Doing so will help to see the different parts of the face, and it will also make it easier to split polygons to get even more resolution.

3 Add divisions

You must now concentrate on splitting and refining only one half of the model. Consider deleting half the model and creating another mirrored instance as shown previously.

• Using the **Split Polygon Tool**, insert new edges where required in order to better define certain areas.

Tip: *As a rule, try to always create four-sided polygons when splitting geometry. Doing so will spare you problems later on.*

4 Extrusions

• **Extrude** faces to create the nostrils.

• **Extrude** faces to create the ears.

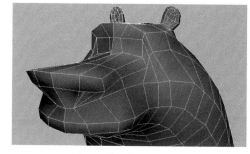

The nostril and ear extrusions

5 Soft normals

The extrusion and polygon splits create hard edges by default.

The following shows how to soften polygonal normals.

• With the *body* geometry selected, select **Normals → Soften Edges.**

Soft and hard edges comparison

6 Mouth

For simplicity reasons, you will not
see how to model the inner mouth
in this lesson. Instead, concentrate
on modeling the lips in order to
clearly define the mouth.

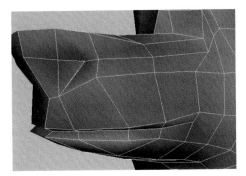

The mouth

7 Merging the model

At this point, you can continue
refining the model, or call it final and
go on with the rest of the project. The
following shows how to mirror and
merge the actual geometry in order
to create a final complete body.

- **Delete** the instanced geometry.

- Select the *body* geometry.

- Select **Mesh** → **Mirror Geometry** → ❑.

- In the options, specify the Mirror Direction to be **–X.**

- Click the Mirror button.

  The geometry is mirrored and then merged together to create a full body.

8 Merging edges

It is possible that through the process
of modeling, you moved central vertices
off the mirror plane, causing the
geometry to have opened edges
along the central axis. The following
shows how to merge those edges:

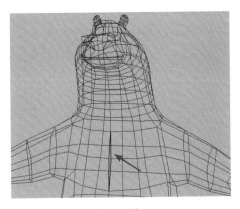

An open edge

- Select the *body* geometry.

- Select **Display** → **Polygons** →
  Border Edges.

  *Doing so causes border edges to be
  displayed with a thicker wireframe line.*

- Press **4** to see your model in
  wireframe.

- Select **Edit Mesh** → **Merge Edge Tool**.

  This tool allows you to choose two edges and force them to merge together.

- **Choose** any of the opened thicker edges.

  Possible edges to be merged with are highlighted in pink.

- **Choose** the pink edge located on the other half of the model.

- Hit **Enter** to merge the edges.

  The edges should not be closed.

- **Repeat** the previous steps for any other open edges.

9 **Final steps**

- With the *body* geometry selected, select **Normals** → **Soften Edges**.

- Select **Edit** → **Delete All by Type** → **History**.

10 **Save your work**

- Save your scene as *07-boog_04.ma.*

Proportions

Sometimes when modeling, you sit back and look at your work thinking you could improve the proportions of the model. An easy way to change a model's proportions is to create and modify a lattice deformer. A lattice surrounds a deformable object with a structure of points that can be manipulated to change the object's shape. Once you are happy with the new proportions, you can simply delete the history, thus freezing the deformations on the models.

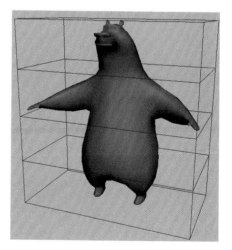

The lattice deformer

1 **Create a lattice deformer**

- Select the *body* geometry.

- From the **Animation** menu set, select **Deform** → **Create Lattice**.

  A large lattice box is created around your model.

- In the Channel Box with the lattice selected, set the *ffd1LatticeShape* node as follows:

  S Divisions to 5;

  T Divisions to 5;

  U Divisions to 3.

  Doing so will change the amount of subdivisions in the lattice deformer, which in turn adds more lattice points to deform the surface with. This will allow more control over the deformations.

Tip: *You may adjust those settings to better fit your geometry and divide the model into body part sections.*

2   Deform the lattice box

- **RMB** on the lattice object in the viewport to bring up the lattice context menu and select **Lattice Point**.

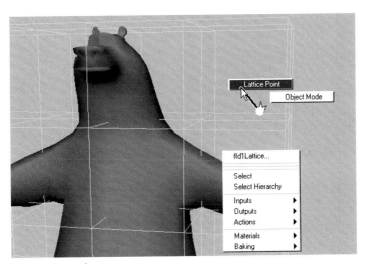

The lattice context menu

- Select lattice points and **transform** them just like you would do with vertices.

  Notice how the lattice points deform the geometry.

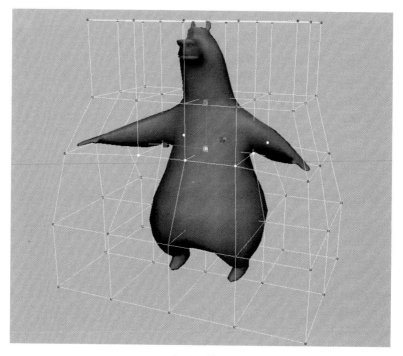

Lattice effect

- Find the best proportions possible.

Tip: *This is a good time to place the character's feet on the world grid, if they are not already. Also, make sure to place the model's center of gravity centered on the Z and X-axes.*

3 Delete the deformer

If you would simply delete the lattice deformer, the geometry would snap right back to its original shape. In order to keep the deformation and freeze the geometry with that shape, you need to delete its history, which will automatically delete the deformer.

- Select the body geometry.

- Select **Edit** → **Delete by Type** → **History.**

Final touches

The body of the bear looks great, but Boog is still missing key components such as eyes and claws. Those objects will be created starting from NURBS primitives.

Just like the rest of this lesson, you will model only half the geometry and then mirror it over to the other side.

1   **Eyeball**

- Select **Create** → **NURBS Primitives** → **Sphere**.

- **Rename** the sphere to *eyeball*.

- **Translate** and **scale** the *eyeball* to the proper eye location.

- **Rotate** the *eyeball* by **90** degrees on its **X-axis**.

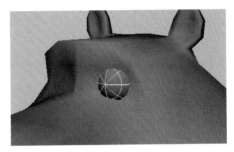

The eyeball in place

2   **Eyelid**

- With the *eyeball* selected, select **Edit** → **Duplicate Special** → ❑.

- In the shown window, select **Edit** → **Reset Settings**, then turn on the **Duplicate input graph** option.

  This option duplicates the geometry along with all its inputs, such as construction history, which will be used here.

- Click the **Duplicate Special** button.

- **Rename** the duplicate to *eyelid*.

- From the Channel Box, **rotate** the eyelid by **-90** degrees on its **Y-axis**.

- **Scale** the *eyelid* so that it is a little bigger than the *eyeball*.

- In the Channel Box, highlight the *makeNurbsSphere2* input node.

- Set the **Start Sweep** to **20** and the **End Sweep** to **340**.

  The eyelid will use its construction history in order to simplify the eye blinks.

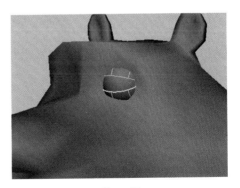

The eyelid

3 Claws

- **Create** a NURBS cone primitive.

- Set the makeNurbsCone input node as follows from the Channel Box:

  Radius to 0.2;

  Sections to 4;

  Spans to 2;

  Height Ratio to 10.

- **Rename** the cone to *claw1*.

- **Place** and **tweak** the claw's shape as in the adjacent image:

- **Duplicate** the claw in order to create all the other ones for the hand and foot.

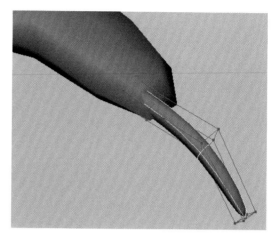

The first claw

 Tip: *You can go in the duplicate options and select Edit → Reset Settings before duplicating the first claw since the construction history is not required.*

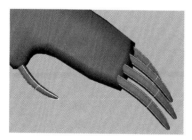

Hand claws

Foot claws

4 Mirror the objects

- Select the *eyeball*, *eyelid* and all the *claws*.

- Press **Ctrl+g** to group them all together.

- With the *eyeball* selected, select **Edit** → **Duplicate Special** → ❑.
- In the shown window, turn on the **Duplicate input** graph option.

  Doing so will duplicate the required construction history on the eyelid.

- Click the **Duplicate Special** button.
- In the Channel Box with the duplicated group still selected, set **ScaleX** to **-1**.

  You now have all the objects for both sides of the character.

The full character

5 **Save your work**

- Save your scene as *07-boog_05.ma*.

Conclusion

In this lesson, you learned how to model a complete character out of basic polygonal primitives. In the process, you used several polygonal modeling tools to create the shape and details. As you noticed, each tool created an input node for which you were able to modify the construction history. You also used the lattice deformer, which is a great deformer to know about.

In the next lesson, you will texture the bear. This will allow you to experiment with polygonal texture tools and techniques.

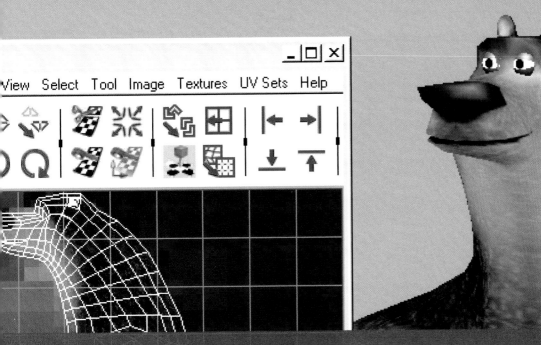

Lesson 08
Polygonal texturing

You now have a polygonal mesh that requires texturing. Even though polygons have a default setting for UV parameters onto which textures can be applied, in this lesson you will adjust these to get the best possible result. You can use special polygon tools to assign and modify these kinds of values on the model.

You will first apply texture projections in order to create UV coordinates on the mesh. Then, you will texture map the bear using textures imported as file textures.

In this lesson you will learn the following:

- How to project textures on polygons;

- How to manipulate projections;

- How to use the UV Texture Editor;

- How to grow and reduce the current selection;

- How to assign and paint textures using the 3D Paint Tool;

- How to remove unused shading groups.

Texturing polygonal surfaces

The bear will be textured using multiple shading groups and texture maps. You will start by texturing the eyes and claws of the character. Once that is done, you will texture the main body geometry. Positioning the texture on the surface will be accomplished using useful polygon texturing tools. Feel free to continue using your own file, or start with *07-boog_05.ma* from the last lesson.

1 UV Texture Editor

The UV Texture Editor is where you can see the UVs of your model. UVs are similar to vertices except that they live in a flat 2D space. The UVs determine the coordinates of a point on a texture map. In order to properly assign a texture to a polygonal model, the UVs need to be unfolded somewhat like a tablecloth.

- Select the *body* geometry.

- Select **Window → UV Texture Editor**.

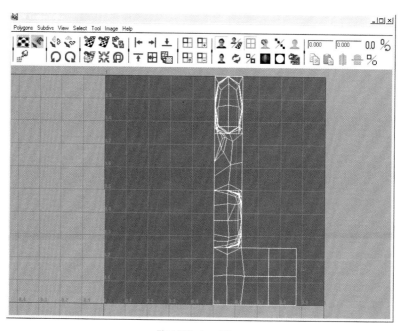

The UV Texture Editor

Displayed in the UV Texture Editor are the UVs for the selected geometry. Those UVs are now irregular and will result in a very poor texture mapping.

2 Create and assign a body shader

- **Open** the Hypershade window.

- **Create** a *blinn* material node.

  Blinn is the material that once properly set-up can look the most like fur.

- **Rename** the material node to *bodyM*.

- **Assign** the *bodyM* material to the *body* geometry.

- Turn on the **Hardware Texturing** in the Perspective view to see your work in the upcoming steps.

3 Map a checker to the color

- Open the **Attribute Editor** for the *bodyM* material.

- **Map** the **Color** attribute with a **Checker** texture node.

Irregular texture placement due to poor UVs

Note: *The checker texture is just a temporary texture in order to better see the UV placement on the model.*

4 Planar mapping

In order to start correcting the texture mapping of the character, you will use a planar projection.

- With the *body* geometry selected, select **Create UVs → Planar Mapping → □** from the Polygons menu set.

- In the option window, select **Project from X-axis.**

- Click the Project button.

  A large projection plane icon surrounds the object, which projects the texture map along the X-axis. You can see the texture mapped onto the surface with hardware texturing.

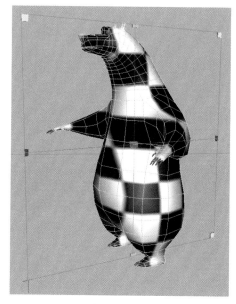

Planar projection

5 Projection manipulators

The projection manipulator allows you to transform the projection to better suit your geometry.

You can toggle the manipulator type for a conventional all-in-one manipulator by clicking on the *red T*.

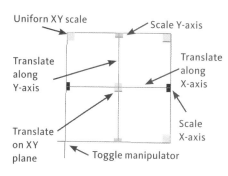

Planar projection manipulator

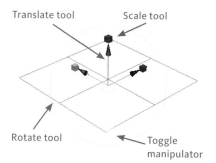

Other planar projection manipulator

Note: *If the projection manipulator disappears, reselect the geometry, click on the polyPlanProj input node in the Channel Box and select the Show Manipulator Tool, or press the t hotkey.*

6 UV Texture Editor

If you look in the UV Texture Editor, you will see that the UVs of the model have been updated to be projected in the same way as the projection in the viewport.

- In the UV Texture Editor menu bar, select **Image** → **Display Image** to toggle the display of the checker texture to **Off**.

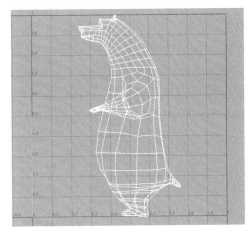

The projected UVs

Note: *The view of the object and the loaded texture are both initially displayed in the Texture Editor with a square proportion – regardless of the proportion of the planar projection positioned in the 3D space of the model and the proportion of the texture image file.*

Modifying UVs

It is important to prevent overlapping with the UVs where it is not wanted. For instance, if you make a planar projection from the front of the model, the UVs would overlap on the front and back of the model. If you make the belly of the character another color, the back would also change.

In this example, you made the projection from the side because the character should be symmetrical on its X-axis. The problem with the current UVs is that the arms are overlapping with the belly and could cause unwanted texture results later in this lesson.

Since UVs can be tweaked as needed through the UV Texture Editor, you will now alter the UVs manually.

1 Select the arm UVs

- In the UV Texture Editor with the bear's UVs displayed, **RMB** and select **UV** from the context menu.

Doing so sets the current selection mask to UVs only.

- **Click+drag** a selection rectangle over the bear's paw.

  The UVs of both paws are now selected because their UVs are overlapping.

- From the main Maya interface, select **Select → Grow Selection Region**.

  The neighbor UVs on the model are selected, which increases the current selection.

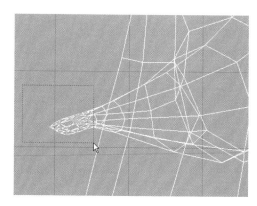

Selecting the paw UVs

Tip: You can press **Shift+>** to increase the selection and **Shift+<** to shrink the current selection.

- Select **Select → Grow Selection Region,** or press **Ctrl+>** a few more times until you have the entire arm selected.

2 Unfolding the arm UVs

The goal of this step is to minimize the arm overlapping from the rest of the body. You could do this entire step manually by moving the UVs one by one, but in order to speed up the process, you will automatically unfold the selected UVs.

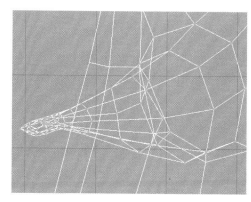

All of the entire arm UVs selected

- From the UV Texture Editor, select **Polygons → Unfold → ❒.**

- In the Unfold options, make sure that **Pin UVs** is enabled and that **Pin Unselected UVs** is chosen.

  By setting those options, you specify to the tool that you want only the selected UVs to be unfolded.

- Click the **Apply and Close** button.

3   Moving UVs

- Press **r** to evoke the **Scale Tool** and tweak the UVs in the UV Texture Editor.

- You can press **Ctrl+<** to shrink the current selection in order to scale up the other row of UVs.

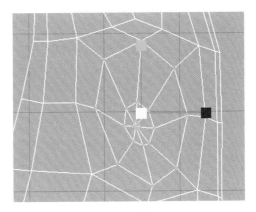

Scaling the resulting UVs

Note: *The placement of the UVs doesn't need to be perfect since the arms will be the same color overall.*

- Close the UV Texture Editor and go in Object mode.

4   **Save your work**

- Save your scene as *08-boogTxt_01.ma*.

3D Paint Tool

A great way to create custom texture is to paint a texture directly on a model in the viewport. The 3D Paint Tool allows you to paint using default paintbrushes or Paint Effects brushes. You can use the tool to outline details to be painted in separate software, or to create a final texture directly in Maya.

Tip: *As you are working with the 3D Paint Tool, you might want to change the way the UVs are laid out to minimize texture stretching and overlapping.*

1   **Set the 3D Paint Tool**

- Select the *body* geometry.

- Select the **Rendering** menu set by pressing **F6.**

- Select **Texturing → 3D Paint Tool → □**.

  This will open the tool's option window.

- Scroll down to the **File Textures** section.

- Make sure **Attribute to Paint** is set to **Color**.

- Click the **Assign/Edit Textures** button.

  This will open the new texture creation options.

- Set **Image Format** to **Tiff (tif)**.

- Set both the **Size X** and **Size Y** to 512.

Tip: *For more definition in your textures and (and if your computer can handle it), you might want to boost up the texture resolution to 1024 x 1024 or even 2048 x 2048.*

- Click the **Assign/Edit Textures** button.

  Doing so will duplicate the currently assigned texture and save it in your project in the 3dpainttextures folder. As you paint on the geometry, only this new texture will be automatically updated.

2 Set the initial color

You will now paint a color over the old checker pattern.

- In the 3D Paint Tool settings, change the **Color** attribute in the **Flood** section to be a **dark brown**.

- Click on the **Flood Paint** button.

  The bear is now totally brown.

3 Set erase image

To make sure that you can erase your drawing and come back to the original texture, you need to set the erase image as the current texture.

- Scroll to the **Paint Operations** section and click on the **Set Erase Image** button.

4 Paint on geometry

- Under the **File Texture** section, turn **On** the **Extend Seam Color** option.

This option will make sure that there are no seams visible when painting.

- Scroll at the top of the 3D Paint Tool and make sure the second **Artisan** brush is enabled in the **Brush** section.

- When you put your mouse cursor over the geometry in the viewport, if the brush size is too big or too small for painting, set its **Radius (U)** in the option window, or hold the **b** hotkey and drag the radius of the brush in the viewport.

- Change the **Color** attribute from the **Paint** section to a **light brown**.

- **Paint** directly on the geometry to change the color of the bear's belly.

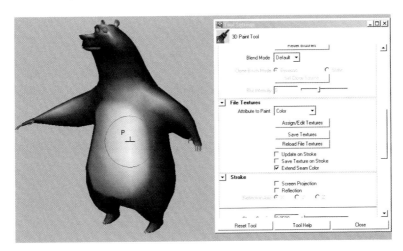

The painted belly

- Continue painting the bear with different colors on the different parts of his body such as the neck, nose, eye sockets, mouth, ears and paws.

Fully painted bear

> **Note:** It is possible that sometimes painting directly on the geometry creates artifacts. This can be due to things such as seams, color, texture resolution, UV placement, overlapping, etc. One way of correcting this is by editing the texture later on in a paint program.

5 Paint options

Under the Paint Operations section, you can set various paint operations like Paint, Erase, Clone, Smear and Blur. You can also set the Blend Mode, which affects the way new strokes are painted to your texture. Those options can be very useful to tweak your texture.

6 Paint Effects

- Scroll to the **Brush** section of the tool and enable the first **Paint Effects** brush.

- To choose a template brush, click on the **Get Brush** button to invoke the Visor.

Get Brush button

- In the Visor, scroll to the **Hair** directory and choose the brush called **furKodiakBear.mel**.

- Experiment painting on the geometry.

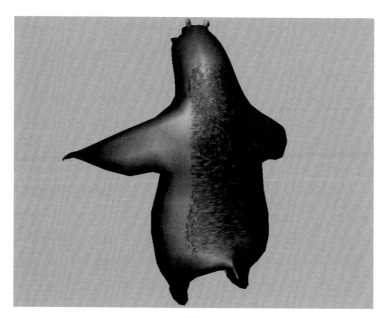

Paint Effects fur

7 Screen projection

When painting with a Paint Effects brush, you will notice that the brush icon in the viewport looks stretched. This is because the brush bases itself on the object's UVs, which are stretched. To correct the problem, you need to enable the screen projection option.

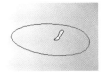

Stretched brush

- Expand the **Stroke** section in the 3D Paint Tool window.

- Turn **On** the **Screen Projection** attribute.

- **Paint** on geometry.

Note: *When painting with Screen Projection, you are painting using the current camera view. This can be very useful in some cases, but can also create stretched textures when painting on geometry parallel to the view.*

8 Reference strokes

You might find it easier to draw only reference strokes in Maya and then use a paint program to refine the look of the texture. To do so, you will draw where you want to add texture details on the object, and then open the texture in a paint program. Once you are done with the texture, you can reload it in Maya.

9 Save textures

You have not yet saved the texture just drawn to disk, making it inaccessible to another program.

- To save the texture manually, click the **Save Textures** button in the **File Textures** section.

OR

- To save the texture automatically on each stroke, turn **On** the **Save Texture on Stroke** checkbox in the **File Textures** section.

10 Edit the texture

You can now edit your texture from the *3dpainttextures* directory in a paint program. When you are done modifying the texture, save the new image out.

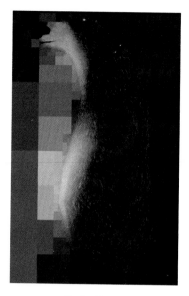

The final texture

The final texture on the model

- Back in Maya, in the texture's Attribute Editor, click the **Reload** button to update the fur texture for the new version.

Tip: *If you saved the file under a different name or in a different location, browse to get the modified texture.*

Final touches

Since the character's geometry consists of several other objects as well, you should also be texturing those. Note that the eyes and claws were made out of NURBS surfaces so they will not require extra UV steps. The texturing of NURBS surfaces will be shown more in-depth in the third project.

1 Create and assign an eye shader

- **Open** the Hypershade window.

- **Create** a *phong* material node.

  Phong is the material that suits the shiny eyes best.

- **Rename** the material node to *eyeM*.

- **Assign** the *eyeM* material to both *eyeballs*.

2 Map a ramp to the color

- Open the Attribute Editor for the *eyeM* material.

- **Map** the **Color** attribute with a **Ramp** texture node.

Tip: *Make sure that the Normal option is selected at the top of the Create Render Node window.*

- **Rename** the ramp node to *eyeColor*.

3 Tweak the ramp

- In the Attribute Editor for the *eyeColor*, set the following:

  Type to **U Ramp**;

  Interpolation to **None**.

- **Tweak** the ramp's colors to the right:

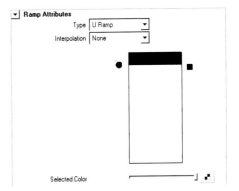

4 Create and assign a eyelid shader

- **Create** a *blinn* material and **rename** it to *eyelidM*.

- Set the **Color** of the material to be a brown similar to the surrounding fur color of the bear.

Tip: *Use the Teardrop Tool in the Color Picker window to directly select the color you need on the model.*

- **Assign** the *eyelidM* to the *eyelid* objects.

5 Create and assign a claw shader

- **Create** a *Phong* material and **rename** it to *clawM*.

- Set the **Color** of the material to **black**.

- **Assign** the *clawM* to all the *claw* objects.

Optimizing the scene

To maintain a good workflow, you should clean up your scene once texturing is complete. For instance, you might want to delete all unused shading network in the scene.

1 **Delete unused nodes**

- From the Hypershade window, select **Edit** → **Delete Unused Nodes**.

  Maya will go through the list of render nodes and delete anything that is not assigned to a piece of geometry in the scene.

2 **Optimize scene size**

- Select **File** → **Optimize Scene Size**.

  Maya will go through the entire scene and remove any unused nodes.

3 **Delete the history**

- Select all the objects except the *eyelids*.

- Select **Edit** → **Delete by Type** → **History**.

4 **Save your work**

- The final scene *08-boogTxt_02.ma* can be found in the support files. Boog's texture is called *body.tif* and is located in the *3dpainttextures* directory.

Conclusion

You now have a good understanding of texturing polygons. You have experimented with a projection and some polygonal tools and actions. There is much more to learn concerning polygon texturing, so feel free to experiment on your own.

In the next lesson, you will learn about creating joint chains, which is the first step for animating a character.

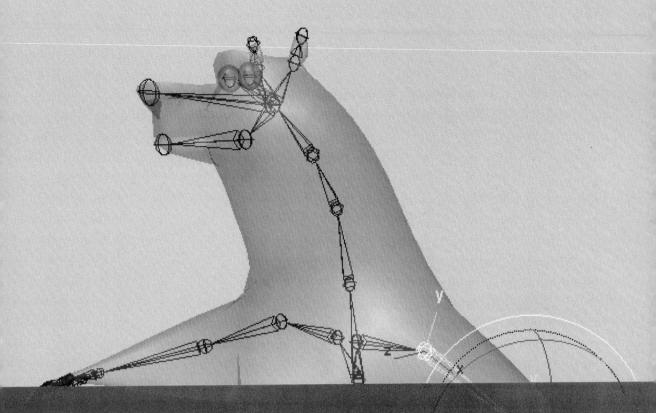

Lesson 09
Skeleton

In this lesson you will create the skeleton hierarchy to be used to bind the geometry and to animate the bear character. In order to create a skeleton, you need to draw joints to match the shape of your character. The geometry is then bound to the skeleton and deformations are applied.

In this lesson you will learn the following:

- How to create skeleton joints;
- How to navigate around a joint hierarchy;
- How to edit joint pivots;
- How to mirror joints;
- How to reorient joints;
- How to edit the joint rotation axis.

Drawing a skeleton chain

In this exercise, you will draw skeleton chains. Even if this operation appears to be simple, there are several things to be aware of as you create a joint chain.

1 Joint Tool

- Open a new scene and change the view to the side Orthographic view.

- From the **Animation** menu set, select **Skeleton** → **Joint Tool** → ⃞.

  The tool's option window is displayed.

- Change the **Orientation** attribute to **None**.

Note: *This attribute will be explained later in this exercise.*

- Click the **Close** button to close the tool window.

- In the side view, **LMB+click** two times to create a joint chain.

- Press **Enter** to exit the tool.

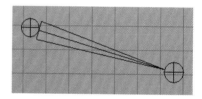

A simple joint chain

2 Joint Hierarchy

- Open the Hypergraph.

  Notice the joint hierarchy, which is composed of two nodes.

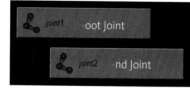

Joint hierarchy

3 Adding joints

- Click on the **Joint Tool** icon in the Toolbox or press the **y** hotkey to invoke the last tool used.

- **LMB** on the end joint of your previous chain.

  The tool will highlight the end joint.

- **LMB+click** two times to create a Z-like joint chain.

  The new joints are children of the joint selected in the previous step.

- You can **MMB+drag** to change the last joint placement.

- Press **Enter** to exit the tool.

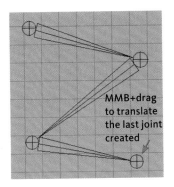

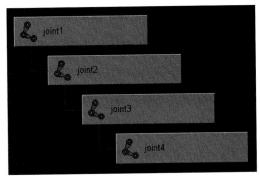

New joint chain   Joint hierarchy

4 **Automatic joint orientation**

When using the automatic orientation, all three joint axes are aligned according to the right-hand rule. For example, if you select an orientation of XYZ, the positive X-axis points into the joint's bone and towards the joint's first child joint, the Y-axis points at right angles to the X-axis and Z-axis and the Z-axis points sideways from the joint and its bone.

Note: *If you look closely at the joints in the Perspective view, you can see these axes and where they are pointing.*

- **Double-click** on the **Joint Tool** icon in the Toolbox.

  The tool's option window is displayed.

- Change the **Orientation** attribute to **XYZ**.

- **Close** the tool window.

- Create a second joint chain similar to the first one.

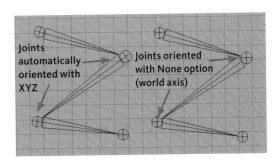

Joint orientation

Notice that as you draw the joints, they are automatically oriented toward their child.

5 Joint rotation axis

To better understand the effect of the joint orientation, you need to rotate in local mode and compare the two chains you have created.

- **Double-click** on the **Rotate Tool** icon in the Toolbox.

  The tool's option window is displayed.

- Select **Local** as the **Rotation Mode**.

  This specifies that you want to rotate nodes based on their local orientation rather than using the global world axis.

- **Close** the tool window.

- Select the second joint of both chains and see the difference between their rotation axes as you rotate them.

  Notice that when the joint is properly oriented, it moves in a more natural way.

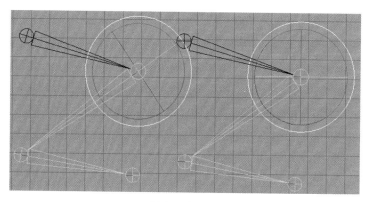

Joint rotation axis

Complex joint chain

When you create a complex joint chain, you can use some features intended to simplify your work. For instance, you can navigate in a hierarchy of joints as you create them. You can also use a command to reorient all the joints automatically.

1 Navigate in joint hierarchy

- **Delete** all the joint chains in your scene.

- Make the *top* view active.

- Press the **y** hotkey to invoke the **Joint Tool**.

Note: *Make sure the tool* **Orientation** *is set to* **XYZ.**

- **Draw** three joints as indicated on the right:

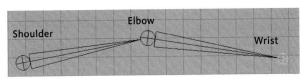

Arm chain

- **Draw** a thumb made of two joints.

- Press the **up arrow** twice on your keyboard to put the selection on the wrist joint.

  The arrows let you navigate in the hierarchy without exiting the Joint Tool.

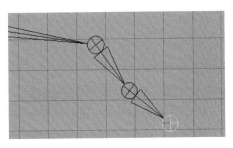

Thumb joints

- **Draw** the index joints and press the **up arrow** again.

- **Draw** the remaining fingers as indicated on the right:

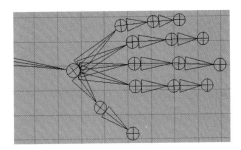

Completed hand

2 Snap to grid

- Press the **up arrow** until the selection is on the shoulder joint.

- Hold down the **x** hotkey to snap to grid and add a spine bone.

- Press **Enter** to exit the Joint Tool.

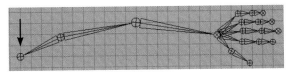

Spine bone

3 **Reroot a skeleton**

In the last step, you created a spine bone that is the child of the shoulder bone. This is not a proper hierarchy, since the spine should be the parent of the shoulder. There is a command that allows you to quickly reroot a joint chain.

- Select the *spine* bone, which was the last joint created.

- Select **Skeleton** → **Reroot Skeleton**.

The spine is now the root of the hierarchy.

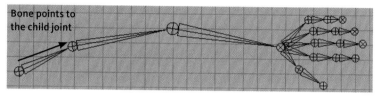

Spine joint as root

4 **Mirror joints**

Another very useful feature is the ability to mirror a joint chain automatically.

- Select the *shoulder* bone.

- Select **Skeleton** → **Mirror Joint** → ❑.

- In the option window, specify **Mirror Across** the **YZ** plane.

- Click the **Mirror** button.

Both arms

Bear skeleton

You are now ready to create a skeleton for the bear from the last lesson. To do so, you need to determine the proper placement of each joint. Once that is done, you will need to set a proper joint orientation so that when you rotate a joint, it rotates in an intuitive manner. If you do not take great care for placement and orientation, you will have difficulty later on animating the character.

1 **Open scene**

- Open the file *08-boogTxt_02.ma*.

2 Character spine

In this step, you need to determine a good placement for the pelvis bone, which will be the root of the hierarchy. Once that is done, it will be easy to create the rest of the spine bones.

- Select **Skeleton** → **Joint Tool**.

- Make the *side* view active.

- **LMB** to create the *pelvis* joint.

  It is recommended that the pelvis joint be aligned with the hips.

- **LMB** to draw three equally spaced joints, which will represent the *spine1*, *spine2* and *neck* joints.

- **LMB** to draw three equally spaced joints, which will represent the *neck1*, *neck2*, *head* and *nose* joints.

- Hit **Enter** to complete the joint chain.

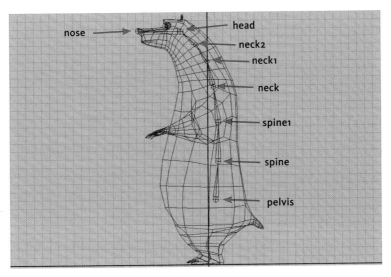

Pelvis, spine and head joints

Note: *A spine could be made of more bones, but this is not required in this example. The nose joint would normally be used only to get a visual representation of the head when the geometry is hidden, but you might use it to deform the nose when the bear will sniff as well.*

- Rename each joint properly.

3 Create a leg

You now need to create the legs of the character. The new joint chain will be in a separate hierarchy, but you will connect it to the pelvis later on.

- Select **Skeleton → Joint Tool**.

- **Click+drag** the *hip* joint to its proper location.

  The hip joint should be centered on the hip geometry and very close to the pelvis joint.

- **Draw** the remaining *knee*, *ankle* and *toe* joints, and create an extra joint on the tip of the foot, which should be called *toesEnd*.

- Press **Enter** to exit the tool.

- Change the current view to the *front* view.

  Notice that all the bones you created were drawn centered on the X-axis. That was correct for the spine, but not for the leg.

- **Translate** the *hip* joint on the X-axis to fit the geometry as indicated to the right:

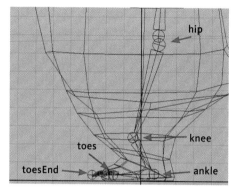

Leg joints

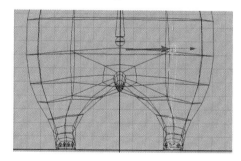

Front view

4 Connect and mirror the leg

- Select the *hip* joint, then **Shift-select** the *pelvis* joint.

- Select **Skeleton → Connect Joint → ☐**.

- Change the **Mode** option to **Parent Joint**.

- Hit the **Connect** button.

  The leg is now parented to the pelvis.

Note: *You could also parent using the **p** hotkey.*

- Select the *hip* joint.

- Select **Skeleton** → **Mirror Joint** → ❐.

- Make sure the **Mirror Across** option is set to **YZ**.

- Click on the **Mirror** button.

  If your character was modeled symmetrically, it should now have two legs properly placed.

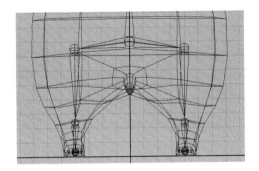

Completed lower body

- Rename all the joints appropriately.

Note: *Make sure to prefix the joints on the left side with l, and the ones on the right side with r. For example, if you name the ankle, you may want to call it lAnkle.*

5 **Arm and hand joints**

- Select **Display** → **Animation** → **Joint Size...**

- Set the **Joint Size** to **0.25**.

  Doing so will reduce the display size of the joints in the viewport, making it easier to place joints close together, such as the finger joints.

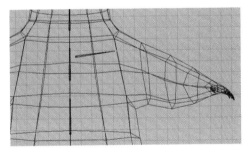

- From the *front* view, **draw** a joint to represent the *clavicle* between the last *spine* and *neck* joints, then **draw** the *shoulder* joint.

The clavicle and shoulder joints

- Change the current view to the *top* view.

- Create the character's *elbow*, *wrist* and *hand*.

Tip: *Don't forget to use the **up arrow** to navigate the joint hierarchy.*

- While in Smooth Shaded mode, select **Shading** → **X-Ray** from the panel menu.

- From the *Perspective* view, **translate** the joints down to fit the geometry correctly.

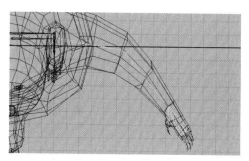

The arm and hand joints

 Tip: *It is a better workflow for joint placement to rotate the joints rather than translate them.*

- **Rename** all the joints correctly.

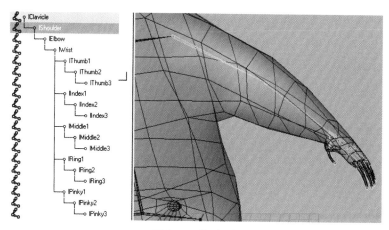

Joints correctly placed

 Tip: *It might be easier to set the display in the viewport as X-Ray with Wireframe on Shaded.*

6 Joint pivot

In some cases, you might want to adjust the position of a joint without moving all of its children. You can use the **Insert** key (**Home** key on Macintosh) to move a joint on its own.

For instance, if the angle defined by the shoulder, elbow and wrist joints is not appropriate, you can correct the problem by moving a joint on its own.

- Select the *elbow* joint.

- Select the **Move Tool**.

- Press the **Insert** key (**Home** on Macintosh).

- **Move** the pivot of the *elbow* joint.

- Press the key again and exit the Move Pivot manipulator.

7 Connect and mirror the arm

- **Repeat** step **4** to connect the *clavicle* joint to the *spine1* joint and mirror it.

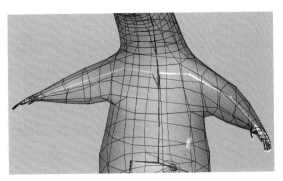

Proper arms

8 Details

- Select the **Joint Tool**.

- From the *side* view, click on the *head* joint to highlight it.

  Doing so tells the tool that you want to start drawing joints from the head joint.

- **Draw** two joints for the ear, one for the eye and two for the mouth as indicated on the right:

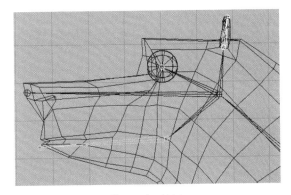

The new head joints

- **Draw** two joints for the tail starting from the *pelvis*.

- **Rename**, translate and mirror the new joints.

Joint orientation

Now that the bear has a skeleton, you need to double-check all the joint orientations using the Rotate Tool. In this case, most of the joint orientations will be good by default, but there will be times when you will need to change some orientations to perfect your skeleton.

1 Hide the geometry

- From the *Perspective* view, select **Show → Polygons** and **Show → NURBS Surfaces** to hide them.

2 Default rotation values

It is recommended that all rotations of a joint hierarchy be zeroed out. This means that when the skeleton is in the current default position, all the joint rotations are zero.

- Select the *pelvis* joint.

- Select **Modify → Freeze Transformations**.

  If you rotated bones in previous steps, their rotations are now zeroed out.

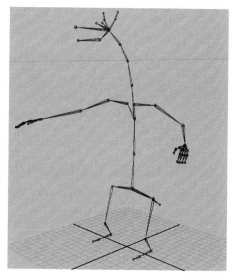

Complete skeleton

Note: *Unlike geometry, joint translations cannot be zeroed or else they would all be at the origin.*

3 Reorient all joints

You can reorient all the joints in a hierarchy automatically to your preferred orientation, such as XYZ.

- Select the *pelvis* joint.

- Select **Skeleton → Orient Joint → ❑** .

- Make sure the **Orientation** is set to **XYZ**, then click the **Orient** button.

  All the joints are now reoriented to have the X-axis pointing toward their children.

4 Local rotation axes

The automatic orientation of the joints is not always perfect. Depending on how your skeleton was built, it can flip certain local rotation axes and you need to manually fix those pivots.

Local rotation axes mask

- Select the *pelvis* joint.

- Press **F8** to go in Component mode and enable the **?** mask button.

  All the local rotation axes are displayed in the viewport for the selected joints.

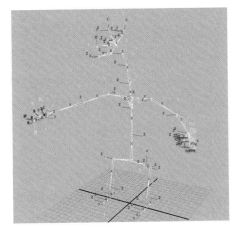

Local rotation axes in the viewport

5 Manually set the local rotation axes

It might seem confusing at the moment, but changing the local rotation axes is quite easy. There is one axis per joint, and if you dolly closer to a joint, you will see that the axis respects the left-hand rule, where the **X-axis** points toward the first child joint.

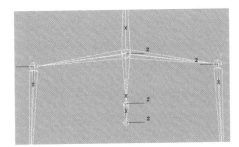

Pelvis and hips' local rotation axes

In certain cases, you will not want the automatic orientation setting. The problems usually arise when you select multiple bones and rotate them at the same time. For instance, if you select the entire spine and neck joints you would notice an odd rotation, since their rotation axes are not aligned.

X rotation on the upper body is not in the same orientation as the X rotation of the lower body since Z points in different directions

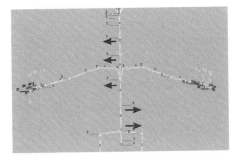

Bad rotation axes

To fix the problem, manually select an incorrect local rotation axis and rotate it into a good position.

• Still in Component mode with the local rotation axis displayed, select the *spine* and *neck* local rotation axes by clicking on them and holding down the **Shift** key.

• Select the **Rotate Tool** by pressing the **e** hotkey.

• **Rotate** on the X-axis by about **180 degrees**.

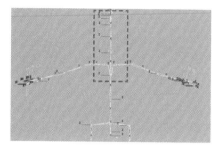
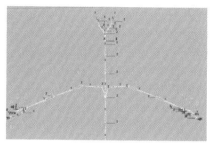

The selected head rotation axis   *The corrected rotation axis*

Note: When using the Rotate Tool, you will notice a greyed zone defining the angle you are currently defining. In order to rotate by about 180 degrees, make sure that the greyed area defines a straight line.

• Go back in Object mode and try rotating the spine and neck together.

The problem seen earlier is now solved.

Note: It is normal that mirrored joints have an inverted local rotation axis. This is a welcome behavior set in the Mirror Joint command, which allows animation to be mirrored from one limb to another.

6 Test the skeleton

You should now test your skeleton to see if everything is rotating as expected. If you notice incorrect local rotation axes, attempt to correct them manually by following the steps outlined above. Typical problematic areas are the knees and ankles, since the joint chains are made in a Z shape.

> **Note:** It usually doesn't matter how an end joint's local rotation axis is since it might not be intended for animation.

7 Save your work

- Save your work as *09-boogSkeleton_01.ma*.

Conclusion

You now have greater experience creating skeleton chains and navigating skeleton hierarchies. You learned how to move and rotate joints, and how to use joint commands such as reroot, connect, mirror and orient. Finally, you manually changed local rotation axes, which is the key to creating a good skeleton.

In the next lesson, you will bind the bear geometry to the skeleton and explore different techniques and tools used for character rigging.

Lesson 10
Skinning

For your character's geometry to deform as you move joints, you must bind it to the skeleton. There are many skinning techniques to bind a surface. In this lesson, you will first experiment with basic examples, which will help you to understand the various types of skinning. You will then use this understanding to bind the bear character.

In this lesson you will learn the following:

- How to bind using parenting;
- How to use rigid binding;
- How to use the Edit Membership Tool;
- How to edit rigid bind membership;
- How to use flexors;
- How to use lattice binding and smooth binding;
- How to access skin influences;
- How to set and assume a preferred angle;
- How to set joint degrees of freedom and limits.

Parent binding

Perhaps the simplest type of binding is to parent geometry to joints. This type of binding is very fast and needs no tweaking, but requires the pieces of a model to be separate. For instance, an arm would need to be split into two parts: an upper arm and a lower arm. There are other scenarios where parenting is appropriate, for example, a ring on a finger, or the eyes of a character.

1 **Create a simple scene**

- Open a new scene and change the view to the top Orthographic view.

- Draw three joints defining an arm.

- Change the view to the *Perspective* view.

- Create two polygonal cylinders and place them over the bones, as follows:

Basic parenting setup

2 **Parent the geometry**

- Select the *left cylinder*, then **Shift-select** the *left bone*.

- Press the **p** hotkey to **Parent** the cylinder to the bone.

- Repeat the last two steps to **Parent** the *right cylinder* to the *right bone*.

Note: *Notice that the geometry is now a child of the joints in the Outliner.*

3 **Test joint rotations**

- Select the bones and rotate them to see the result of the parenting.

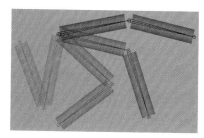

Joints' rotation

> **Note:** Notice that when selecting, bones have a higher selection priority than geometry. To select a bone, simply make a bounding box selection over the bone and geometry.

Rigid binding

Rigid binding works basically like the parenting method, except that it affects the geometry's components. By rigid binding geometry on bones, the vertices closer to a certain bone will be instructed to follow that bone. This type of binding usually looks good on low resolution polygonal geometry or NURBS surfaces, but can cause cracking on dense geometry. Following are two examples using rigid binding:

1 **Create a simple scene**

- Open a new scene and change the view to the *top* Orthographic view.

- **Draw** three joints defining an arm.

- Select the first joint and press **Ctrl+d** to duplicate the joint chain.

- **Move** the joint chains side by side.

- From the *Perspective* view, create a *polygonal cylinder* and a *NURBS cylinder*.

- Place each cylinder to entirely cover a joint chain.

- Set the polygonal cylinder's **Subdivisions Height** to **10**.

- Set the NURBS cylinder's **Spans** to **10**.

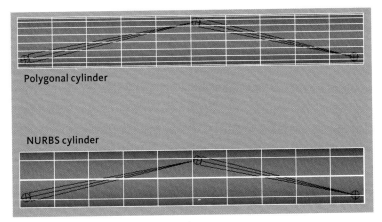

Example scene setup

2 Rigid bind

- Select the *first joint chain*, then **Shift-select** the *polygonal cylinder*.

- Select **Skin** → **Bind Skin** → **Rigid Bind**.

- Select the *second joint chain*, then **Shift-select** the *NURBS cylinder*.

- Select **Skin** → **Bind Skin** → **Rigid Bind**.

3 Test joint rotations

- Select the bones and rotate them
  to see the result of the rigid binding
  on both geometry types.

  *The polygonal object appears to
  fold in on itself, since a vertex
  can only be assigned to one bone.
  The NURBS object seems much
  smoother because the curves of
  the surface are defined by the CVs,
  which are bound to the bones just
  like the polygonal object.*

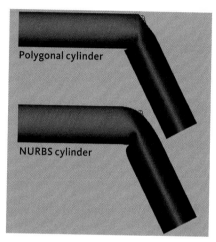

Rigid binding

Note: *Notice in the Outliner that the geometry is not parented. The binding connects the
geometry's vertices to the joints.*

4 Edit Membership Tool

When using rigid bind, you might want to change the default binding so that certain points
follow a different bone. The Edit Membership Tool allows you to specify the cluster of points
affected by a certain bone.

- Select **Deform** → **Edit Membership Tool**.

- Click on the *middle bone* of the first joint chain.

  *You should see all the vertices affected by that joint highlighted in yellow. Vertices affected by
  other bones are highlighted using different colors to distinguish them.*

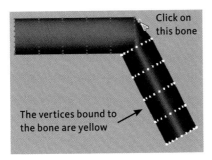

The Edit Membership Tool

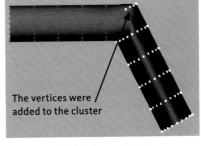

Added polygon vertices

- Using the same hotkeys as when you select objects, toggle points from the cluster using **Shift**, remove points from the cluster using **Ctrl** and add points to the cluster using **Shift+Ctrl**.

- **Repeat** the same steps for the NUBRS geometry to achieve a better deformation.

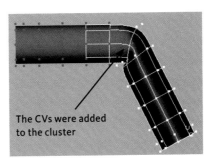

Added NURBS vertices

Flexors

Flexors are a type of deformer designed to be used with rigid bound surfaces. By creating a flexor for a joint, you can smooth out the binding region between two bones, thus preventing geometry from cracking. Flexor points can also be driven by Set Driven Keys to modify their positions as the bone rotates. For instance, you can refine an elbow shape when the elbow is folded.

1 Creating flexors

- From the previous scene, reset the rotations of the bones to their default positions.

- Select the *middle joint* for the first joint chain.

- Select **Skin → Edit Rigid Skin → Create Flexor...**

  An option window is displayed.

- Make sure the **Flexor Type** is set to **Lattice**.

- Turn **On** the **Position the Flexor** checkbox.

- Click the **Create** button.

  A flexor is created at the joint's position and is selected so that you can position it correctly.

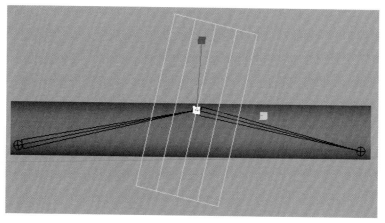

The flexor deformer

- **Translate** and **scale** the flexor to cover the bending region.

2 Test joint rotations

- Select the *middle bone* and rotate it to see the result of the flexor on the geometry.

  Notice that the bending area of the polygonal geometry is now much smoother.

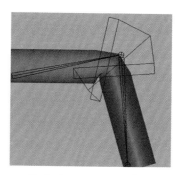

The bent geometry using a flexor

Tip: *If necessary, hide the flexor object by toggling* **Show** → **Deformers***, so you can see the deformations more clearly.*

3 Set Driven Keys

- **Zero** the rotation of the bones.
- Select **Animate** → **Set Driven Key** → **Set** → ❐.
- In the **Driver** section, load the *middle joint* and select the **Rotate Y** attribute.

- Select the *flexor* and press **F8** to display its points.

- Select all the flexor's lattice points and click the **Load Driven** button in the Set Driven Key window.

- Highlight all the driven objects in the **Driven** section and highlight the **XYZ values** on the right side.

- Click the **Key** button to set the normal position.

- Go back in Object mode and **rotate** the *middle joint* on the **Y-axis** by about **80** degrees.

- Select the *flexor* and press **F8** to display its points.

- **Move** the flexor points to confer a nice elbow shape to the cylinder.

- Click the **Key** button to set the bent position.

Note: *The points on the flexor might not move exactly as expected since they are using the local space of the middle bone.*

4 Test joint rotations

- Select the *middle bone* and rotate it to see the result of the driven flexor on the geometry.

  Notice that you can achieve a much better crease by using a driven flexor.

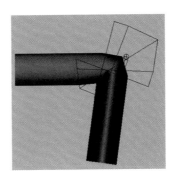

Driven flexor

Lattice binding

Another way to achieve nice skinning using rigid bind is to create a lattice deformer on the geometry and rigid binding the lattice to the bones. This technique can achieve a very smooth binding, using the simplicity of the rigid binding to your advantage.

1 Detach a skin

- Select the *polygonal cylinder* from the previous exercise.

- Select **Skin** → **Detach Skin**.

The geometry returns to the original shape and position it was in before being bound.

- Select the *middle joint* and zero its rotation.

- Select the *flexor* and press **Delete** on your keyboard, as it is no longer required.

2 Create a lattice

- Select the *polygonal cylinder*, then select **Deform** → **Create Lattice**.

A lattice is created and fits the geometry perfectly.

- Increase the number of lattice subdivisions by going to the **Shapes** section in the Channel Box and setting its **T Divisions** attribute to **9**.

3 Rigid bind the lattice

- With the lattice still selected, **Shift-select** the *first bone* of the joint chain.

- Select **Skin** → **Bind Skin** → **Rigid Bind**.

4 Test joint rotations

- Select the *middle bone* and rotate it to see the result of the lattice on the geometry.

At this time, the binding is not much different than a normal rigid binding.

The bones deform the lattice, which in turn deforms the geometry

The bound lattice

5 Adjust the lattice

- Select the *lattice* object.

- In the **Outputs** section of the Channel Box, highlight the *ffd1* node.

- Set the following:

    Local Influence S to **4**;

    Local Influence T to **4**;

    Local Influence U to **4**.

The deformation of the geometry is now much smoother.

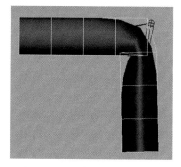

The smoothed influences of the lattice

6 **Edit membership**

It is now much easier to edit the membership of the lattice points rather than the dense geometry vertices.

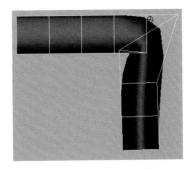

The edited rigid bind membership

7 **Driven lattice**

If the Edit Membership Tool does not provide enough control over the deformation of the geometry, you can use driven keys to achieve a much better deformation for the elbow and the elbow crease, just like in the previous flexor exercise. You can also use driven keys to bulge the bicep.

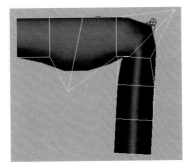

Driven lattice

Smooth binding

The most advanced type of skinning is called *smooth binding*. Smooth binding allows an object vertex or CV to be influenced by multiple bones, according to a certain percentage. For instance, a vertex's influence can follow a particular bone at 100%, or that influence can be spread across multiple bones in varying percentages, such as 50%-50% or 25%-75%. Doing so will move the vertex accordingly between all the influence bones.

1 **Set-up the scene**

- Using the scene from the previous exercise, set the *middle joint* rotation to zero.

- Select **Edit → Delete All by Type → History** to remove the lattice object.

2 **Smooth bind**

- Select the *first joint*, then **Shift-select** the *polygonal cylinder*.

- Select **Skin → Bind Skin → Smooth Bind**.

3 Test joint rotations

- Select the *middle bone* and rotate it to see the result of the smooth binding on the geometry.

Default smooth binding

4 Edit smooth bind influence

Modifying the influences of each bone on each vertex can be a tedious task, but you can use the Maya Artisan Tool to actually paint the weights of the vertices directly in the viewport. The *Paint Skin Weight Tool* will display an influence of 100% as white, an influence of 0% as black and anything in-between as grayscale. This makes it easier to visually edit the influence of bones on the geometry.

- Select *polyCylinder* and go to **Shading → Smooth Shade All**.

- Select **Skin → Edit Smooth Skin → Paint Skin Weights Tool → ☐**.

  The painting option window opens and the geometry gets displayed in grayscale.

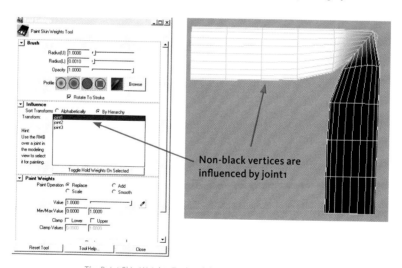

Non-black vertices are influenced by joint1

The Paint Skin Weights Tool and the weights on the geometry

Painting skin weights requires a solid understanding of bone influences. Since the tool is based on the Artisan Tool, you can edit the skin weighting on your own. Smooth binding, along with its various related tools, will be covered in greater detail in the intermediate *Learning Maya 8 | Modeling & Animation Handbook*.

Binding the bear

Since the bear is mostly composed of deformable skin objects, you will bind its geometry using smooth binding. You will also use binding for the eyes and claws. You could parent those objects directly to the skeleton, but it is an easier workflow to keep geometry in one hierarchy and the character skeleton in another.

1 Open the last lesson scene

- Open the file *09-boogSkeleton_01.ma.*

- **Save** the file as *10-boogSkinning_01.ma.*

2 Set Preferred Angle

When binding geometry on a skeleton, you need to test the binding by rotating the bones. By doing so, you should be able to replace the skeleton back to its default position quickly. Maya has two easily accessible commands called *Set Preferred Angle* and *Assume Preferred Angle*. Those commands allow you to first define the default skeleton pose, and then return to that pose whenever you want.

Note: *The preferred angle also defines the bending angle for IK handles.*

- Select the *pelvis* joint.

- In the viewport, **RMB** over the *pelvis* joint to pop the contextual Marking Menu.

- Select **Set Preferred Angle**.

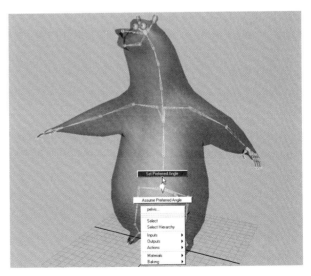

Joint Marking Menu

Note: *These commands are also available in the **Skeleton** menu.*

3 Assume Preferred Angle

- **Rotate** several joints to achieve a pose.

- Select the *pelvis* joint.

- In the viewport, **RMB** over the *pelvis* joint and select **Assume Preferred Angle**.

  The skeleton should return to its preferred angle (set in the previous step).

4 Bind the body

- Select **Skin → Bind Skin → Smooth Bind → ⬜**.

- In the smooth bind options, change **Bind To** to **Selected Joints**.

Tip: *It is recommended to select the joints to which you want to bind the geometry for simplicity reasons. You can thus avoid having unwanted influence on unwanted bones.*

- Select the following joints, which should play an important role in the binding of the bear:

pelvis	*lShoulder*	*rShoulder*	*lKnee*
spine	*lElbow*	*rElbow*	*lAnkle*
spine1	*lWrist*	*rWrist*	*lToes*
neck	*lThumb1*	*rThumb1*	*rHip*
neck1	*lIndex1*	*rIndex1*	*rKnee*
neck2	*lMiddle1*	*rMiddle1*	*rAnkle*
head	*lRing1*	*rRing1*	*rToes*
tail	*lPinky1*	*rPinky1*	
lClavicle	*rClavicle*	*lHip*	

Note: *For simplicity reasons, the head will only be influenced by the head joint.*

- **Shift-select** the *body* geometry.
- Click the **Bind Skin** button in the smooth bind option window.

  You will notice that the wireframe of the bound geometry is now purple, which is a visual cue to show the connection to the selected joint with history.

- **Rotate** the *pelvis* joint to see if the geometry follows correctly.

5   Smooth bind the eyeballs

- Select the *lEyeball* geometry, then **Shift-select** the *lEye* joint.
- Select **Skin → Bind Skin → Smooth Bind**.
- **Repeat** the previous steps to bind the right eye.
- **Rotate** the *eye* joints to see if the geometry follows correctly.

6   Rigid bind the eyelids

- Select the *lEyelid* and *rEyelid* geometry, then **Shift-select** the *head* joint.
- Select **Skin → Bind Skin → Rigid Bind → ❑.**
- In the rigid bind options, change **Bind To** to **Selected Joints**.
- Click the **Bind Skin** button.
- **Rotate** the *head* joints to see if the geometry follows correctly.

7   Rigid bind the claws

You can now rigid bind all the remaining claw geometry on its respective bones.

- Select the *pelvis* joint, then select **Skeleton → Assume Preferred Angle**.

  Doing so will ensure all the skeleton rotations are set to their preferred values.

Note: *Do not translate bones. The preferred angle command only keeps rotation values.*

- **Rigid bind** all the remaining geometry to the skeleton.

8 **Ensure everything is bound**

- To ensure all the geometry is bound, select the *pelvis* joint and **translate** it.

  You will easily notice if a piece is left behind.

- **Undo** the last movement to bring the skeleton back to its original position.

The entirely bound character

Joint degrees of freedom and limits

A character is usually unable to achieve every possible pose. In this case, the bear's articulation works in a similar way to the human body. Some joints cannot be rotated a certain way or exceed a certain rotation limit. Bending joints too much or in the wrong way might cause the geometry to interpenetrate or appear broken. Joints have many options to let you control how they are bent by the animator.

1 **Degrees of freedom**

By default, all three rotation axes on a joint are free to rotate. If you need to, you can limit the degrees of freedom on a joint. In the case of the bear, the elbows and knees cannot bend in all three directions due to the nature of a biped skeleton. Therefore, you need to limit these joints' rotations to a single axis.

- Select the *lElbow* joint.

- Notice on which axis the joint should be allowed to bend.

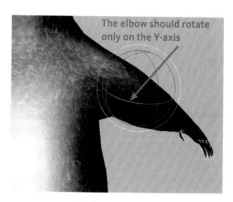

The elbow should rotate only on the Y-axis

The elbow rotation axes

Tip: *The Rotate Tool must be in Local mode.*

- Open the Attribute Editor and scroll to the **Joint** section.

- Turn **Off** the **X** and **Z** checkboxes for the **Degrees of Freedom** attribute.

    Notice that the **Rotate X** *and* **Rotate Z** *attributes in the Channel Box are now locked.*

2 Joint limits

A joint limit allows you to specify the minimum and maximum values allowed for a joint to rotate. In this case, the elbow joint needs to stop rotating when it gets fully bent or fully extended.

- Select the *lElbow* joint.

- **Rotate** the joint to bend it on the **Y-axis** and stop just before it interpenetrates with the upper arm.

- In the Attribute Editor, open the **Limit Information** section.

- In the **Rotate** section, turn **On** the **Rot Limit Y Min** attribute.

- Click on the **<** button to put the **Current** value in the **Min** field.

- **Rotate** the *lElbow* joint on the **Y-axis** the other way and stop when the arm is perfectly straight.

- Back in the Attribute Editor, turn **On** the **Rot Limit Y Max** attribute.

- Click on the **>** button to put the **Current** value in the **Max** field.

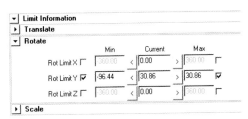

The lElbow rotation limits

3 Remainder of skeleton limits

You can now set the freedom and limitations on the bear skeleton as you would like them to be.

4 Save your work

The completed version of the bound bear can be found in the support files as *10-boogSkinning_01.ma*.

Conclusion

You have now explored the various skinning types required to bind a character to its skeleton. You also learned how to change joints' degrees of freedom and set limit information.

In the next lesson, you will refine your character setup by using IK handles, constraints and custom attributes. You will also create a reverse foot setup that will help maintain the robot's feet on the ground.

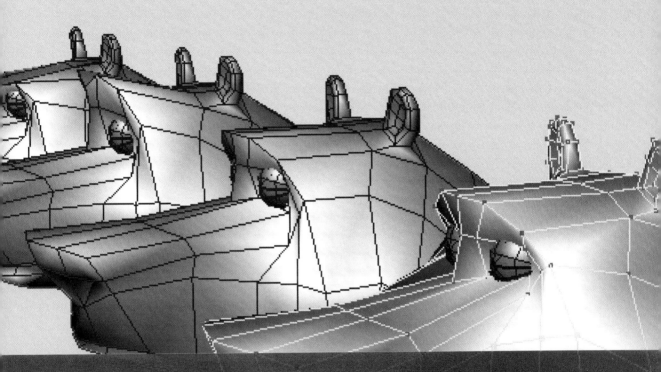

Lesson 11
Blend shapes

In this lesson you will create a blend shape deformer, which is a type of deformer that
blends between different geometry shapes. This will allow you to model facial expressions
for the bear to be used for animation.

In this lesson you will learn the following:

- How to sculpt surfaces by painting with the Artisan tool;

- How to use different brush operations;

- How to create blend shapes;

- How to access blend shapes.

Sculpting a surface

You will now test the Artisan Sculpt Tool. You will use the tool on a sphere to get a feel for it. Once you are more familiar with the tool, you will apply brush strokes to the bear geometry.

1 **Make a test sphere**

- **Create** a polygonal primitive sphere.

- Set its construction history for both **Subdivisions Axis** and **Subdivisions Height** to 60.

- To better see the effect of your painting in the viewport, assign a new *phong* material to the sphere by selecting **Lighting/Shading** → **Assign New Material** → **Phong**.

2 **Open the Sculpt Polygons Tool**

- With the *pSphere* selected, select **Mesh** → **Sculpt Geometry Tool** → ❐.

  This opens the **Tool Settings** *window, which includes every Artisan sculpting option.*

- Click on the **Reset Tool** button to make sure that you are starting with the Artisan default settings.

- Set the following attributes:

  Under **Brush**:

  Radius (U) to 0.2.

  Under **Sculpt Parameters**:

  Max Displacement to 0.1.

- Place the Tool Settings window to the right of the *sphere*.

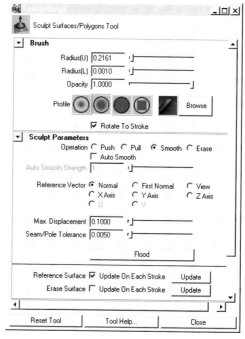

Tool Settings window

3 **Paint on the surface**

- Move your cursor over the *pSphere* geometry.

  The cursor icon changes to show an arrow surrounded by a red circular outline. The arrow indicates how much the surface will be pushed or pulled, while the outline indicates the brush radius. The Artisan brush icon is context sensitive. It changes as you choose different tool settings.

- **Click+drag** on the *sphere*.

  You are now painting on the surface, pushing it toward the inside.

Tip: *Artisan works more intuitively with a tablet and stylus, since the input device mimics the use of an actual paintbrush.*

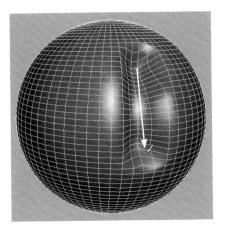

First brush stroke

4 **Change the Artisan display**

- Click the **Display** tab in the Tool Settings window.

- Click on **Show Wireframe** to turn this option **Off**.

  Now you can focus on the surface without displaying the wireframe lines.

5 **Paint another stroke**

- **Paint** a second stroke across the mask surface.

  Now it is easier to see the results of your sculpting.

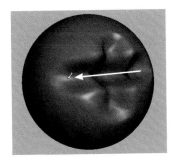

Second brush stroke

The sculpting tools

You will now explore some of the Artisan sculpting operations to see how they work. So far, you have been pushing on the surface. Now you will learn how to pull, smooth and erase.

1 **Pull on the surface**

- In the Tool Settings window, scroll to the **Sculpt Parameters** section.

- Under **Operation**, click on **Pull**.

- **Tumble** around to the other side of the sphere.

- **Paint** on the surface to create a few strokes that pull out.

2 **Smooth out the results**

- Under **Operation**, click on **Smooth**.

- Under **Brush**, change the **Radius (U)** to **0.6**.

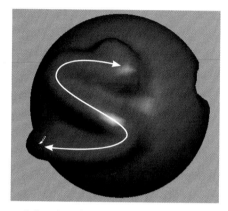

Pulling the surface with several brush strokes

This increases the size of your brush. You can see that the red outline has increased in size. This is the brush feedback icon.

Tip: *You can hold the **b** hotkey and **click+drag** in the viewport to interactively change the brush size.*

- **Paint** all of the strokes to smooth the details.

  If you stroke over an area more than once, the smoothing becomes more evident.

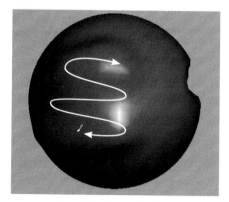

Smoothing the brush strokes

3 **Erase some of the brush strokes**

- Under **Operation**, click on the **Erase** option.

- **Paint** along the surface to begin erasing the last sculpt edits.

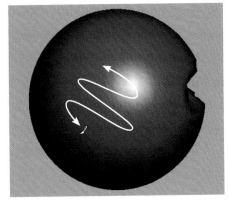

Erasing the brush strokes

4 **Flood erase the surface**

- Under **Operation**, click on the **Pull** option.

- In the **Sculpt Parameters** section, click on the **Flood** button.

  This uses the current operation and applies it to the entire surface using the current opacity setting.

- Under **Operation**, click on the **Erase** option.

- In the **Sculpt Parameters** section, click on the **Flood** button.

  The sphere comes back to its original shape.

Fully erased surface

Updating the reference surface

When you paint in Artisan, you paint in relation to a *reference surface*. By default, the reference surface updates after every stroke so that you can build your strokes on top of one another. You can also keep the reference surface untouched until you decide to update it manually.

1 **Change the brush attributes**

- Under **Operation**, click on **Pull**.

- Set the following attributes:

  Under **Brush**:

  Radius (U) to o.2.

  Under **Sculpt Parameters**:

  Max Displacement to o.2.

2 Pull the surface with two strokes

- **Paint** on the surface to create two crossing strokes that pull out.

  The second stroke is built on top of the first stroke. Therefore, the height of the pull is higher where the two strokes intersect.

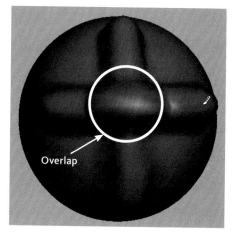

Painting with reference update

3 Change the reference update

- In the Tool Settings window, scroll down in the **Sculpt Parameters** section, and turn **Off** the **Reference Surface: Update On Each Stroke**.

4 Paint more overlapping strokes

- **Paint** on the surface to create a few strokes that pull out.

  *This time, the strokes do not overlap. The reference surface does not update, therefore the strokes can only displace to the **Maximum Displacement** value. You cannot displace beyond that value until you update the reference surface.*

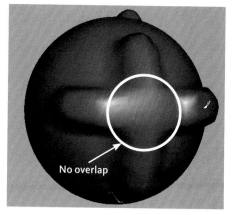

Painting with no reference update

5 Update the reference layer

- Still in the **Sculpt Parameters** section, click on the **Update** button next to **Reference Surface**.

6 Paint on the surface

- **Paint** another stroke over the last set of strokes.

The overlapping strokes are again building on top of each other.

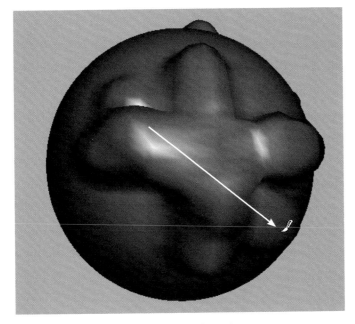

Painting on updated reference layer

7   **Flood erase the surface**

   - Under **Operation**, click on the **Erase** option.

   - Click on the **Flood** button.

Sculpting the bear

You will now use the Artisan Sculpt Tool to create a few facial shapes for the bear. You will first duplicate the body of the bear in order to have multiple copies to use for the blend shape deformer. Feel free to use your previously saved bear, or continue with *10-boogSkinning_01.ma*.

1   **Skin envelope**

   Before you start making blend shapes, you must ensure that the geometry is in its original position. One way to get the skin back to its exact original position is to turn off the skin's influence.

   - Select the bear's *body*.

- In the Channel Box, highlight the *skinCluster1* node.

- Set **Envelope** to o.

  Doing so temporarily turns off the skinCluster, thus removing any influence of the skeleton and placing the geometry back to its exact original position.

2 Duplicate the bear

The blend shape deformer requires the original untouched bear and bear duplicates to be deformed.

- Select all of the bear's geometry.

- Press **Ctrl+d** to **Duplicate** it.

 Tip: *Make sure the duplicate options are back to their default values.*

- **Rename** the new *body* geometry to *smile*.

- Highlight the *smile's* locked attributes in the Channel Box, then **RMB** and select **Unlock Selected**.

- **Move** the new geometry next to the original one.

- **Repeat** the previous steps to create the following duplicates:

        sad;
        browUp;
        browDown.

Highlight and unlock the attributes

The duplicates

Tip: *It is good to duplicate the other objects like the eyes, since you will be able to use them as reference for when you model the blend shapes.*

- Select the bear's *body*.

- In the Channel Box, highlight the *skinCluster1* node.

- Set **Envelope** to 1.

3 Sculpt the smile shape

You will use Artisan to paint and deform the smile geometry.

- With the *smile* body geometry selected, select **Mesh → Sculpt Geometry Tool → ❒** from the Polygons menu set.

- Click on the **Reset Tool** button to make sure that you are starting with Artisan's default settings.

- Set the following attributes:

Under **Brush**:

  Radius (U) to 0.5.

Under **Sculpt Parameters:**

  Operation to **Pull**;

  Reference Vector to **Y-axis**;

  Max Displacement to 0.1.

Under **Stroke:**

  Reflection to **On**.

This option allows you to sculpt only one side of the geometry to create the complete shape.

Under **Display:**

  Show Wireframe to **Off**.

This last option will turn off the display of the wireframe on the geometry. It is up to you to turn this on or off.

Note: In the previous test sphere example, you were painting using the normals of the surface as the direction to be pushed and pulled. In this case, you will pull along the **Y-axis**, which will move the vertices up.

- **Paint** directly on the model to get a shape similar to the following:

Smile shape

4 Sculpt the other shapes

- **Repeat** the previous steps to sculpt the three other shapes and any other shape you would want.

Sad shape

Brow up shape   Brow down shape

Blend shape deformer

In order to make character animation more realistic, you need a deformer that will blend between the original bear geometry and the geometry displaying emotion that you just created. That kind of deformer is called a *blend shape deformer*. Blend shapes are very useful in 3D, especially to animate facial expressions on characters, but they can also be used for plenty of other things.

1   Creating the deformer

- Select in order the *smile*, *sad*, *browUp* and *browDown* shapes and then **Shift-select** the original *body* shape.

Note: *It is important to select the original object last.*

- From the **Animation** menu set, select **Deform** → **Create Blend Shape** → ❐.
- In the blend shape option window, make sure to set **Origin** to **Local**.
- Select the **Advance** tab and make sure **Deformation Order** is set to **Front of chain**.
- Click the **Create** button.

Note: *The Front of Chain option tells Maya that you need the blend shape deformer to be inserted before any other deformers, such as the skinCluster.*

2 Testing the deformer

- Select the original *body* geometry.

  In the Channel Box, you should see a blendShape1 node and its construction history.

- **Highlight** the *blendShape1* node.

  Notice that the attributes have the same names as the geometry you duplicated earlier. Those attributes control the blending between the original shape and the sculpted ones.

INPUTS
skinCluster1
blendShape1
tweak25
  Envelope 1
  smile 0
  sad 0
  browUp 0
  browDown 0

The blendshape node

- **Highlight** the *smile* attribute's name.

- **MMB+drag** from left to right to invoke the virtual slider and see the effect of the deformer on the geometry.

- Experiment blending more than one shape at a time to see its effect.

Sad and browDown shapes mixed together

3 Tweaking the blend shape

Since construction history links the blend shape with the deformed surface, you can still tweak the sculpted geometry as needed.

- Make modifications on any of the sculpted geometry with the Artisan Sculpting Tool.

Tip: *Your changes must be made on the sculpted blend shape geometry and not on the original geometry.*

4 Delete targets

- Select all the duplicated geometry used to create the blend shapes.

- Press **Backspace** or **Delete** to dispose of them.

Note: *When you delete blend shape targets, Maya keeps the blend values in the blend shape node instead of using the geometry in the scene. Because of this, it is important to not delete the history on the model unless you want to get rid of the blend shapes.*

5 Save your work

- Save your scene as *11-boogBlendshapes_01.ma*

Conclusion

You are now more familiar with the very useful blend shape deformer, as well as the Artisan Sculpting Tool. You also learned about locators, custom attributes, connections and Set Driven Keys, which are essential for understanding any basic animation setup.

In the next lesson, you will use the animation locators to animate the orb into your scene.

Lesson 12
Inverse kinematics

In this lesson, you will add IK (inverse kinematics) handles and constraints to the existing bear skeleton in order to make the character easier to animate. You will also create a reverse foot setup, which simplifies floor contact when animating, and hand manipulators, which will help lock hands upon contact with the environment. Last, you will learn about pole vector constraints.

In this lesson you will learn the following:

- How to add single chain IK handles;

- How to add rotate plane IK handles;

- How to create a reverse foot setup;

- How to use point, orient and parent constraints;

- How to use pole vector constraints.

IK HANDLES

There are several types of IK handles and you will experiment with two types in this lesson: the *Single Chain IK* and the *Rotate Plane IK*. The difference between these two is that the single chain IK handle's end effector tries to reach the position *and* orientation of its IK handle, whereas the rotate plane IK handle's end effector only tries to reach the position of its IK handle.

Single Chain IK

A single chain IK handle uses the single chain solver to calculate the rotations of all joints in the IK chain. Also, the overall orientation of the joint chain is calculated directly by the single chain solver.

1 **Open the last bear scene**

- **Open** the file *11-bookBlendshapes_01.ma*.

- **Save** the file as *12-boogIK_01.ma*.

2 **Joint rotation limits**

For better results using IKs, it is not recommended to have rotation limits on joints that are part of an IK handle. Limiting joint rotations will prevent the IK solver from finding good joint rotations and may cause it to behave unexpectedly.

- **Remove** rotation limits and enable all degrees of freedom for the *shoulder, elbow* and *wrist* joints, if any.

- **Remove** rotation limits and enable all degrees of freedom for the *hip, knee, ankle* and *toe* joints, if any.

Note: *Rotation limits and degrees of freedom are especially useful on joints intended to be animated manually.*

3 **Single Chain IK**

- Select **Skeleton → IK Handle Tool → ❏**.

  The tool's option window will be displayed.

- Change the **Current Solver** for the **ikSCsolver**.

- Click on the **Close** button.

- In the viewport, click on the *IShoulder* bone.

  The joint will be highlighted. This is the start joint.

- Click on the *IWrist* bone.

  The IK handle gets created, starting at the shoulder and going down to the wrist of the character.

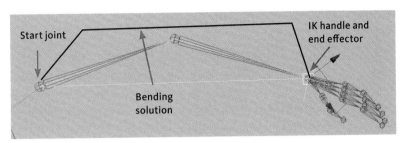

Single chain IK

In the Hypergraph, you can see the end effector connected into the hierarchy and the IK handle to the side. The end effector and the IK handle are connected along with the appropriate joints at the dependency node level. When you control the handle, you control the whole IK chain.

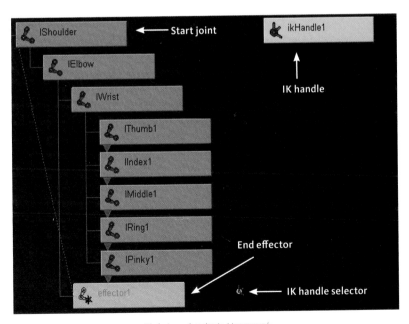

IK chain and nodes in Hypergraph

4   **Experiment with the IK handle**

- Press **w** to enter the **Translate Tool**.

- **Translate** the IK handle and notice the resulting bending of the arm.

Tip: *If the IK handle does not bend the arm or if it bends it the wrong way, it is because the angle in the arm joint chain was not appropriate. To remedy the situation, delete the IK handle, bend the arm appropriately and then recreate the IK.*

- Press **e** to enter the **Rotate Tool**.

- **Rotate** the IK handle and notice the resulting bending of the arm.

  Rotating the IK handle will change the bending solution, but will not affect the wrist's rotation. You will create a hand setup in a later exercise.

- **Rename** the IK handle *lArmIk*.

5   **Preferred angle**

- With the IK selected, **RMB** in the viewport and select **Assume Preferred Angle**.

  The arm joints and the IK handle will move back to the preferred angle set in the previous lesson.

6   **Right arm IK**

- **Create** another single chain IK for the right arm and rename it *rArmIk*.

Tip: *IK handles have a higher selection priority than joints and geometry. To pick an IK handle, simply make a selection bounding box over it.*

Rotate Plane IK

A rotate plane IK handle uses the rotate plane solver to calculate the rotations of all joints in its IK chain, but not the joint chain's overall orientation. Instead, the IK rotate plane handle gives you direct control over the joint chain's orientation via the pole vector and twist disk, rather than having the orientation calculated by the IK solver.

Note: *The twist disc is a visual representation showing the vector defining the chain's overall orientation. You will experiment with the twist disk in the following steps.*

1 Rotate Plane IK

- Select **Skeleton** → **IK Handle Tool** → ❑.

- Change the **Current Solver** for **ikRPsolver**.

- Click on the **Close** button.

- In the viewport, click on the *lhip* bone.

- Click on the *lAnkle* bone.

  The IK handle gets created, starting at the hip and going down to the ankle of the character.

2 Experiment with the IK handle

One differentiating feature of this type of IK handle is the ability to control the twist of the solution using the *Twist* and *Pole Vector* attributes.

- **Move** the IK handle up.

- Press **t** to show the IK handle manipulators.

- **Move** the pole vector manipulator located next to the twist disk.

  This manipulator affects the pointing direction of the IK chain.

- Highlight the **Twist** attribute in the Channel Box and **MMB+drag** in the viewport.

  This attribute also affects the pointing direction of the IK chain, but overrides the pole vector attributes.

- **Rename** the IK handle *lLeglk*.

3 Reset the IK handle's position

- With the IK selected, **RMB** in the viewport and select **Assume Preferred Angle**.

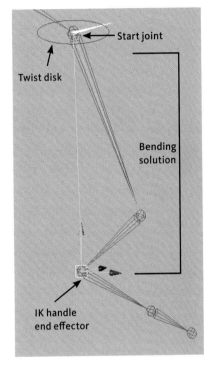

Rotate plane IK

Lesson 12: Inverse kinematics

4 **Right leg IK**

- **Create** another rotate plane IK for the right leg.

- **Rename** the IK handle *rLegIk*.

5 **Save your work**

Reverse Foot

When you animate a walking character, you need one of the character's feet to plant itself while the other foot is lifted into position. In the time it is planted, the foot needs to roll from heel to toe. A reverse foot skeleton is the ideal technique for creating these conditions.

1 **Draw the reverse foot skeleton**

- Change the viewport for a *four view* layout.

- Dolly on the feet of the bear in all views.

- Select **Skeleton → Joint Tool**.

  The **Orientation** *of the tool should be set to* **XYZ**.

- In the *side* view, create the first joint on the heel of the bear's foot.

- In the *front* view, **MMB+drag** the new joint to align it with the rest of the foot joints.

- In the *Perspective* view, turn **Off** the geometry display by selecting **Show → NURBS Surfaces** and **Show → Polygons**.

- Hold down the **v** hotkey to enable **Snap to Point**.

- **Draw** three other bones, snapping them to the *toesEnd, toes* and *ankle* joints respectively.

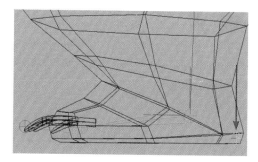

The heel joint

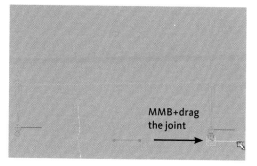

MMB+drag
the joint

Move the heel joint

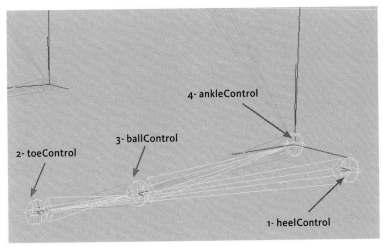

The complete reverse foot

- Press **Enter** to exit the tool.

2 Rename the joints

- **Rename** the joints as shown to the right:

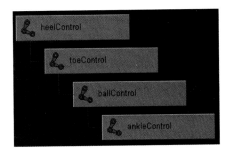

Renamed joints

Set-up the reverse foot

To control the foot and have a proper heel to toe rotation, you will now constrain the IK handle, ankle and toe joints to the reverse foot chain. This will allow you to use the reverse foot chain to control the foot and leg.

1 Point constrain the IK handle

- Select the *ankleControl* joint on the reverse foot chain.

- **Shift-select** the IK handle.

- Select **Constrain → Point**.

  The point constraint forces an object to follow the position of a source object. The IK handle is now positioned over the reverse foot's ankleControl joint.

Tip: *You may want to use the Hypergraph panel to help you select the joint.*

2 Test the reverse foot chain

- Select the *heelControl* joint.

- **Move** the joint to test the foot setup so far.

  The ankle moves with the reverse foot chain, but the joints do not stay properly aligned.

- **Undo** your moves.

3 Orient constrain the toes

To align the rest of the foot, you will orient constrain the *toes'* joint to the reverse foot.

- Select the *toeControl* joint on the reverse foot chain.

- **Shift-select** the *toes'* joint from the leg chain.

- Select **Constrain → Orient → ❑** .

- In the orient constraint options, turn **On** the Maintain Offset option.

- Click the **Add** button.

  The orient constraint forces an object to follow the rotation of a source object. The Maintain Offset option forces the constrained object to keep its position.

- **Move** the *heelControl* joint to test the foot setup so far.

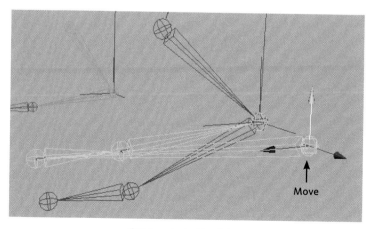

Orient constrained toes' joint

- **Undo** your moves.

4 Orient Constrain the ankle joint

You will now repeat these last few steps for the *ankle* joint.

- Select the *ballControl* joint on the reverse foot chain.

- **Shift-select** the *ankle* joint from the leg chain.

- Select **Constrain → Orient**.

  Now the foot joints and reverse foot joints are aligned.

5 Test the movement of the reverse foot

- **Rotate** the different joints of the foot setup to test them.

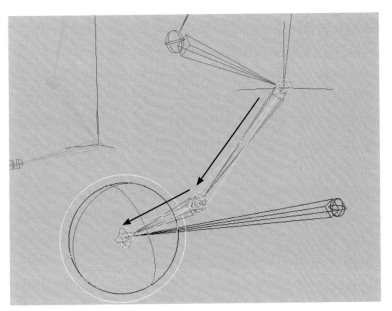

Orient constrained ankle joint

- **Undo** your moves.

- Select the *heelControl* joint.

- **Move** the joint to test the motion.

  If you pull the reverse foot further than the leg chain will allow, the leg will pull away from the reverse foot. This is the desired effect.

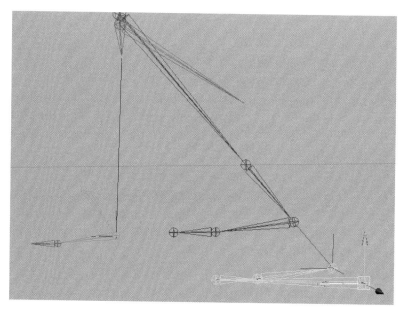

Moving the reverse foot chain

- **Undo** the last movement to bring the reverse foot back to its original position.

Creating the heel to toe motion

You can now control the rotation of the foot by rotating the various control joints on the reverse foot. Instead of requiring the rotation of several joints to achieve a heel to toe motion, you will use Set Driven Key to control the roll using a single attribute on the *heelControl* joint.

1 **Add a Roll attribute**

- Select the *heelControl* joint.

- Select **Modify** → **Add Attribute**.

- Set the following values in the Add Attribute window:

    Attribute Name to roll;

    Data Type to **Float**;

    Minimum to -5;

    Maximum to 10;

    Default to 0.

- Click **OK** to add the attribute.

  You can now see this attribute in the Channel Box. The minimum and maximum values give reasonable boundary values for the roll.

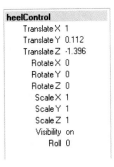

The roll attribute in the Channel Box

2 Prepare the Set Driven Key window

- Select **Animate** → **Set Driven Key** → **Set…**

- Select the *heelControl* joint and click **Load Driver**.

- In the **Driver** section, highlight the **Roll** attribute.

- Select the *heelControl*, *ballControl* and *toeControl* joints and click **Load Driven**.

Set Driven Key window

3 Key the heel rotation

- In the **Driven** section, highlight **heelControl** and the **rotate Z** attribute.

- Click on the **Key** button to set the starting rotation.

- In the Channel Box, set the **Roll** value to **-5**.

- Set the **Rotate Z** to **20**.

- Again, click on the **Key** button.

Foot rotated back on heel

- You can now test the **roll** attribute by clicking on its name in the Channel Box and MMB+dragging in the viewport. You can see that the foot rolls from the heel to a flat position.

- Set the **Roll** attribute to 0.

4 Key the ball rotation

- In the **Driven** section, click on **ballControl** and then on **rotate Z**.

- Click on the **Key** button to set the starting rotation.

- Click on **heelControl** in the **Driver** section and set the **Roll** value to 10.

- Click on **ballControl** and set the **Rotate Z** to 30.

- Again, click on the **Key** button in the Set Driven Key window.

- Click on **heelControl** and set the **Roll** value back to 0.

 Tip: *When working with Set Driven Key, always set the value of the driver before setting the driven. If you set the driver second, it will reset your driven value because of earlier keys.*

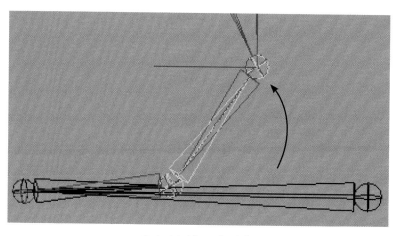

Foot rotated forward on ball

5 Key the toe rotation

- In the **Driven** section, click on **toeControl** and then on **rotate Z**.

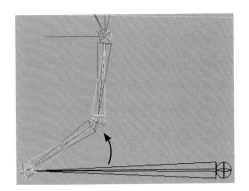

Foot rotated forward on toe

- Click on the **Key** button to set the starting rotation.

- Click on **heelControl** and set the **Roll** value to **10**.

- Click on **toeControl** and set the **Rotate Z** to **30**.

- Again, click on the **Key** button.

6 **Test the foot roll**

- Select the *heelControl* joint.

- Click on the **Roll** attribute name in the Channel Box and **MMB+drag** in the viewport to test the roll.

- Set the **Roll** back to **0**.

- Click the **Close** button in the Set Driven Key window.

7 **Right foot setup**

Create another reverse foot setup for the right leg.

- Select the *heelControl* joint.

- Select **Edit** → **Duplicate Special** → .

- In the options, turn **On** the Duplicate input graph option.

- Click the **Duplicate Special** button.

  By duplicating the input graph, you will keep the driven keys you have just made.

- In the Channel Box, change the value of the **TranslateX** attribute to be the same value, but **negative**.

- **Recreate** the different constraints on the right foot.

- **Rename** all the joints appropriately with their left and right prefixes.

8 **Test the setup**

- Select the *pelvis* joint.

- **Move** and **rotate** the *pelvis* to see the effect of the constrained IK handles.

Moving the pelvis joint

- **Undo** the last step to bring the pelvis back to its original position.

9 Save your work

Hand Setup

It is good to be able to plant the feet of your character, but it would also be good to control the hand rotations. In this exercise, you will create a basic hand setup that will allow you to control the hand rotations.

1 Change the arm IK type

Single plane IKs are best used when you don't need to bother with the hands' rotation. This means that they are not ideal for the type of control you are looking for in this case. You will need to delete the ones you have on the arms and create new rotate plane IKs.

- Select the two arm IK handles.

- Press **Delete** on your keyboard.

- Select **Skeleton → IK Handle Tool**.

  The IK type should already be set to ikRPsolver.

- **Create** IK handles for both arms.
- **Rename** the IK handles properly.

2 Create a hand manipulator

- Select **Show → NURBS Surfaces** to hide all the NURBS surfaces in the viewport.
- Select **Create → NURBS Primitives → Circle**.
- **Rename** the circle *lHandManip*.
- Press **w** to enter the **Translate Tool**.
- Hold down the **v** hotkey and snap the *circle* to the *lWrist* of the skeleton.
- **Rotate** and **scale** the circle to fit the wrist.

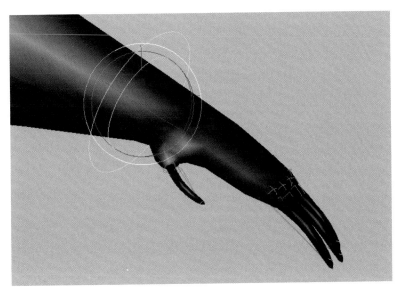

The hand manipulator

- Select **Modify → Freeze Transformations**.

3 Constrain the IK handle

- With the *circle* still selected, **Shift-select** the *lArmIk* handle.
- Select **Constrain → Parent**.

  The parent constraint forces the constrained object to follow a source object just as if it parented to it.

4   Constrain the wrist

- Select the *circle*, then **Shift-select** the *lWrist* joint.

- Select **Constrain** → **Orient**.

5   Test the wrist manipulator

- **Move** and **rotate** the *lHandManip* to see how it affects the arm and hand.

- **Move** and **rotate** the *pelvis* joint to see how it affects the arm and hand.

  Notice the hand stays planted wherever it is. This is exactly the behavior you are looking for.

- **Undo** the last steps to place the *pelvis* and *lHandManip* in their original locations.

6   Create a pole vector constraint

- Select **Create** → **Locator**.

- Hold down **v** to enable **Snap to Point**, then snap the locator on the *lElbow* joint.

- **Move** the *locator* back on the **Z-axis** by about **5 units**.

- With the *locator* selected, **Shift-select** the *lArmlk* handle.

- Select **Constrain** → **Pole Vector**.

  The pole vector constraint will connect the locator's position into the IK handle's **Pole Vector** *attribute. By doing this, you can now control the rotation of the arm using a visual indicator.*

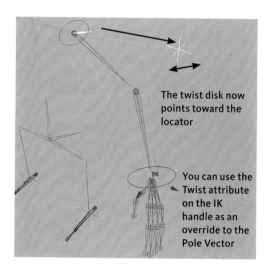

The twist disk now points toward the locator

You can use the Twist attribute on the IK handle as an override to the Pole Vector

A pole vector locator

- **Rename** the locator to *lArmPv.*

7   Right hand manipulator

- **Create** the same type of manipulator on the right hand.

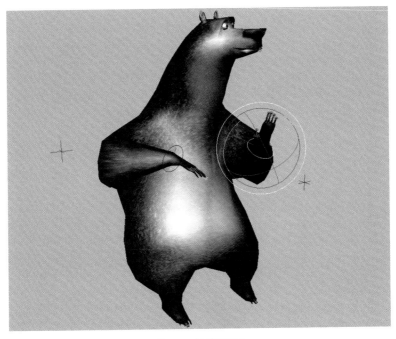

The completed IK setup

8 **Save your work**

- The final scene is named *12-boogIK_01.ma*.

Conclusion

In this lesson, you learned the basics of how to use IK handles in a custom setup. You experimented with some of the most popular tricks, such as the reverse foot setup and manipulators. You also used the twist attribute and pole vector constraints, which are required for any good IK handle animation.

In the next lesson, you will refine the current character setup even more. Steps will include creating an eye setup, locking and hiding non-required attributes, adding and connecting custom attributes and creating a character set. Doing so will make your character rig easier to use, limiting manipulation errors that could potentially break it. Last, you will generate a higher resolution version of the geometry.

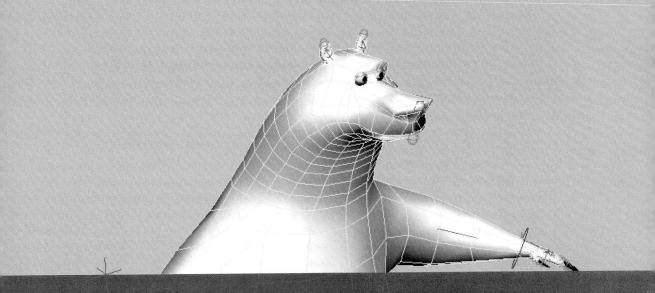

Lesson 13
Rigging

Character rigging requires a thorough knowledge of the Maya objects and lots of experimentation. The more you experiment with creating and animating character rigs, the better you will become at producing first-rate setups.

In this lesson, you will finalize the bear rig by making it animator friendly. This means that you will make the various useful setups and attributes easy to find, as well as hiding unnecessary ones. You will also create a high-resolution polygonal version of the bear, in order to get better visualization once you are done animating.

In this lesson you will learn the following:

- How to organize the rig's hierarchy;

- How to create selection sets and create visibility layers;

- How to strategically place attributes;

- How to use aim constraints and the jiggle deformer;

- How to lock and hide nodes and attributes;

- How to create a smooth node and hook it to the rig and a character set for keyframing.

Rig hierarchy

When you look in the Outliner, your character's hierarchy should be clean, well named and simple to understand. For instance, all the setup nodes should be parented together under a master node. You could then use that master node for the global placement of the character in a scene.

1 Open the last setup scene

- **Open** the file *12-boogIK_01.ma.*

- **Save** the scene as *13-boogRig_01.ma.*

2 Geometry group

- Select all the bound geometry in your scene.

Tip: *It might be simpler to select geometry groups from the Outliner.*

- Press **Ctrl+g** to group it all together.

- **Rename** the group *lores* (low resolution).

- Select the *lores* group and press **Ctrl+g** again.

- **Rename** the group *geo.*

3 Create a master node

- Change the current view for the *top* view.

- Select **Create →
  EP Curve → ❑**.

- Change the **Curve Degree** for **1 Linear**.

- Click the **Close** button.

- Hold down **x** and draw a four-arrows shape as indicated:

- Hit **Enter** to complete the curve.

- **Rename** the curve *master.*

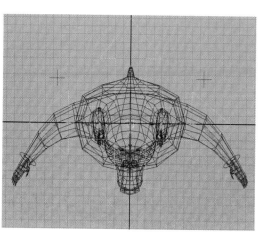

The master node curve

4 **Hierarchy**

- Select **Panels** → **Saved Layouts** → **Persp/Outliner**.

- In the Outliner, select all character setup nodes and **Parent** them to the *master* node.

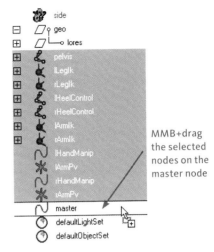

MMB+drag the selected nodes on the master node

Parent setup nodes to master

Note: *Do not parent bound geometry or the geometry group to the master node.*

There should now be only two main groups in the Outliner, which are geo *and* master.

5 **Node names**

- Make sure all nodes are named correctly.

Note: *It is recommended to have unique names for all your objects.*

6 **Character rig layer**

- In the Layer Editor, click on the **Create new layer** button.

- **Rename** the new layer *setupLayer*.

- Select the *geo* node in the *Perspective* view, then **RMB** on the *setupLayer* and select **Add Selected Objects**.

All the character rig nodes can now be hidden by hiding the setupLayer.

Selection sets

Selection sets are meant to simplify the selection process of multiple objects. In the bear setup, it would be nice to select all the finger joints at once in order to be able to open or close the hand easily.

1 Select the fingers

- Select the *lWrist* joint.

- Select **Edit → Select Hierarchy.**

  This will select all the child joints of the lWrist joint.

- **Ctrl+click** on the *lWrist* bone to deselect it.

- Put the cursor over the Outliner and press **f** to frame the selected objects.

  You should see that all the fingers and the lWrist_orientConstraint are selected.

- **Ctrl+click** on the *lWrist_orientConstraint* to deselect it.

2 Create a set

- Select **Create → Sets → Quick Select Set...**

- In the Create Quick Select Set window, enter the name *lFingersSet.*

- Click the **OK** button.

  If you scroll down in the Outliner, there will be a set called lFingersSet.

  lFingersSet

The new set

3 Use the selection set

- Select *lFingersSet* in the Outliner.

- **RMB** to pop a contextual menu and select **Select Set Members.**

  All the objects in the set are selected.

- Press **e** to enter the **Rotate Tool.**

- **Rotate** all the joints simultaneously.

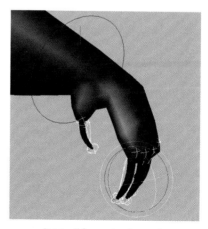

Rotate all fingers simultaneously

Tip: *If you notice that some joint local rotation axes are not aligned to close the fingers correctly, you can go in Component mode and adjust them.*

4 **Edit a selection set**

- **Undo** the last rotation.

- Select **Window** → **Relationship Editors** → **Sets**.

- On the left side of the Relationship Editor, click on the **+** sign next to the *lFingersSet* to expand it.

  All the objects in that set are displayed.

- Still in the left side of the Relationship Editor, highlight the *lThumb1*, *lThumb2* and *lThumb3* joints from the set *lFingersSet*.

- Select **Edit** → **Remove Highlighted from Set**.

Note: *When you highlight a set in the Relationship Editor, its members are highlighted on the right side of the panel. Toggle objects on the right side to add or remove them to the current set.*

- **Close** the Relationship Editor.

5 **Create a set for the right hand**

6 **Save your work**

- **Save** your scene as *13-boogRig_01.ma*.

Custom attributes

As you will notice by working in the current rig, some attributes are not easy to access. You should place useful attributes on strategic nodes for easy access.

Since you control the arms and legs' IK handles using custom setups, it is a good idea to place useful IK attributes on the hands, manipulator and the reverse foot bones.

1   Add new attributes

- Select the *lHandManip*, the *rHandManip*, the *lHeelControl* and the *rHeelControl*.

- Select **Modify** → **Add Attribute**.

- Set the following:

    Attribute Name to **twist**;

    Data Type to **Float**;

    Default to **o**.

- Click the **Add** button.

    This will add the **Twist** *attribute to all selected nodes. The Add Attribute window will remain open for further attribute additions.*

- Set the following:

    Attribute Name to **ikBlend**;

    Data Type to **Integer**;

    Minimum to **o**;

    Maximum to **1**;

    Default to **1**.

- Click the **OK** button.

2   Connect the new attributes

- Select **Window** → **General Editors** → **Connection Editor**.

- Select the *lHandManip*.

- In the Connection Editor, click on the **Reload Left** button.

- Scroll down and highlight the **Twist** attribute.

- Select the *lArmIk*.

- In the Connection Editor, click on the **Reload Right** button.

- Scroll down and highlight the **Twist** attribute.

    You have just connected the **Twist** *attribute of the hand manipulator to the left arm IK handle* **Twist** *attribute.*

- Highlight the **ikBlend** attribute on the left side of the editor.

- Highlight the **ikBlend** attribute on the right side of the editor.

  *The **ikBlend** attribute of the hand manipulator is now connected to the left arm IK handle **ikBlend** attribute.*

3 Repeat

- **Repeat** the previous steps in order to connect the remaining *rHandManip*, *lHeelControl* and *rHeelControl* attributes to their respective IK handles.

- Click the **Close** button to close the Connection Editor.

4 Hide the IK handles

Since you have connected the *Twist* and *IK Blend* attributes of the IK handles to their manipulators, the IK handles can now be hidden since they are no longer required to be visible or selected.

- Select the *lArmIk*, the *rArmIk*, the *lLegIk* and the *rLegIk*.

- Set the **Visibility** attribute in the Channel Box to **Off** by typing **o** in the Channel Box.

  All the IK handles are now hidden.

- Highlight the **Visibility** attribute's name.

- **RMB** in the Channel Box and select **Lock Selected**.

  *Doing so will prevent the IK handles from being displayed, even when using the **Display → Show → All** command.*

Selection handles

There are several nodes that you will need to select when animating the character. Unfortunately, those nodes can be hidden under geometry or difficult to pick in the viewport. This is where a selection handle becomes helpful.

1 Show selection handles

- Select the *lHeelControl*, the *rHeelControl* and the *pelvis* joints.

- Select **Display → Transform Display → Selection Handles**.

- Clear the current selection.

- **Click+drag** a selection box over the entire character in the viewport.

  Since selection handles have a very high selection priority, only the three selection handles get selected.

2 Move selection handles

- Go in **Component** mode.

- Make sure only the selection handle mask is enabled.

The selection handle mask

- Select the selection handles for the *lHeelControl*, the *rHeelControl* and the *pelvis* joints.

- Press **w** to enable the **Translate Tool**.

- **Translate** the selection handles towards the back of the **Z-axis** until they are outside the geometry.

- Go back in **Object** mode.

3 Save your work

- **Save** your scene as *13-boogRig_02.ma*.

The selection handle outside the geometry

Eye setup

The eyes of the bear need to be able to look around freely. To do so, you will create an aim constraint, which forces an object to aim at another object. You will also need to define a new attribute for blinking.

1 LookAt locator

- A locator will be used to specify a point in space where the eyes will be looking. Select **Create → Locator** and **rename** it *lookAt*.

- **Move** the locator in front of the bear about **20 units** on the **X-axis** and about **30 units** on the **Y-axis**.

- **Parent** the *lookAt* locator to the *master* node.

The lookAt locator

2 Freeze transformations

In order to easily place the *lookAt* locator at its default position, you should freeze its transformations.

- Select the *lookAt* locator.

- Select **Modify → Freeze Transformations**.

3 Aim constraint

- Select *lookAt*, then from the Outliner, **Ctrl-select** the *lEye* joint from the Outliner.

Note: *You might have to expand the hierarchy in the Outliner using the **+** sign to reach the desired node.*

- Select **Constrain → Aim → ❑**.

- Turn **On** the **Maintain Offset** checkbox, then click the **Add** button.

- **Repeat** for the *rEye* joint.

4 Experiment with lookAt

- Select the *lookAt* locator and **move** it around to see how the *eyeball* reacts.

The eyes looking at the locator

5 Eye blink attribute

It would be good to have a *blink* attribute on the locator, to make it easy to blink the bear's eyes.

- Select the *lookAt* locator and select **Modify** → **Add Attribute...**

- Set the following in the new attribute window:

  Attribute Name to *blink*;

  Data Type to **Float**;

  Minimum to 0;

  Maximum to 2;

  Default to 1.

- Click the **OK** button to add the new attribute.

6 Eye blink driven keys

- Select the **Animate** → **Set Driven Key** → **Set**.

- Load the *lookAt* node and the *blink* attribute as the driver.

- Select both *eyelid* geometry, then highlight the *makeNurbsSphere* in the Channel Box.

- Click on the **Load Driven** button.

- Highlight the two *makeNurbsSphere* nodes and highlight their *startSweep* and *endSweep*.

- Click the **Key** button.

- Set the **blink** attribute to 0, then set the **sweep** attributes to set the eye closed.

- Click the **Key** button.

- Set the **blink** attribute to 2, then set the **sweep** attributes to set the eye wide open.

- Click the **Key** button.

7 Test the eye blink

- Test the **Blink** attribute using the virtual slider.

Jiggle deformer

The jiggle deformer will make vertices jiggle as the geometry is moving. You will use a jiggle deformer on the belly of the bear so that it wobbles as he is walking.

1 Paint Selection Tool

- Select the *body* geometry.

- In the Toolbox, **double-click** on the **Paint Selection Tool**.

- **Paint** on the *body* geometry to easily select the belly vertices.

Tip: *Use the Unselect paint operation to select unwanted vertices.*

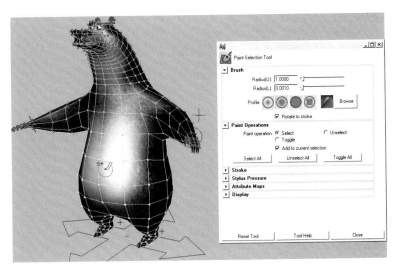

The vertices to be used with the jiggle deformer

2 Create a jiggle deformer

- Select **Deform** → **Create Jiggle Deformer** → **Regular**.

- In the option window, set the following:

 Ignore Transform to **On**;

 Stiffness to 0.2;

 Damping to 0.2.

- Click the **Create** button.

 The jiggle1 deformer will be added to the bear's input history in the Channel Box.

3 Smooth the jiggle influence

As it is right now with default value, all the vertices selected are fully affected by the jiggle deformer. It is possible to create a nice gradient effect by smoothing the jiggle's weight.

- Select **Deform** → **Paint Jiggle Weights Tool** → ☐.

- Change the **Paint Operation** to **Smooth**.

- Click on the **Flood** button repetitively 5 or 6 times to get the image on the right:

- Close the tool window.

The jiggle influence

4 Test the jiggle deformer

In order to test the jiggle deformer, take some time to keyframe some rough animation and playback the scene. The attributes of the jiggle deformer to tweak can be found in the Channel Box, when the *body* geometry is selected.

Once testing is over, remove the animation and make sure all the joints are at their preferred angle.

5 Save your work

- **Save** your scene as *13-boogRig_03.ma*.

Hide and lock nodes and attributes

Many nodes and attributes in the character rig are not supposed to be animated or changed. It is recommended that you double-check each node and attribute to see if the animator requires them. If they are not required, you can hide and lock them.

The Channel Control window allows you to quickly set which attributes are displayed in the Channel Box and which ones are locked.

1 Lock geometry groups

Since all the geometry is bound to the skeleton, it must not be moved. All the geometry attributes should therefore be locked.

- Select **Window** → **Hypergraph Scene Hierarchy**.

- Make sure all nodes are visible in the Hypergraph by setting **Options** → **Display** → **Hidden Nodes** to **On**.

- Select the *geo* group.

- Select **Edit** → **Select Hierarchy**.

- In the Channel Box, highlight the **Translate**, **Rotate** and **Scale** attribute names.

- **RMB** in the Channel Box and select **Lock and Hide Selected**.

2   Channel Control Editor

- Select **Window** → **General Editors** → **Channel Control**.

  Under the **Keyable** *tab, all the keyable attributes shown in the Channel Box are displayed. If you highlight attributes and then click on the* **Move >>** *button, the selected attributes will be moved in the* **Nonkeyable Hidden** *column. Notice that only the* **Visibility** *attribute is still visible in the Channel Box.*

  In the same manner, under the **Locked** *tab, you can move the wanted attributes from the* **Locked** *column to the* **Non-Locked** *column and vice versa.*

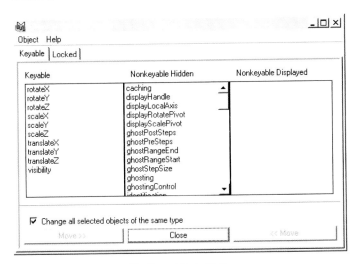

The Channel Control Editor

3   Hide end joints

End joints are usually not animated.

- **Lock and hide** all the end joints on your skeleton.

An end joint is the last joint in a joint chain. They are usually created only for visual reference and often never used.

Tip: *Try using* **Edit** → **Select All by Type** → **Joints***, then press, the down arrow repetitively until all the end joints are selected.*

4 **Lock joints**

Joints can usually rotate, but should not be translated or scaled. There are exceptions, such as *joint roots*, that usually need to be able to translate.

- **Lock and hide** the **Translate**, **Scale** and **Visibility** attributes for all the joints in the scene, except for *pelvis*, *lHeelControl* and *rHeelControl,* which require translation.

- **Lock and hide** the **Scale** and **Visibility** attributes for the *pelvis*, *lHeelControl* and *rHeelControl.*

5 **Rest of setup**

You should spend some time checking each node in your character rig hierarchy to lock and hide unwanted attributes or nodes. When you don't know what an attribute does, you should at least set it to non-keyable, so that it doesn't appear in the Channel Box. This will prevent it from being keyframed accidentally.

6 **Master scale**

You should make sure to set the *master*'s scaling attributes to non-keyable, but you should not lock these attributes. By doing so, you can be sure no keyframes will be made on the global scaling of the character, but you will still be able to change the bear's scaling to fit its environment.

7 **Save your work**

- **Save** your scene as *13-boogRig_04.ma.*

High resolution model

When animating a character, it is good to have the choice of displaying either the high resolution or low resolution model. In this case, the bear geometry is already quite low resolution and it would be good to have a high resolution version of the model to visualize the final result of your animation.

Here you will use a polygonal smooth node and connect it to a new attribute on the character's master. Once that is done, you will be able to crank up the bear's resolution easily.

1 **Smooth polygons**

- Select the *body* geometry.

- Select **Mesh → Smooth**.

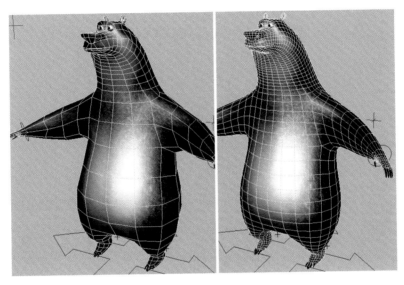

High resolution geometry

2 **Smooth attribute**

- Select the *master* node.

- Select **Modify → Add Attribute…**

- Set the following in the new attribute window:

  Attribute Name to *smooth*;

  Data Type to **Float**;

  Minimum to 0;

  Maximum to 3;

  Default to 0.

- Click the **OK** button to add the new attribute.

- With the *body* still selected, highlight the *polySmoothFace1* node from the Channel Box.

- Using the Connection Editor, connect the new *smooth* attribute to the *polySmoothFace1*'s **Divisions** attribute.

- **Test** the new attribute.

  You can now easily increase or decrease the resolution of the model.

3 Layer

- Click the **Create a new layer** button in the Layer Editor.

- **Rename** the layer *geometryLayer*.

- Add the *geo* group to the new *geometryLayer*.

  The layers will allow you to quickly toggle between the setup and the models.

Creating character sets

In the next lesson, you will use keyframing techniques to make the bear walk. To organize all animation channels needed for keyframing, you can create character sets. These sets let you collect attributes into a single node that can then be efficiently keyed and edited as a group.

1 Create a main character node

- Select the *master* node.

- Select **Character** → **Create Character Set** → **o** from the Animation menu set.

- Set the following:

  Name to *bear*;

  Hierarchy below selected node to **On**;

  All keyable to **On**.

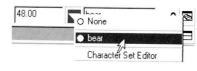

Character menu

- Click **Create Character Set.**

  This character is now active and visible next to the Range Slider. It was created with all the keyframable attributes for the entire master hierarchy.

2 Remove unnecessary attributes from the character set

- Select the *bear* character set from the Outliner.

  All the character's attributes are listed in the Channel Box.

 bear

The character node

If you scroll in the Channel Box, you will notice that some attributes are already connected (colored). They are being driven by constraints, therefore, they are not needed in the character.

- Use the **Ctrl** key to highlight all of the colored attributes in the Channel Box for the bear character set.

- Select **Character → Remove from Character Set**.

Those attributes are now removed from the character set.

3 **Save your work**

- **Save** your scene as *13-boogRig_05.ma.*

Conclusion

You now have a biped character all hooked up and ready for a stroll. You made your character rig simpler for an animator to use and virtually unbreakable. You also created an attribute to set the resolution of the model, which will be very useful for visualizing animation.

In the next lesson, you will animate the bear using the character rig and character set. It will put both your rig and animation skills to the test.

Lesson 14
Animation

The character you built is now ready to be animated. To create a walk cycle, you will build up the motion one part at a time. Starting with the sliding of the feet, you will then lift the feet, use the roll attribute and set the twist of the pelvis. When that is done, you will animate the upper body accordingly.

In this lesson, you will learn the following:

- How to reference a scene;
- How to animate the character's legs and arms;
- How to animate the roll of the foot;
- How to animate the twist of the pelvis;
- How to create a cycle using the Graph Editor;
- How to bake animation channels;
- How to create a Trax clip;
- How to export a Trax clip.

Reference

Instead of working with the file from the last lesson, you will reference the bear. A reference refers to another scene file that is set to read-only. It allows you to animate the character, leaving the rig file untouched. That way, if you update the rig file, the animation file will also get updated.

1 Create a reference

- Select **File → New Scene**.

- Select **File → Create Reference → □**.

  Doing so will open the Create Reference options.

- Under **Name Clash Options**, set **Resolve all nodes** with this string: *bear*.

  This will prefix all the reference nodes with the string bear.

Note: *For simplicity reasons, the bear prefix will not be cited.*

- Click on the **Reference** button.

- In the browse dialog that appears, select the file *13-boogRig_05.ma*, then click **Reference**.

  The file will load into the current one.

  Notice the small diamond icon in the Outliner and the red names in the Hypergraph. This means that the bear nodes are loaded from a reference file as read-only.

Referenced nodes in the Outliner and Hypergraph

Note: *If you need to bring changes to the character setup from the last lesson, you will need to open the rig file, make your changes, then save the file. Once that is done, you will need to open the animation file again to reload the new referenced rig. Be careful; if you remove nodes or attributes that are animated in the animation file, their animation will be lost.*

2 Layers

- Turn the visibility **On** for the *geometryLayer* and the *setupLayer*.

- Make sure the **smooth** attribute on the *master* node is set to **0**.

  You should now see only the low resolution model along with its rig.

3 Change the view panels

- Select **Panels** → **Layouts** → **Two Panes Stacked**.

- Change the top panel to a *side* view and the bottom panel to a *Perspective* view.

- For the *side* view, select **View** → **Predefined Bookmarks** → **Left Side**.

- In the *side* view, turn **Off** both **Show** → **NURBS Surfaces** and **Show** → **Polygons**.

  This panel will be used to watch the movements of the rig.

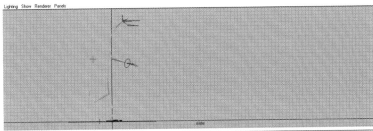

View panel layout

ANIMATING A WALK CYCLE

To create a walk, you will start with a single cycle. To create a cycle, you will need the start position and end position to be the same. There are several controls that need to be keyed, including the position of the feet, the roll of the feet, and the rotation of the pelvis.

Animate the feet sliding

You will now key the horizontal positions of the feet to establish their forward movement. This will result in a sliding motion of the feet.

1   Set your time range

- Set the **Start Time** and **Playback Start Time** to 1.

- Set the **End Time** and **Playback End Time** to 20.

    This will give you a smaller time range to work with as you build the cycle.

2   Active character

- In the **Current Character** menu next to the Range Slider, select *bear*.

    Now any keys you set will be set on all the attributes of this character node.

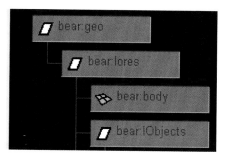

Active Character menu

3   Position and key the lower body start pose

You will key the starting position of the character in the position of a full stride.

- Go to frame 1.

- Select the *lHeelControl* selection handle and **translate Z** to 5 units.

- Select the *rHeelControl* selection handle and **translate Z** to 0 units.

Tip: *Make sure the Translate Tool is set to be in World coordinates.*

- Set the *pelvis* **translate** Z to **4** units.
- **Move** the *pelvis* down until the knees bend.

Note: *Leave the arms behind for now. Later, you will add secondary animation.*

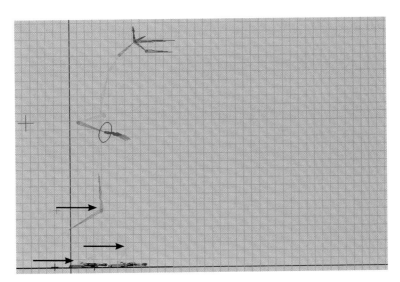

Lower body position

- Press **s** to set a key on all the channels of the *bear* character.

4 Position and key the right foot

- Go to frame **10**.
- Set the *rHeelControl* **translate** Z to **10** units.

  This value is exactly double the value of the initial left foot key. This is important to ensure that the two feet cycle together later.

- Set the *pelvis* **translate** Z to **9** units.

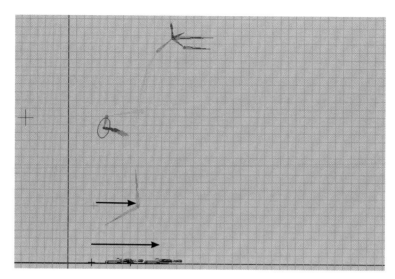

Right leg position

- Press **s** to set a key on all the channels of the *bear* character.

5   Position and key the left foot

You will move the left foot into a position that is similar to the starting position.

- Go to frame **20**.

- Set the *lHeelControl* **translate Z** to **15** units.

  Again, the value is set using units of 5. This will ensure a connection between cycles later.

- Set the *pelvis* **translate Z** to **14** units.

- Press **s** to set a key on all the channels of the *bear* character.

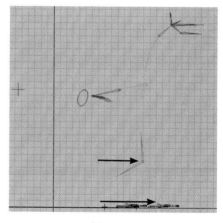

Left leg position

Edit the animation curves

To refine the in-between motion of the feet, you can use the animation curves to view and change the tangent options for the feet.

1   **View the curves in the Graph Editor**

You will edit the animation curves produced by the keys in the Graph Editor.

- Clear the selection.

- Select **Windows** → **Animation Editor** → **Graph Editor**.

- In the Graph Editor, highlight the *bear* character.

- Select **View** → **Frame All**.

- Press the **Ctrl** key to select *lHeelControl.TranslateZ* and *rHeelControl.TranslateZ* in the Outliner section of this window.

- Select **View** → **Frame Selection**.

The pattern of the animation curves you have created should look as follows:

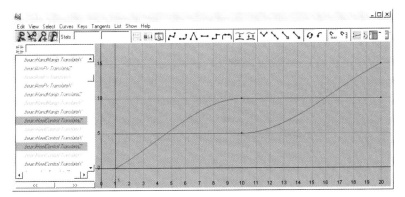

Animation curves in Graph Editor

- **Playback** the animation to see the motion.

> **Note:**   *If you open the Graph Editor when the feet are selected, you will see an animation channel with keys set in the negative direction. This is the animation curve connecting the Rotate Z of the foot to the Roll attribute.*

2   **Edit the curve tangents on the feet**

The curve tangent type should be changed so that the steps cycle smoothly. The default tangent type is clamped.

- Select the two animation curves for *lHeelControl.TranslateZ* and *rHeelControl.TranslateZ*.

- Select **Tangents → Flat**.

The visual difference between clamped and flat tangents in the Graph Editor is subtle. Look at the start and end keyframes on the curves. The flat tangents will create a smooth hook-up for the cycle between the start frame and end frame.

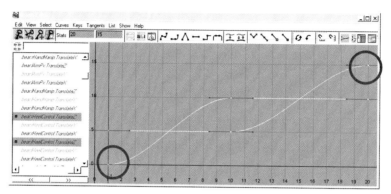

Flat tangents

Animate the feet up and down

You will now key the vertical raising and lowering of the feet to establish the stepping action.

1 Turn on Auto Key

You will now use **Auto Key** to help with the raising of the feet.

- Click on the **Auto Keyframe** button in the right side of the Time Slider to turn it **On**.

- Open the **Animation Preferences** window, using the button just to the right of the **Auto Keyframe** button.

- In the **Timeline** category, make sure the **Playback speed** is set to **Play every frame**.

- Click on the **Animation** category and set the following under the **Tangents** section:

  Default in tangent to **Flat**;

  Default out tangent to **Flat**.

  This will set all future tangents to flat.

- Click on the **Save** button.

2 Raise the right foot at midstep

Key the high point of the raised foot at the appropriate frame.

- Go to frame **5**.

- Select the *rHeelControl*.

- **Translate** the foot about **0.5** units up along the **Y-axis**.

  This sets a new key for the Y-axis channel of the foot using Auto Key.

3 Raise the left foot at midstep

- Go to frame **15**.

- Select the *lHeelControl*.

- **Move** the foot about **0.5** units up along the **Y-axis**.

  Again, a key is automatically set.

- **Playback** the results.

The character is walking

4 Save your work

Tip:	*Leave Auto Key set to On.*

Animate the pelvic rotations

To create a more realistic action, the pelvis' position and rotation will be set to work with each step. You will again set keys for the translation and rotation of the pelvis using Auto Key.

1 **Select the pelvis Y rotation**

You will now animate the pelvis' rotation to give the walk a little more motion.

- Go to frame **1**.

- Select the *pelvis* node using its selection handle.

- In the *top* view, **rotate** the *pelvis* using the rotation handle in a clockwise direction by about **-10 degrees**.

This points the left hip towards the left foot and the right hip towards the right foot.

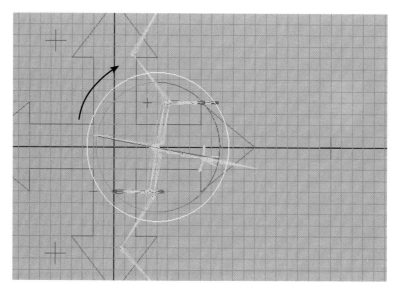

Rotate pelvis toward left foot

2 **Rotate in the opposite direction**

- Go to frame **10**.

- **Rotate** the pelvis in the opposite direction by about **10 degrees**.

3 **Copy the first Y rotation**

- Go to frame **1**.

- In the Time Slider, **MMB+drag** the current time to frame **20**.

  The display has not changed, but the time has changed.

- With the *pelvis* still selected, highlight the **Rotate X** attribute in the Channel Box, then **RMB** and select **Key Selected**.

  By doing so, you have manually set a keyframe on the rotateX value of the pelvis from frame 1 to frame 20.

- **Refresh** the Time Slider by dragging anywhere in the time indicator.

  Notice that the pelvis' rotateX attribute has the exact same value at frame 20 that it does at frame 1.

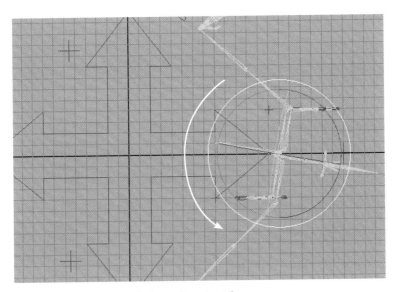

Copied rotation value at frame 20

4 Pelvis in front view

- Go to frame **5**.

- In the *front* view, **Rotate** the *pelvis* so that the right hip is raising with the right leg.

- **Translate** the *pelvis* on the **X-axis** so that the weight of the bear is on the left leg.

- Go to frame **15**.

- **Rotate** the *pelvis* in the opposite direction as the left foot raises.

- **Translate** the pelvis on the **X-axis** so that the weight of the robot is on the right leg.

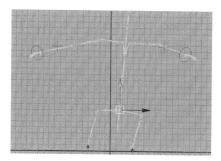
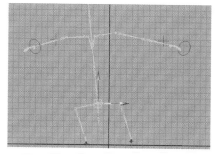

Offset pelvis with right foot raised   *Offset pelvis with left foot raised*

5   Edit the keys

To prepare the file for creating cycles later, you will need to ensure that the rotations match at the start and end of the cycle.

- Make sure the pelvis is selected.

- In the Graph Editor, press the **Ctrl** key and highlight the **Translate X**, **Rotate X** and **Rotate Y** attributes.

- Select **View → Frame All**.

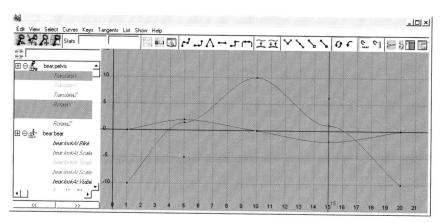

Pelvis curves

Since you copied frame 1 of the pelvis' X rotation onto frame 20 in Step 4, the start and end values of the animation curve are a perfect match. If they were different, you could have fixed the curve in the Graph Editor so that the cycled motion is smooth.

Add a bounce to the walk

To create a bouncing motion for the walk, you will add keyframes to the Y translation of the *pelvis* node.

1 Edit the pelvis height

- In the Graph Editor, highlight the *pelvis.TranslateY* channel.

2 Insert keys

- Select the **Insert Keys Tool** found in the Graph Editor.

- Select the **translateY** curve, then with your **MMB** insert a key at frame **5** and frame **15**.

3 Edit the Y translation value of the keys

- Press **w** to select the **Move Key Tool**.

- Select the new keys at frame **5** and frame **15**.

- Hold down **Shift** and select the two new keyframes.

- Press **w** to invoke the **Move Tool**.

- **Click+drag** with the **MMB** to move these keys to a value of about **8.2** to add some bounce to the walk.

- Press **a** to frame the curve.

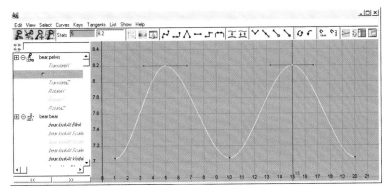

Pelvis Y Translate channel

Note: *Make sure the value you are using doesn't hyperextend the legs.*

Animate the heel rotation

When you created the reverse foot setup, you spent a great deal of time preparing the foot for the *heel to toe* motion that occurs when walking. You are now going to keyframe the foot rotations to take advantage of this work.

1   Set a key on the right foot's roll

- Go to frame 1.

- Select the *rHeelControl* using its selection handle.

- Set the *rHeelControl*'s **Roll** attribute to 5.

2   Set a second roll key

- Go to frame 10.

- Set the *rHeelControl*'s **Roll** attribute to -5.

3   Set a third key on the right foot's roll

- Go to frame 20.

- Set the *rHeelControl*'s **Roll** attribute to 5 again.

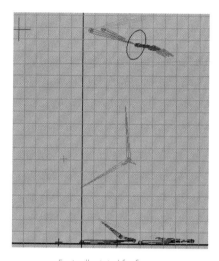

Foot roll rotated for frame 1

4   Set an in-between key on the right foot's roll

- Go to frame 13.

- Set the *rHeelControl*'s **Roll** attribute to 0.

5   Set a key on the left foot's roll

- Use the same technique to set the *lHeelControl*'s **Roll** attribute as follows:

    At frame 1, set **Roll** to -5;

    At frame 3, set **Roll** to 0;

    At frame 10, set **Roll** to 5;

    At frame 20, set **Roll** to -5.

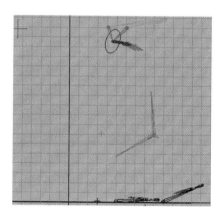

Foot rotated backward for frame 10

6   Playback the results

7 **Save your work**

- **Save** your scene as *14-boogWalk_01.ma*.

Animate the arm swing

The character needs some motion in his arms. To do this, you will animate the translation of the arm manipulators to create an animation that can be cycled.

To add some secondary motion, you will also set keyframes on the rotation of the head.

1 **Set keys for the start position**

- Go to frame **1**.

- **Move** and **rotate** the *lHandManip* behind the body and low down.

- **Move** and **rotate** the *rHandManip* in front of the body and up.

  Now the arms are opposite to how the feet are set-up. This makes the swinging motion work with the feet.

- Select the *head* joint and **rotate** it around the **Y-axis** by around **10-degrees**.

  This has the head and hips moving in opposite directions.

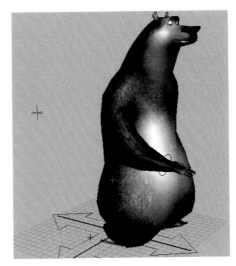

Arm positions

2 **Copy keys for the end position**

In order to create a smooth transition for the arm cycle, you must have matching values at the start and end of the cycle.

- Select the *lHandManip* and *rHandManip* nodes.

- In the timeline, **MMB+drag** and move the Time Slider to frame **20**.

  *The character will not move when you scrub along the timeline with the **MMB** depressed.*

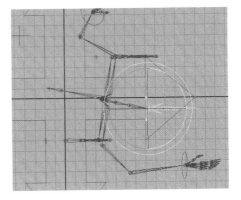

Top view of head rotation

- Highlight the **translation** and **rotation** attributes in the Channel Box.

- **RMB** and select **Key Selected** from the pop-up menu.

  This sets keyframes only on the attributes you have selected in the Channel Box.

  Because you also have the rHandManip node selected, you can see three dots after the lHandManip name in the Channel Box. This indicates that the rHandManip node is active, and that it has also received the keyframes.

- **Refresh** the Time Slider at frame **20**.

  You will see that you have set keyframes at the current position on the manipulators, but they are not following the robot.

Note: *You can also use the Dope Sheet to copy and paste selected keyframes, or you can cut and paste keyframe values from the Graph Editor.*

3 Add to attributes

You must now set the right offset to the values already in the Translate Z attributes of the left and right hand manipulators. The Channel Box can allow you to enter a simple mathematical expression in the attribute value field.

- With the *lHandManip* and *rHandManip* manipulator selected, type **+=10** in the **Translate Z** attribute in the Channel Box, then hit **Enter**.

4 Set keys for the head

Use the method outlined in Step 2 to set the last keyframe for the head rotation.

- Select the *head*.

- **MMB+drag** the Time Slider from frame **1** to frame **20**.

- **LMB** over the *head* **Rotate Y** attribute in the Channel Box to highlight it.

- **RMB** and select **Key Selected** from the pop-up menu.

5 Set keys for the middle position

- Go to frame **10**.

- **Move** the arm manipulators opposite to the *legs*.

- **Rotate** the head joint opposite to the *hips*.

Arm positions at frame 10

6 · Keyframe the in-between

- Make sure to set a good position for the arms at frames **5** and **15**.

7 Fix the arm manipulator curves

- In the Graph Editor, select the arm manipulators' **translate** and **rotate** attributes.

- Select all keyframes between frame **5** and **15**.

- Select **Tangents** → **Spline**.

8 Delete the static channels

If a curve is flat its whole length, the value of the attribute it represents isn't changing. Thus, this attribute is a *static channel*. Static channels slow Maya processing, so it's beneficial to remove them.

- Select **Edit** → **Delete All By Type** → **Static Channels**.

9 Turn off Auto Key

10 Save your work

- **Save** your scene as *14-boogWalk_02.ma*.

Cycle the animation

So far, you have animated one full step for the walk cycle. Next, you will use the Graph Editor to complete the cycle.

1 Set your time range

- Set the **Start Time** and **Playback Start Time** to 1.

- Set the **End Time** and **Playback End Time** to 300.

2 View all curves in the Graph Editor

- Select **Windows → Animation Editor → Graph Editor.**

- Select *bear* from the Outliner portion of the window to see all the animation curves for the character.

3 View the cycle

In order to check if the cycle works smoothly, you can display the curves' infinity and set it to cycle.

- In the Graph Editor, select **View → Infinity.**

- Select all the animation curves.

- Select **Curves → Pre Infinity → Cycle with Offset.**

- Select **Curves → Post Infinity → Cycle with Offset.**

  Cycle with Offset appends the value of the last key in the cycled curve to the value of the first key's original curve. You can now see what the curves are like when cycled.

- **Play** the animation.

4 Adjust the curves

- Zoom on the curves and adjust the tangents so that the connection between the curves and cycle is smooth.

- If needed, adjust the tangency of the keyframes on frames 1 and 20.

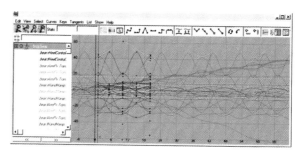

Bear animation cycles

> **Tip:** If you play the animation up to frame 300, you should clearly see if there are any problems with your cycle.

Bake the keyframes

Ultimately, you will use this animation inside the Trax Editor, so you will bake the keyframes of the post infinity onto the curves. The Trax Editor cannot use post infinity curves from the Graph Editor, so you will generate the actual keyframes by baking them.

1 Select the bear character

- In the Graph Editor, select *bear*.

2 Bake the keyframes

- In the Graph Editor, select **Curves → Bake Channel → ☐**.

- Set the following options:

  Time Range to **Start/End**;

  Start Time to **1**;

  End Time to **115**;

  Sample by **5**;

  Keep Unbaked Keys to **On**;

  Sparse Curve Bake to **On**.

- Click the **Bake** button.

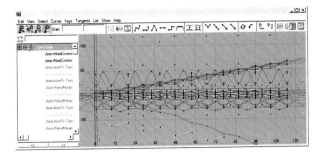

Baked curves

3 Save your work

- **Save** your scene as *14-boogWalk_03.ma*.

Create a Trax clip file

The animation is done, but since you will be working with the Trax Editor later in this book, you will now create a Trax clip file and export it for later use.

1 Open the Trax Editor window

- Select **Window** → **Animation Editor** → **Trax Editor**.

- Make sure the *bear* character is set as current.

- In the Trax Editor, enable **List** → **Auto Load Selected Characters**.

2 Create a clip

- From the Trax Editor, select **Create** → **Animation Clip** → ❑.

- Set the following options:

   Name to *walk*;

   Leave Keys in Timeline to **Off**;

   Clip to **Put Clip in Trax Editor and Visor**;

   Time Range to **Animation Curve**;

   Include Subcharacters in Clip to **Off**;

   Create Time Warp Curve to **Off**;

   Include Hierarchy to **On**.

- Click the **Create Clip** button.

- Press **a** in the Trax Editor to frame all.

   A clip is created and placed in the Trax timeline. A corresponding clip source file called walkSource is also placed in the Visor.

   Until you export the clip, it can only be accessed through this scene file.

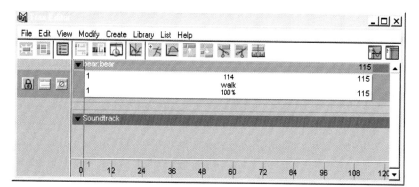

Walk clip in Trax Editor

3 Export the clip

- Select **File** → **Visor...**

- Select the **Character Clips** tab to see the clip source.

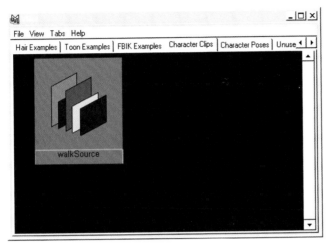

Walk source clip in Visor

- Select the *walkSource* clip.

- **RMB** on the clip and select **Export.**

  A pop-up menu will browse to the clips directory of your current project.

- **Save** the clip as *boogWalkExport.*

  Now you can import this clip into another scene.

- **Close** the Visor.

4 Save your work

- **Save** your scene as *14-boogWalk_04.ma.*

Conclusion

Congratulations, you have completed a walk cycle! You learned how to reference a file, and then you animated the bear using a character set. You produced a perfect cycle and exported a Trax clip.

In the next project you will build a SUV from NURBS, texture it and rig it up so that Boog can interact with it.

IMAGEGALLERY

SONY PICTURES
animation

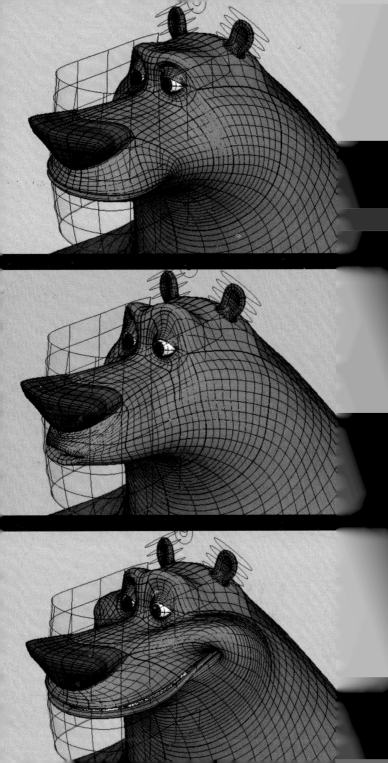

Project 03

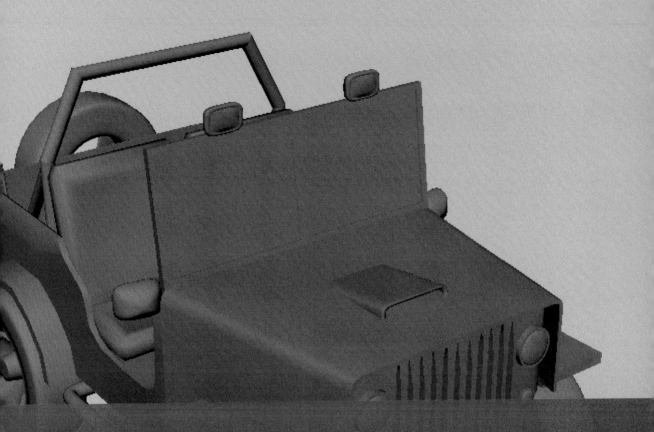

Lesson 15
NURBS modeling

This lesson will introduce you to modeling with NURBS (Non-Uniform Rational B-Spline)
surfaces. With NURBS, you can create curves and surfaces to build up your models.
Since NURBS geometry is perfect for static objects, in this lesson you will build a SUV
for Boog to drive.

In this lesson you will learn the following:

- How to project curves on a surface;

- How to trim a surface;

- How to use loft, revolve and extrude surface tools;

- How to duplicate curves from a surface;

- How to insert isoparms;

- How to make boolean operations.

Set-up your project

Since this is a new project, it is recommended to set a new current project directory.

1   Set the project

- If you copied the support files onto your drive, go to the **File** menu and select **Project → Set...**

  A window opens pointing you to the Maya projects directory.

- Click on the folder named *project3* to select it.

- Click on the **OK** button.

  This sets the project3 directory as your current project.

  OR

- If you did not copy the support files on your drive, create a new project called *project3* with all the default directories.

2   Make a new scene

- Select **File → New Scene**.

Tires

The first step for modeling the SUV is to model the tires. This will be a simple exercise that will introduce several tools to be used throughout this lesson.

1   Rim profile curve

You will now create the rim of the tire by revolving a profile curve.

- Select **Create → EP Curve Tool → □**.

- In the options, make sure **Curve Degree** is set to **1 Linear**.

- From the *front* view, **draw** the curve seen to the right:

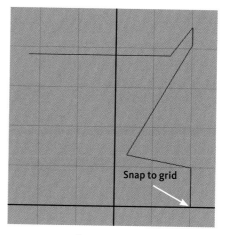

The rim profile curve

Tip: *Make sure to hold down x to snap to grid your first point on the X-axis.*

2 Revolve the rim

- Press **F4** to select the **Surfaces** menu set.

- With the curve selected, select **Surfaces → Revolve → ❑**.

- In the options, make sure to set **Axis Preset** to X.

- Click the **Revolve** button.

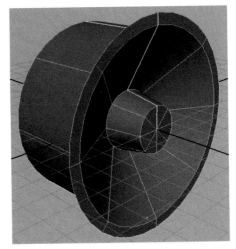

The revolved rim

> **Tip:** *Because of construction history, you can still tweak the shape of the rim by modifying the profile curve.*

3 Rim holes

You will now cut out holes in the inner portion of the rim using projected curves.

- Select **Create → NURBS Primitives → Circle**.

- **Translate** the circle on its **X-axis** and set its **RotateZ** attribute to **90**.

- From the *side* view, press **F9** to display the circle's CVs.

- Select the CVs and **tweak** them to look like the image to the right:

- Go back in Object mode.

- Press **Insert** to move the circle's pivot, then hold down **x** and snap the pivot on to the origin.

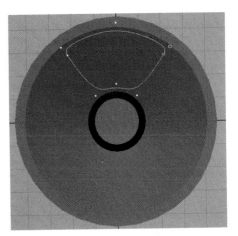

The hole profile curve

Tip: *If you move the CVs rather than moving the circle's transform, the pivot of the circle will remain centered on the X-axis, which is what you want.*

4   Duplicate the hole curve

- Select **Edit → Duplicate Special → □.**

- Set the following:

  Geometry type to **Copy**;

  Rotate X to **120**;

  Number of copies to **2**;

- Click the **Duplicate Special** button.

  You should now have three hole profile curves properly placed.

5   Project the curves

You will now project the curves on the rim geometry. This will allow you to later trim the rim holes out.

- Select all three hole curves.

- **Shift-select** the rim geometry.

- Make sure you are looking through the *side* view.

  This will be the direction in which the curves are projected.

- Select **Edit NURBS → Project Curve on Surface.**

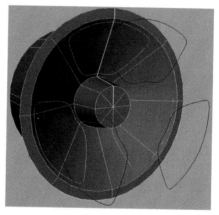

The projected curves

There are now projected curves on the rim surface.

- It is possible that the hole curves were projected on the rear section of the rim. If so, simply select the unwanted projected curves and press **Delete**.

Note: *It is important to do this action from the side view since the projection of the curve is made from the active camera. You can change that behavior in the options of the Project Curve on Surface Tool.*

6 Trim the holes

You will now trim the holes out of the rim.

- With the rim selected, select **Edit NURBS → Trim Tool**.

  The rim geometry is now displayed with white stipple wireframe.

- Using the **LMB**, click all the rim sections that you want to keep.

  Only the holes should be drawn as stipple lines.

- Once all the correct regions are selected, press **Enter**.

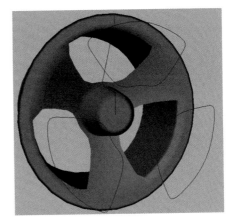

The trimmed surface

Note: *By default, the resolution in the viewport of trimmed surfaces is low. This is only a display issue and should not affect the surface once rendered.*

Tip: *You can still modify the original projection curve to dynamically update the trimmed surface.*

Note: *Trimming a surface does not delete or modify any NURBS components. The surface of the trimmed section is simply not drawn. To display a trimmed surface, select* **Edit NURBS → Untrim Surfaces**.

7 Duplicate the trim edges

You can duplicate the trimmed edges and loft them toward the inside of the rim to give some thickness to the metal.

- **RMB** over a trimmed edge on the rim geometry and select **Trim Edge**.

- Hold down **Shift** and highlight all the trim edges on the rim.

  The trim edges are highlighted in yellow. It is possible that one of the trim edges is divided into two parts due to the closing edge of the revolve surface.

- Select **Edit Curves →
  Duplicate Surface Curves.**

  There are now curves that perfectly match the trim edges.

- **Translate** the new curves toward the inside of the rim.

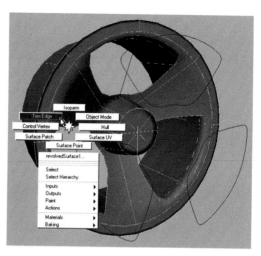

The NURBS context menu

8 Loft the trim edges and curves

By lofting a trim edge and its respective duplicated curve, you can create a thickness appearance on the rim.

- Select any trim edge, then **Shift-select** its respective duplicated curve.

- Select **Surfaces → Loft.**

- **Repeat** for the other trim edges.

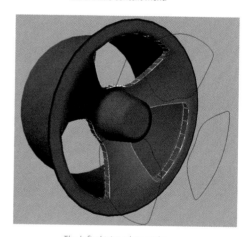

The lofted trim edges and curves

9 Tire profile

- Select **Create → EP Curve Tool → ❑.**

- In the options, make sure **Curve Degree** is set to **3 Cubic.**

- From the *front* view, **draw** the tire profile curve and tweak its shape to look as follows:

10 Revolve the tire

- With the curve selected, select **Surfaces → Revolve.**

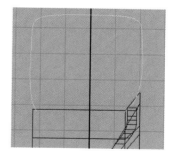

Tire profile curve

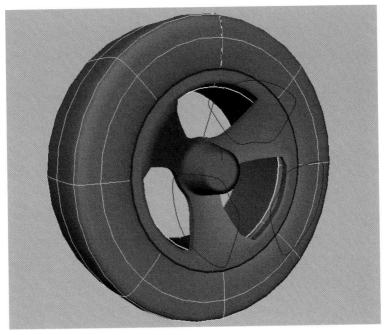

The revolved tire

11 Finish the tire

Since all the tools used thus far created construction history, you must now delete.

- Make sure you like the look of the tire.

- Select **Edit → Delete All by Type → History**.

- Select all the curves and **delete** them.

- **Rename** all the pieces appropriately.

- **Group** the tire all together and name it *wheel*.

12 Save your work

- **Save** your scene as *15-SUV_01.ma*.

Chassis

Now that you have tires, you can build up the SUV chassis. You will do that by first drawing curves and then using lofts to generate the geometry.

1 Duplicate the wheels

- **Move** the *wheel* group on the ground plane.

- **Move** the *wheel* to the front left corner by **13** units on the **X-axis** and **16** units on the **Z-axis**.

- **Duplicate** the *wheel* group to the three other corners of the SUV as **instances**.

The four wheels in place

Tip: *Since the wheel will not be deformed, it is recommended to use instances, which are faster to load and draw.*

2 Chassis curve

- Select **Create → CV Curve Tool**.

- From the *top* view, **draw** the following curve holding down **x** to snap to the grid:

- With the curve selected, select **Edit Curves → Open/Close Curves**.

  Doing so closes the curve, making it periodic. This means that the curve has the same start and end point.

3 Loft

You will now duplicate the curves, place them appropriately and loft them together.

- **Move** the first chassis curve up to about **9** units.

- **Duplicate** the curve and **move** it up to about **20** units.

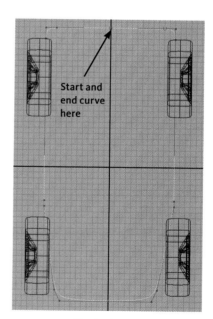

Start and end curve here

The chassis curve

- Select the two curves, then select **Edit Curves → Offset → Offset Curve**.

  Doing so automatically offsets the curves, which will be used to give the chassis some thickness.

- From the Channel Box, adjust the **Distance Attribute** of the *offsetCurve* node to a smaller value such as **0.5**.

- Select the bottom outside curve, then **Shift-select** the top outside curve, the top inside curve and, lastly, the bottom inside curve.

- Select **Surfaces → Loft →** ❑.

- Set **Surface Degree** to **Linear** and turn **On** the **Close** checkbox.

- Click the **Loft** button.

The lofted surface

4 Hood curve

- Select **Create → CV Curve Tool**.

- From the *front* view, **draw** the hood profile curve as follows:

- **Move** the hood curve to the front of the SUV.

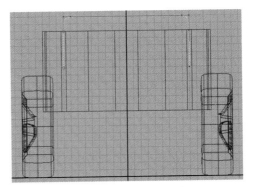

The hood curve

5 Loft the hood

- Select the front hood curve, then select **Edit Curves → Offset → Offset Curve**.

- From the Channel Box, adjust the **Distance Attribute** of the *offsetCurve* node to **0.3**.

- **Duplicate** the two hood curves and **translate** them back to the base of the windshield.

- **Scale** the curves on their **X-axes** to make them a bit larger than the chassis surface.

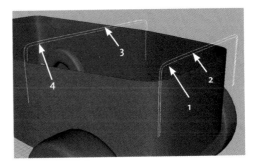

The hood curves selection order

- Select the curves in order, then select **Surfaces → Loft**.

- **RMB** on the lofted surface and select **Isoparm**.

- **Click+drag** on the hood to select an isoparm across its width.

- Hold down **Shift** to select more isoparms.

Note: *When you click directly on an isoparm to select it, the isoparm gets highlighted with a continuous yellow line. If you **click+drag** on an isoparm, a dotted yellow line shows you the isoparm at the cursor's position.*

- Select **Edit NURBS** → **Insert Isoparms** to add the highlighted isoparms to the hood geometry.

6 Adjust the shape

- Select **Edit** → **Delete All by Type** → **History**.

- Select **Edit** → **Select All by Type** → **NURBS curves**.

Note: *The original curves are usually kept for construction history, thus, you need to manually delete the unnecessary curves in order to keep your scene clean.*

- **Delete** the curves.

- Take some time to adjust the shape of the SUV chassis. Make sure that the front of the chassis fits the inside of the hood. Move down the back part of the hood to fit the bottom of the chassis.

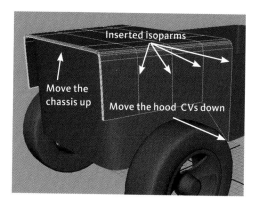

The adjusted shape of the SUV

7 Save your work

- **Save** your scene as *15-SUV_02.ma*.

Booleans

Booleans work in a similar way to the Trim Tool, except that they allow you to unite, subtract or intersect two surfaces together. You will use booleans to create openings for the wheels in the chassis.

1 Create a cylinder

- **Create** a default **NURBS** cylinder.

- **Move** it over the rear wheels and **scale** it a bit bigger than the wheels.

- Make sure that the cylinder is longer than the width of the chassis.

The cylinder to use for boolean

2 Booleans

- Select **Edit NURBS → Booleans → Union Tool**.

- Click on the *chassis* to highlight it, then hit **Enter**.

- Click on the *cylinder* to execute the tool and hit **Enter**.

  The tool is executed and it trimmed the sections intersecting between the cylinder and the chassis.

The rear boolean executed

Note: *It is possible that depending on the selection and orientation of the surface, you might need to change the order of the selection or the boolean operation type.*

3 Door boolean

- **Create** a cylinder as in the previous steps, but this time, make it to represent the door openings.

- Select **Edit NURBS → Booleans → Union Tool**.

- Click on the *chassis* to highlight it, then hit **Enter**.
- Click on the *cylinder* to execute the tool.

The door cylinder shape

Tip: *When you enable the Hull mask in the Status bar, you can see a line connecting all the CVs from the same row and column. Clicking on a hull will select all the CVs connected to that hull.*

The door boolean

Details

You can start contributing details to the SUV by adding tubing around the chassis using the extrude command. You will also build the SUV windshield and interior.

1 Create extrude curves

The extrude command requires two curves to extrude properly. First, it needs a profile curve, which, in this case, will be a simple circle. Second, it needs a path curve to extrude with.

- Select **Create → NURBS Primitives → Circle**.

  This will be the profile curve.

- Select **Create → EP Curve Tool → ❑**.

- Set the **Curve Degree** to **Linear.**

- From the *front* view, **draw** the roll cage tubing to the right:

- Select the profile circle, press **w** to evoke the **Move Tool**, then press **c** to snap to curve and snap the circle to an end point of the extruded curve.

The roll cage curve

- Select the profile curve followed by the extrude curve, and then select **Surfaces → Extrude → ❑**.

- In the options, set the following:

  Style to **Tube**;

  Result Position to **At Path**;

  Orientation to **Path Direction.**

The extruded tube

- Click the **Extrude** button.

- Because of construction history, adjust the used curves to perfect the extrusion.

2 Create other tubing

Create any other tubing that you desire on the SUV, such as bumpers and step bars.

The SUV tubing

 Tip: *Some tubing is simpler to create starting from NURBS cylinder primitives with caps.*

3 Windshield

Since the windshield is square, it is simpler to create it using polygons.

- Use what you have learned in the last project to create the windshield using extrusions.

The windshield

4 Car floor

Because of the complexity of the car interior, it is a good idea to use polygons to build it.

The car floor

5 Spare tire

- Duplicate as an **instance** one of the *wheels* and **place** it as a spare tire on the back of the SUV.

6 Engine grid

- You can use the same boolean technique shown earlier to create a grid pattern on the front of the chassis.

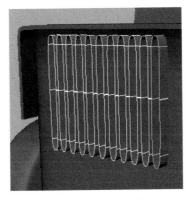

Cylinders to be used for the grid booleans

> **Tip:** The grid booleans might not be displayed correctly since the viewport is keeping the geometry simple for quick interactions. When the geometry is rendered, everything will look good.

7 Steering, gearshift and pedals

- Take some time to model the steering wheel, gearshift and pedals out of your preferred geometry type.

Steering wheel, gearshift and pedals

8 Lights

- **Create** some nice looking headlights, cab lights and tail lights.

Models of lights

 Tip: *Don't forget to mirror symmetrical geometry to speed up your work.*

9 Other details

- **Create** the fenders to cover both the front and rear wheels.

- Add mirrors, seats, antenna, air intake, etc. to your liking.

- Select all the geometry and **freeze** its transformations.

- **Delete** all the history.

- **Optimize** the scene size to delete any unused nodes from the scene.

The final SUV

10 Save your work

- **Save** your scene as *15-SUV_03.ma*.

Conclusion

In this lesson, you experimented with several NURBS curves and surface tools. NURBS modeling for static objects can be straightforward, but modeling organic shapes requires much more experience and planning.

In the next lesson, you will assign materials and textures to the SUV.

Lesson 16
NURBS texturing

In this lesson, you will learn about NURBS texturing, 3D placement projections and shading network conversion. You will start by texturing the SUV using texture projections and learning how to convert a shading network texture. You will also learn about reference objects and the Texture Placement Tool.

In this lesson you will learn the following:

- How to texture a NURBS surface;

- How to project a texture using a projection node;

- How to set colors using RGB values;

- How to convert a shading network to a file texture;

- How to do a second texture projection on a surface;

- How to prevent texture sliding using reference objects;

- How to place a texture using the Interactive Placement Tool.

Texturing Surfaces

Unlike polygonal geometry, UV mapping is not required on NURBS geometry since texture coordinates are determined by the U and V directions of the NURBS surface itself. You will see later in this lesson that the only way to map a texture differently is by using projection mapping.

1 Checker texture

In order to view the default UV maps, you will create both a lambert and checker texture, and then assign them to the wheel geometry.

- In the Hypershade, create a **Lambert** material.

- **Map** the **Color** of the new material with a **checker** texture.

Tip: *Make sure the create option at the top of the Create Render Node window is set to Normal.*

- Press **6** on your keyboard to enable the **Hardware Texturing**.

- **Assign** the new checker material to the wheel group, which will assign it to all its child surfaces.

- See how the texture is mapped.

On equally proportionate surfaces (as close to square as possible), the checker texture won't appear to be too stretched, but on long and thin surfaces, such as the rim thickness lofts, the texture will look stretched. Also, when a NURBS surface has a pole, the texture will look pinched.

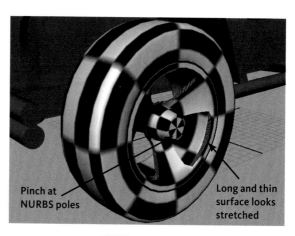

Pinch at NURBS poles

Long and thin surface looks stretched

NURBS texture mapping

2 Assign a file texture

- **Create** a **Blinn** material.

- **Map** the **Color** of the new material with a **File** texture.

- Set the **Image Name** of the file texture to be thread.tif from the sourceimages folder.

- **Assign** the new material to the tire surface.

  When the texture is seamless, you should not see any seam on the geometry.

Thread texture

3 Finish the wheel

- **Create** a **Blinn** material with a grey color and **assign** it to the rim.

- **Create** a **Blinn** material with a black color and **assign** it to the inside surfaces of the rim.

4 Other wheels

- **Assign** the same materials onto the other wheels.

The textured wheel

Tip: *To speed up the display in the viewport, you can select all the geometry in the scene and press 1 to set the NURBS display to coarse.*

Projections

You will now create a shading network to project a logo on the hood of the SUV.

1 Create a projection

First, you will map the hood surface, but since you want to place the logo at a specific location, you will use a projected texture.

- **Create** another **Blinn** material.

- Click on the **map** button for the **color** of the new material.

- Change the create option at the top of the Create Render Node window to **As Projection**.

- Low click on the **File** button to create the file texture along with its projection node.

- Set the **Image Name** of the file texture to be logo.tif from the sourceimages folder.

- **Assign** the new material to the hood surface.

  The projection of the texture is determined by the 3D texture placement node located at the origin.

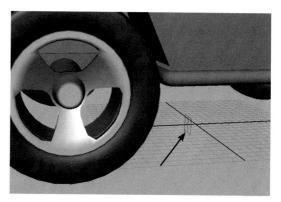

Hood texture placement node

2 Place the projection

- Select the place3dTexture node from the viewport.

- **Rotate** it on the **Y-axis** by **90 degrees**.

- In the Attribute Editor, click on the **Fit to group bbox** button.

  The node will move to fit the bounding box of the surfaces using this texture.

The placement node set to fit the surface

Tip: *To raise the texture display quality, select the material and in the Attribute Editor, set the* **Texture Resolution** *from the* **Hardware Texturing** *section to* **Highest**.

- Use the manipulator to **rotate**, **scale** and **translate** the projection as to the right:

The adequate projection

3   **Fix texture wrapping**

At this time, the texture repeats itself outside the projection box and is projected inverted on the other side of the hood. There is an option you can use to disable this functionality.

- Select the place3dTexture node in the viewport.

- In the Channel Box, highlight the projection node.

- Set **Wrap** to **Off**.

No texture wrapping

Note: *The projection manipulator changes when you set* **Wrap** *to* **Off**. *This is because you can now demarcate the depth of the projection and prevent the texture from being inverted on the other side of the hood.*

- **Scale** the projection manipulator on its **Z-axis**.

- **Translate** it to replace the projection correctly on the side of the hood.

The scaled projection manipulator

Tip: *In the Attribute Editor for the projection node under the* **Extra Attributes** *section, you can set the* **Resolution** *of the textures to be higher or to match your texture size.*

4 Change the default color

The texture is displayed correctly, but the default shader color is displayed outside the texture boundary.

- Open the Attribute Editor for the projection node again.
- Scroll down to the **Color Balance** section.
- Click on the color swatch of **Default Color**.

Note: *The* **Default Color** *is the color underneath the texture that is revealed when coverage is less than 1.0 or when wrapping is off.*

- In the color picker window, under the **Sliders** section, change **HSV** to **RBG**.

  Doing so allows you to set the color using Red, Green and Blue values rather than Hue, Saturation and Lightness.

- Set the **0 to 1** option to **0 to 255**.

  Doing so allows you to set the **RGB** *color using sliders that go from* **0** *to* **255***.*

- Set the **RGB** values to 179, 0 and 0.

  This is the exact background color used in the logo texture.

- Click the **Accept** button.

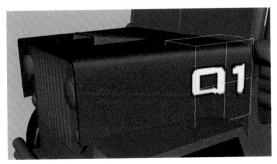

The corrected default color

Convert to texture

Since the logo shading network is becoming fairly complex, you will convert the network as a single file texture.

The shading network will then be much simpler to render since a proper texture will perfectly fit the UVs of the hood geometry.

1 Convert the shading network

Maya can convert a complex shading network into a single texture file.

- Select the hood shader and **Shift-select** the hood geometry.

- From the Hypershade, select **Edit → Convert to File Texture (Maya Software) → ❑.**

- In the option window set the following:

  UV Range to **Entire Range**;

  X Resolution to 512;

  Y Resolution to 512;

  Image Format to **TIF**.

- Click the **Convert and Close** button.

  Maya will convert the network to a texture and will create and assign a new network using only a single texture. The new texture is automatically saved in the current project's sourceimages folder.

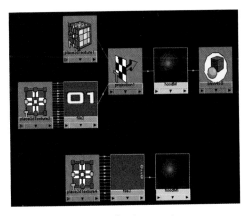

Before and after the conversion

Note: *By converting a shading network to a texture, you do not require a projection and a reference object. The texture fits the geometry perfectly.*

2 Second projection

In order to project another logo on the other side of the hood, you can reuse the old network along with the new converted file texture.

- **Assign** the old shading network back on the hood geometry.

- **Rotate** the projection manipulator to **-90 degrees** on its **Y-axis** and **translate** it on the other side of the hood.

- Rather than using a specific color as the default color, **MMB+drag** the converted texture from the previous step in the **Default Color** attribute in the Attribute Editor.

Doing so establishes a connection that fills the default color with the converted texture.

3 Convert again

- Select the hood shader and **Shift-select** the hood geometry.

- From the Hypershade, select **Edit → Convert to File Texture (Maya Software)**.

The texture generated now contains both logos on either side of the hood.

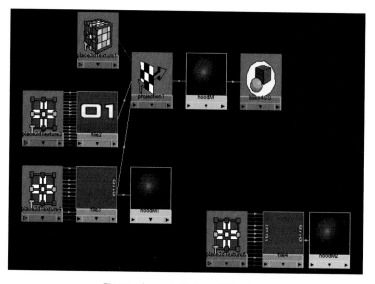

The second converted texture with two logos

Texture reference objects

Projected textures work well on static geometry, but there can be unintended results when the surface is moving or deforming. This is because the object is moving without the projection, which causes a texture sliding problem. To correct this, you can set-up a non-deformed reference object to lock the texture on the geometry.

- Select a surface with a projected texture assigned to it.

- Under the **Rendering** menu set, select **Texturing** → **Create Texture Reference Object**.

  An unselectable object duplicate will appear as wireframe in the viewport. This object is only selectable through the Outliner or the Hypergraph.

Tip: *Using texture reference objects is best when an object is deforming. Otherwise, it might be an easier solution to simply parent the projection node to the model itself.*

Note: *Reference objects are not renderable even if visible in the viewports.*

Interactive Placement Tool

The Interactive Placement Tool is designed to ease the placement of textures onto NURBS surfaces. This tool simply allows you to interactively set the different placement values of a 2D texture via an all-in-one manipulator.

Following is how to use this tool:

- Select a place2dTexture node of a texture used by a NURBS surface.

- In the Attribute Editor, with the file texture's place2dTexture tab selected, click on the **Interactive Placement** button.

  *Doing so will invoke the **NURBS Texture Placement Tool**. This tool displays a red manipulator on the NURBS geometry, which allows you to interactively place the texture in the viewport.*

Note: *You can also access the* **NURBS Texture Placement Tool** *via the* **Texturing** *menu when a NURBS surface is selected.*

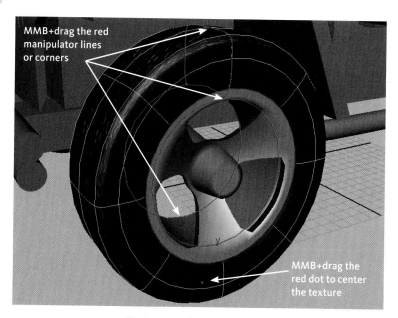

The interactive placement manipulator

Note: *Notice the value of the place2dTexture node update as you drag the manipulator. You could also set the place2dTexture values manually. If you have other surfaces assigned with the same shader, they will also get modified.*

Finish texturing the SUV

You can now spend some time shading and creating textures for the remaining pieces of the SUV. Once you are satisfied with the results, you must make sure your scene is clean of obsolete shading nodes.

1   **Texture the rest of the SUV**

2 Optimize scene size

- Select **File** → **Optimize Scene Size**.

The final SUV

3 Save your work

- **Save** your file as *16-SUVTxt_01.ma*.

Conclusion

You have garnered some experience texturing NURBS surfaces and learned how to use projections and how to convert a projection into a texture. You should take the time to explore the different tools available to you more in-depth to master NURBS texturing.

In the next lesson, you will set-up the SUV for animation.

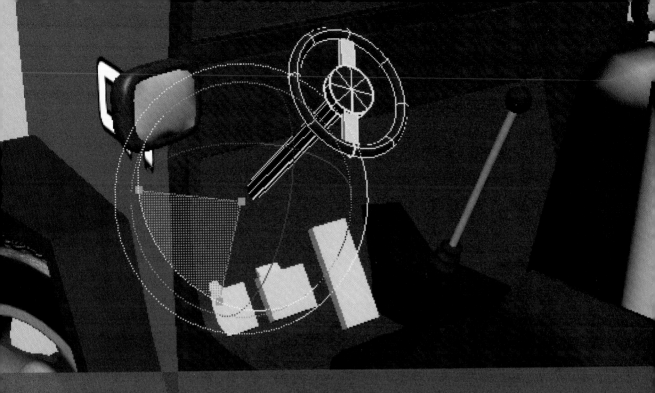

Lesson 17
Rigging

In this lesson, you will rig the SUV for animation. The SUV rig will be slightly different from the bear character since the geometry is more mechanic and, hence, can have some automation built into it. You will first organize the SUV's hierarchy. Once that is done, you will set-up driven keys that will automate some movements, such as having the steering turn the wheels.

In this lesson you will learn the following:

- How to rename multiple objects all at once;
- How to add animation overrides in hierarchies;
- How to set-up reactive driven keys;
- How to change local rotation axis of objects;
- How to set the proper rotate order;
- How to add non-linear deformers.

Hierarchy

The first thing to do before rigging a model is to make sure that all of its nodes are in a good hierarchy where everything is easy to find and well named.

1 Scene file

- **Open** your scene from the last lesson.

OR

- **Open** the scene file named *16-SUVTxt_01.ma* from the support files.

2 Rename multiple objects

When you create content, you should be renaming nodes fairly frequently. Since you usually need to rename all the nodes one by one, you will learn a way to rename several nodes simultaneously.

- Select all the objects that should have similar names, such as the SUV's tubing.

- In the top right corner of the interface, set the **Quick Rename** option as follows:

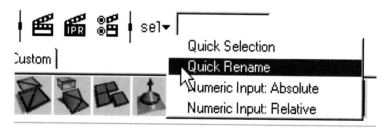

Quick Rename option

- Enter *tube* in the **Quick Rename** field.

Each and every selected object will be assigned a unique name starting with the defined string, followed by a unique number.

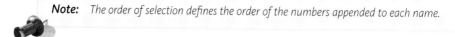

Note: *The order of selection defines the order of the numbers appended to each name.*

- Take some time to appropriately **rename** every node in the scene.

3 **Hierarchy**

- **Group** basic related objects together, such as *lights*, *seats*, *wheel*, *steering*, *antenna*, etc.

- **Repeat** as needed.

- **Group** the remaining sets and objects under their simplest forms, such as *chassis*, *frontWheels*, *rearWheels*, etc.

- Lastly, **group** every top group under a group named *SUV*.

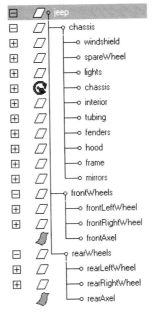

Parts of the SUV hierarchy

Tip: *The idea is to define a hierarchy in which you could animate each object individually without modifying the hierarchy.*

4 **Pivots**

- Make sure every group's pivot is properly placed.

  To do this, make sure you look at every group and determine how it will be moving. Once you know where a group should be rotating from, place its pivot to that location. Doing so will allow you to animate any part of the SUV easily.

Note: *Unlike skinned characters, mechanical geometry and groups can be directly animated without a skeleton structure controlling them.*

5 Overrides

When animating any object as a whole, such as the SUV, it is important to have animation overrides on the top group. These overrides can then be used individually to isolate certain animation. For instance, the top group node will later be animated from path animation. Since this node will be controlled by its connection, you can then use lower overrides to add some custom animation such as rotations or translations.

- Select the *SUV* top group.

- Press **Ctrl+g** to group the hierarchy **three times**.

- **Rename** the top group to *master*.

- **Rename** the group below it to *transOverride*.

- **Rename** the group below *transOverride* to *rotOverride*.

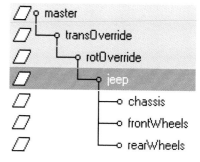

The overrides

6 Save your work

- **Save** your scene as *17-SUVRig_01.ma*.

Automation

Sometimes when creating rigs, you need to add some automation to ease the work of the animator. In this exercise, you will automate the wheel rotations using Set Driven Keys.

Automation is usually considered a good thing from the point of view of the set-up artist, but can also introduce limitations for the animator. For instance, if a wheel movement is automated, the animator doesn't have the ability to spin the wheel or break it manually. Adding animation overrides, however, will allow the animator to gain control over the automation.

Note: *For simplicity reasons, this setup will only work when the SUV is rotated between 0 and 90 degrees on its* **Y-axis** *and translated forward. Having the wheels work in all possible directions would require a more complex exercise. Later in this book you will use a motion path to get automation for the wheels.*

1 Wheel overrides

- Select one of the *wheel* groups.

- Select **Edit → Group → □**.

- In the options, set Group pivot to **Center**.

- Press the **Group** button.

  The wheel is now grouped and the new group's pivot is centered with the wheel geometry.

- **Rename** the new group appropriately with the *auto* prefix to clearly identify this group as being an automated node.

- **Repeat** for the other wheels.

Tip: *Using animation overrides, such as groups, is an inexpensive way to give more control to the artist. Consider adding animation overrides even where it is not required; you will succeed in giving more control over the rig.*

2 Set Driven Keys

You will now animate the wheels to rotate when the SUV moves forward.

- Select **Animate →
  Set Driven Key → Set...**

- Select the *master* node, and then click on the **Load Driver** button.

- Highlight the **master** node and its **translateZ** attribute.

- Select all four wheel *auto* groups, and then click on the **Load Driven** button.

- Highlight all four **wheel** nodes and their **rotateX** attributes.

- Click on the **Key** button in the Set Driven Key window.

  This sets the initial keyframe in the default position.

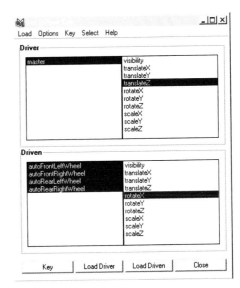

The correct attributes highlighted

3 Mathematics

Trial and error is helpful for determining the proper rotation on the wheels, but you can also use a simple formula to get the proper values.

Following is the formula for finding the distance when rotating a wheel by 360 degrees:

```
pi * diameter = distance
```

You will now use the Distance Tool to get the diameter of a wheel.

- Select **Create** → **Measure Tools** → **Distance Tool**.

  The Distance Tool shows in the viewport the distance between two points. Those two points are defined by locators.

- From the *side* view, click at the center of a wheel and then click on its perimeter to create the distance nodes.

  You now have the radius of the wheel. You need to double that value to get the diameter of the wheel.

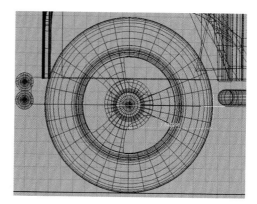

The Distance Tool

- If you solve the above formula with the returned value, you get:

```
3.14 * 14.09 = 44.24
```

- **Note** down this value.

- **Delete** the distance node along with its two locators from the Outliner.

4 Set keys

- Select the *master* node by clicking on it in the Set Driven Key window.

- **Move** the *master* on its **Z-axis** by **44.24** units.

- Select all four wheel groups.

- **Rotate** them on their **X-axes** by **360 degrees**.

- Click the **Key** button.

- **Translate** the *master* on its **Z-axis** to test the setup.

  The wheel should rotate correctly within the translation keys set above.

5 Infinity

The current driven animation curves are finite, and that is why when you translate the SUV, at some point the wheels stop turning. To correct this, you need to change the infinity of the animation curve.

- Select all four wheel groups.

- Open the Graph Editor.

- Select all the animation curves that are visible.

- Select **Curves** → **Pre Infinity** → **Linear**.

- Select **Curves** → **Post Infinity** → **Linear**.

- To make sure the curves are set correctly, select **View** → **Infinity**.

- **Translate** the *master* on its **Z-axis** to test the setup.

  The wheels should no longer stop when you move the master.

6 More driven keys

The wheels are now rotating correctly when you move the master on its **Z-axis**, but odds are that the SUV will not only move in a straight line. For instance, if you rotate the master on its **Y-axis** and translate it, the wheels will now slide or not rotate at all. The following will correct this behavior.

- Make sure to place the *master* back at the origin.

- Set its **rotateY** to **90 degrees**.

  Now if you translate the SUV forward, the wheels will not turn at all. As a result, you need to set new driven keys for the **translateX** *attribute.*

- Still in the Set Driven Key window, highlight **translateX** as the driving attribute.

- Click the **Key** button to set the initial keyframe.

- **Move** the *master* on its **X-axis** by **44.24** units.

- Select all four wheel groups.

- **Rotate** them on their **X-axes** by **360 degrees**.

- Click the **Key** button.

- Set the **infinity** of the new animation curves to **linear**.

- Close the Set Driven Key window.

7 Test the driven keys

The automation you have done so far now allows you to translate the SUV forward in any direction with its wheels moving correctly.

- **Double-click** on the **Move Tool** in the Toolbox.

- Set **Move** to **Object**.

- **Rotate** the SUV *master* and test the wheels by **translating** the SUV on the manipulator **Z-axis**.

8 Steering wheel

Using the same workflow as above, you will now set driven keys to turn the wheels as you rotate the steering wheel.

- Select the *steering* group and the **Rotate Tool**.

The local rotation of the steering group should be oriented just like the steering wheel itself. If it is not, you will need to adjust it as you would when adjusting the local rotation axis of joints.

- Go in **Component** mode and enable the **Local Rotation Axes** mask.

- Select the local rotation axis for the steering group and rotate it appropriately so that one of its axes follows the steering shaft.

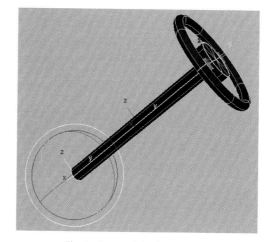

The steering group's local rotation axis

- Go back to **Object** mode and open the Attribute Editor for the steering group.

- Set the **Rotate Order** to start with the same axis you set to point in the direction of the steering shaft. If you made the **Y-axis** point in the direction of the shaft, select either **YXZ** or **YZX**.

Doing so ensures that only the appropriate rotation axis changes when you rotate the steering wheel.

- **Test** rotating the steering wheel to see if the wheels are turning accordingly.

The steering automation

10 **Save your work**

- **Save** your work as *17-SUVRig_02.ma*.

Non-linear deformers

The antenna of the SUV will require some deformation when the SUV will be moving. This is a perfect opportunity to use a non-linear deformer. Non-linear deformers will deform objects according to a mathematical formula such as bend, sine, wave, squash, etc.

In this exercise, you will use a bend deformer to bend the antenna.

1 **Unbend the antenna**

In order to bend the antenna with a deformer, it is recommended to start from straight geometry.

- Select the antenna group, then go in Component mode and select the CVs and hulls mask.

The CVs and hulls mask

- If you model the antenna already bent, straighten it from the *side* view.

The straight antenna

- Go back in **Object** mode.

2 Assign a bend deformer

- Select the *antenna* group.

- Select **Deform → Create Nonlinear → Bend**.

  The bend deformer is created and displayed as a single straight line.

- In the Channel Box, highlight the *bend1* node.

- To make the tweaking of the deformer easier, set **Curvature** to 1.

  The deformer doesn't deform as intended just yet.

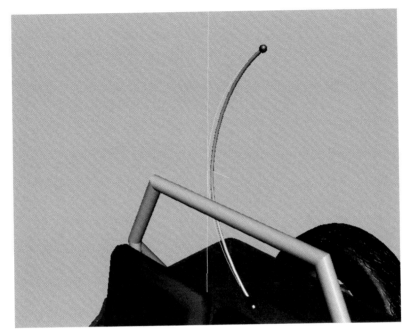

The effect of the bend deformer

3 Tweak the deformer

- Rotate the bend deformer handle by **90** degrees on its **Y-axis**.

- Set **Low Bound** in the Channel Box for the *bend1* to **0**.

- **Translate** the bend deformer handle down to match the anchor of the antenna.

- **Increase** the **High Bound** attribute so that it is longer than then antenna geometry.

- Test the Curvature attribute to see if it bends the antenna correctly.

The final bending effect

4 Custom attribute

When an attribute is hard to find, it is a good idea to make sure it is easily accessible. Select the antenna group.

- Select **Modify → Add Attribute...** and set the following:

    Attribute name to *bend*;

    Data Type to **Float**;

    Default to 0.

- Click on the **OK** button.

- **RMB** on the new **bend** attribute in the Channel Box and select **Connection Editor**.

    This is simply another way of opening the Connection Editor.

- Click **Reload Left** with the *antenna* group selected.

- Click **Reload Right** with the *bend1* node highlighted in the Channel Box.

- Highlight the **bend** attribute in the left column, then highlight the curvature attribute in the right column.

    *Doing so connects the **bend** attribute to the **curvature** attribute.*

- **Close** the Connection Editor.

5 Parent the deformer

In order for the bend deformer to act as intended, its handle needs to be parented into the SUV hierarchy.

- Select the bend deformer handle, then **Ctrl-select** the *chassis* group from the Outliner.

- Press **p** to **parent** the handle to the chassis.

- Hide the deformer using **Ctrl+h**.

Tip: *Deleting the history on the antenna would delete the bend deformer. Make sure to keep the history on the antenna.*

6 Lock and hide attributes

- Make sure to **lock and hide** attributes that are not required to be changed by the animator.

7 Visibility layer

- **Create** a new layer and **rename** it *setupLayer*.

- Select the *master* node and add it to the *setupLayer*.

8 Save your work

- **Save** your scene as *17-SUVRig_03.ma*.

Conclusion

The SUV is now ready to be animated. You have created some automation, but you also made sure that the animator could override that animation. As well, you used a non-linear deformer, which is much easier to use than any other setup.

In the next lesson, you will animate Boog hopping into the driver's seat.

Lesson 18
More animation

Since you have created the SUV model, you can now practice animation skills from a more artistic point of view. In this lesson, you will animate Boog hopping in the SUV's driver seat. This time, rather than approaching animation from a mathematical standpoint, you will have to establish key poses based on artistic knowledge to generate the animation.

In this lesson, you will learn the following:

- How to reference multiple scenes;
- How to establish key poses;
- How to refine in-betweens;
- How to playblast an animation;
- How to fix the timing of your animation.

References

When you first animated Boog, you saw how to create a reference. You will now open that same animation file, but this time you will also reference the SUV and the garage.

1   **Create references**

- **Open** the scene file *14-boogWalk_04.ma* from the second project directory.

- Select **File → Create Reference → ❑.**

- Set **Resolve all nodes with this string:** *SUV.*

  This will prefix all the reference nodes with the string SUV.

- Click on the **Apply** button.

- In the browse dialog that appears, select the file *17-SUVRig_03.ma*, then click **Reference**.

  The file will load into the current one.

- Set **Resolve all nodes with this string:** *garage.*

- Click on the **Reference** button.

- In the browse dialog that appears, select the file *04-animation_01.ma* from the first project, and then click **Reference**.

> **Note:**   *You may have to relink textures that are not automatically found. To do so, simply open the Hypershade, select the Texture tab and change the path of the texture through the Attribute Editor.*

2   **Scaling**

Looking at the three elements in your scene, you can clearly see that there is a scaling issue with the garage geometry.

- Select the *garageGroup* top node.

- Set its **scale X, Y** and **Z-axes** to **5**.

  The garage should not be proportionate to the other elements.

The entire scene

Note: *If the top node's scale attributes are non-keyable and unlocked, they will not show in the Channel Box, but the Scale Tool will still work. Alternatively, you can access the scale attributes in the Attribute Editor. If the scale attributes of the node are locked, you need to unlock them in the referenced file and re-open this file again.*

3 Save your work

- **Save** this scene to *18-jumpAnimation_01.ma* in the current project's *scene* directory.

Jump animation

Now that your scene is properly set-up, you will animate Boog jumping into the SUV. Once this is done, the new sequence will be saved as another Trax clip.

1 Bear character

- In the **Active Character** menu next to the Range Slider, select the *bear* character set.

2 Set the time range

- Set the **Start Time** and **Playback Start Time** to 1.

- Set the **End Time** and **Playback End Time** to 30.

3 Current time

- Move the current time indicator to 1.

4 Clear the Trax Editor

As you may notice, Boog is already animated in this scene. This is because the Trax Editor still contains the Trax walk cycle clip you create earlier. You will now clear the Trax Editor and start a new animation.

- Open the Trax Editor by selecting **Windows → Animation Editors → Trax Editor**.

- If the walk clip is not visible, make sure to turn On the **List → Auto Load Selected Characters** options.

- Click on the *walk* clip to highlight it.

- Press **Delete** to remove it.

  All the animation has now been removed, but the character has kept its initial step position which will be used as the starting pose of the jump animation.

Project 03

- Close the Trax Editor.

5 **Keyframe the start pose**

- Press the **s** hotkey to keyframe the entire *bear* character.

- Enable the **Auto Key** button.

- **Translate** and **rotate** the bear *master* so it is next to the driver's door.

The start pose

6 **Set keys for the anticipation**

- Go to frame **5**.

- Bring the *rHeelControl* forward, next to the *lHeelControl*.

- Place the character as follows to the right:

- Press the **s** key to set a key on the bear character at this new position.

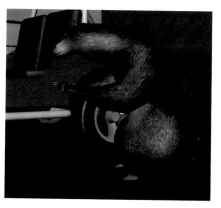

Anticipation pose

7 Set keys for the pushing motion

- Go to frame 10.

- Place the character as follows to the right:

- Press the **s** key to set a key on the bear character at this new position.

Pushing pose

8 Set keys for the jump pose

- Go to frame 15.

- Place the character to the right in mid air over the door opening.

- Press the **s** key to set a key on the bear character at this new position.

Jump pose

9 Fix jump pose tangents

- **RMB** in the Time Slider at frame 15 and select **Tangents → Spline**.

10 Set keys for the landing anticipation pose

- Go to frame 20.

- Place the character as follows:

Press the **s** key to set a key on the bear character at this new position.

Landing anticipation

11 Set keys for the landing pose

- Go to frame **25**.

- Place the character as follows to the right:

- Press the **s** key to set a key on the bear character at this new position.

Landing pose

12 Set keys for the end pose

- Go to frame **30**.

- Place the character comfortably in the SUV with one hand on the steering and the other on the gearshift.

The final pose

Note: *It is possible that Boog's legs are too short to reach the pedals. You can minimize this by lowering the pelvis in the seat.*

13 Tweak the animation

- Scroll the timeline and tweak the poses to make them more fluid with each other.

- Make sure you brought everything along when you moved the character.

- **Playback** the animation.

14 Playblast your animation

A playblast is a movie reflecting your scene animation. When making a playblast, Maya generates the animation by grabbing the image directly from the active viewport, so make sure to display only what you want to see in your playblast.

- Frame the scene in the Perspective view to see it in its entirety.

- From the Show menu in the Perspective panel, hide object types that you do not want in your playblast such as **grids**, **NURBS curves**, **lights**, **locators** and **handles**.

- Press **6** if you want the textures to appear in your playblast.

- Select **Window** → **Playblast**.

  Maya will render every frame, recording it into the playblast. Once the scene has been entirely played through, the playblast is displayed in your default movie player.

Note: *For more options on the playblast, select* **Window** → **Playblast** → □.

15 Animation refinement

Once you have seen the playblast and animation at its real speed, you can concentrate on correcting the motion and timing.

- Note an area that appears to be too fast or too slow in the playblast.

- To move a pose to a different frame, hold down **Shift** and click on a keyframe in the Time Slider.

- **Click+drag** the keyframe to the left to change the pose faster, and to the right to change the pose later.

Note: *You might have to redo your playblast and perform some trial and error before finding the perfect animation speed.*

Tip: *Beginner animators tend to make everything slow motion when animating. Don't be afraid to have only 2 or 3 frames between your poses. An entire jump motion should take about one second, which is only 24 frames.*

16 Save your work

- **Save** this scene to *18-jumpAnimation_02.ma*.

Create a Trax clip file

The animation is done, so you will now create a Trax clip file.

1 Open the Trax Editor window

- Make sure that *bear* is the current character set.

- Select **Window → Animation Editor → Trax Editor**.

2 Create a clip

- From the Trax Editor, select **Create → Animation Clip → ❑**.

- In the Trax window, select **Edit → Reset**.

- Set the following options:

  Name to *jump;*

  Leave Keys in Timeline to **Off**;

  Clip to **Put Clip in Trax Editor and Visor**;

  Time Range to **Animation Curve**;

  Include Subcharacters in Clip to **Off**;

  Create Time Warp Curve to **Off**;

  Include Hierarchy to **On**.

- Click the **Create Clip** button.

- Press **a** in the Trax Editor to frame all.

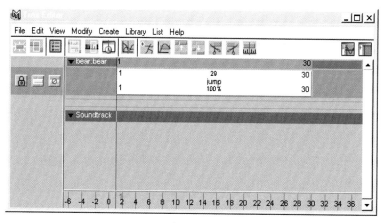

Jump clip in Trax Editor

3 **Export the clip**

- Select **File → Visor...**

- Select the **Character Clips** tab to see the clip source.

- Select the *jumpSource* clip.

- **RMB** on the clip and select **Export.**

- **Save** the clip as *boogJumpExport.ma*

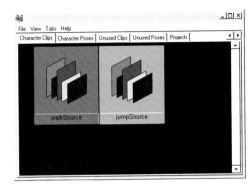

Jump source clip in Visor

Note: *Since you are in a new project, you can either copy the other* boogWalkExport.ma *file or export it again from here.*

- **Close** the Visor.

4 **Save your work**

- **Save** this scene to *18-jumpAnimation_03.ma.*

Conclusion

You have now completed another type of animation that required much more artistic input. As you saw here, a lot of practice is required to achieve good animation in an efficient manner.

In the next lesson you will use the Trax Editor to combine the clips and create a new animated sequence.

Lesson 19
Trax Editor

So far in this book, you have animated the bear and created two Trax clips from the
animated sequences. In this lesson, you will create a more complex motion by joining the
walk clip with the jump clip in the Trax Editor.

The advantage of working with non-linear animation lies in the ability to move, edit,
connect and reuse multiple clips freely, without having to edit multiple time curves.
You can also add numerous sound files to the scene using Trax.

In this lesson, you will learn the following:

- How to work with relative and absolute clips;

- How to clip, split, blend and merge clips;

- How to use time wrap;

- How to layer non-destructive keys over clips;

- How to redirect animation;

- How to use sound in Trax;

- How to animate a two-node camera.

Initial set-up

1 **Scene file**

- **Open** the file you saved at the end of the last lesson.

OR

- **Open** the scene file *18-jumpAnimation_03.ma*.

2 **Set up the work area**

- Set the **Playback Frame Range** to go from 1 to 140.

- From the menus in any modeling window, select **Panels** → **Saved Layouts** → **Persp/Trax/Outliner**.

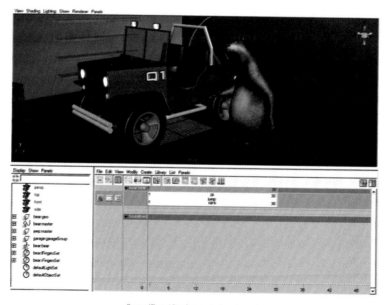

Persp/Trax/Outliner window layout

Generate the animation

The following exercise uses several Trax commands that will establish the animation of the bear. The animation you want to achieve in the scene goes like this:

Boog walks in the garage towards the SUV. As the garage door slowly opens, Boog jumps in his SUV. Once he is comfortably seated, he manipulates the steering wheel and the gearshift, ready to leave the garage.

1 Load the first two clips

- Select the *bear* character from the **Current Character** menu at the bottom right of the interface.

  The Trax Editor will update, showing the jump from the last lesson.

- Select **Library → Insert Clip → walkSource**.

  Both the walk and jump clips are now in the Trax Editor.

- Press **a** to frame all.

- **Click+drag** each clip in the Trax Editor so that the *walk* clip starts at frame **1** and the *jump* clip starts at frame **115**.

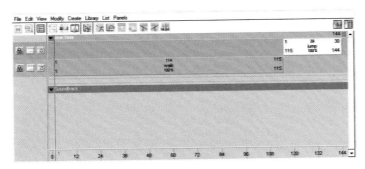

Walk and jump clips

2 Trim the walk clip

- Scrub to frame **58** in the timeline.

  This is a good place to match the jump clip, since it is a pose similar to the start pose.

- Select the *walk* clip.

- Select the **Trim After** icon from the Trax menu to **Trim** the clip after frame **58**.

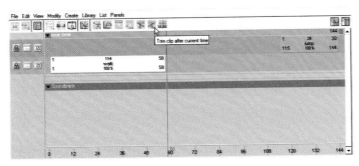

Trim the walk clip after frame 58

- **Move** the *jump* clip to its new starting position at frame 58.

3 View the clips with absolute offset

- **Play** the animation by dragging the vertical time indicator in the Trax window.

  As the walk clip switches to the jump clip during playback, you will see the bear jump back to the original keyframed values of the jump animation, or absolute offset.

4 Change the jump clip to relative offset

- Select the *jump* clip, then press **Ctrl+a** to open its Attribute Editor.

- Scroll to the **Channel Offsets** section and click the **All Relative** button.

- **Play** the animation.

  Now, as the walk clip switches to the jump clip during playback, you will see that the bear keeps jumping from the end walk position. This is because the clip's animation is relative to the end position of the clip preceding it.

5 Ease out the walk clip

At this point, you might notice a drastic speed change between the end of the walk clip and the start of the jump. The following steps will help smooth this.

- Select the *walk* clip.

- **RMB** on the clip and select **Create Time Wrap**.

  A time wrap is a curve that controls the speed of the clip animation. Using this, you will slow down the walk to have the bear come to a complete stop.

- Click on the **Open Graph Editor** button located at the top right corner of the Trax Editor.

- Scroll down in the Graph Editor Outliner and highlight the **Time Wrap** attribute.

- Select the last keyframe and set its **Tangent** to **Flat**.

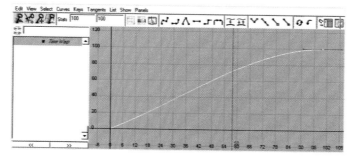

The time wrap curve

- Click on the **Open Trax Editor** button located at the top right corner of the Graph Editor.

- If you scrub in the animation, you will notice that the bear is now smoothly coming to a stop.

6 Blend between the two clips

- Select the *walk* clip, then **Shift-select** the *jump* clip.

- Select **Create → Blend → □**.

- In the option window, set **Initial Weight Curve** to **Ease In Out**.

- Click the **Create Blend** button.

- Select the *jump* clip on its own and **drag** it so that it starts at frame **50**.

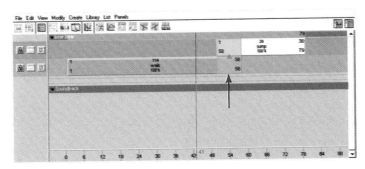

The newly created blend area

- **Playback** the animation. You will notice that the animation is now much more fluid.

> **Tip:** To frame the animation from the Trax Editor in the main Time Slider, **RMB** in the
> Time Slider and select **Set Range To → Enabled Clips**.

7 Merge all the clips

- Select all the clips by **click+dragging** a selection box over the clips in the Trax Editor.

- Select **Edit → Merge → □**.

- In the Merge option window, set the following:

  Name to *bearAnim*;

  Merged Clip to **Add to Trax**.

- Click the **Merge Clip** button.

  The new merged clip is now in the Trax Editor, and has replaced all the previous clips.

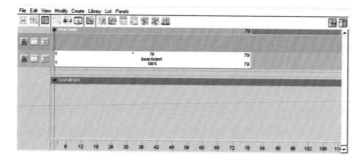

The new merged clip

Redirect the animation

Next, you will change Boog's position so that he fits in the driver's seat perfectly.

1   Change the animation orientation

- Select the bear's *master* node.

- From the Animate menu set, select **Character** → **Redirect** → ❒.

- Select the Translation only option, then click the **Redirect** button.

  Doing so creates an override that allows you to move the animation to the proper place.

The redirect node

- Go to frame **79**.
- Set the following:

  Translate X to **41**;

  Translate Y to **0**;

  Translate Z to **-44**.

- Highlight all **translate** attributes in the Channel Box, then **RMB** and select **Key Selected**.

  Doing so will change the placement of the entire animation.

The correctly placed animation

2   **Save your work**

- **Save** the scene as *19-trax_01.ma*.

Non-destructive keys

You have already experienced the flexibility of working with non-linear animation clips. To further refine the motion, you will add some non-destructive keys to the animation.

1   **Add a start and end key on the head and eyes**

When setting keyframes over a Trax clip, you need to set default keys before and after the region where you want to alter the animation. If you don't set those keys, the offset you keyframe will remain throughout the animation.

- Select the *head* joint.
- Go to frame **1**.

- Press **Shift+e** to keyframe this rotation.

- Go to frame **45**.

- Press **Shift+e** again to keyframe this rotation.

  You will notice some new keys being placed in the timeline.

2 **Add keys to modify the head rotation**

- Go to frame **10** and rotate the *head* joint so the bear looks at the SUV.

- Press the **Shift+e** to keyframe the head.

- Go to frame **30** and rotate the *head* joint so the bear keeps looking at the SUV.

- Press the **Shift+e** to keyframe the head.

> **Note:** If Auto Key is On, you don't have to manually key the rotation after you have set
> a key once.

- Select the keyframes at frames **10** and **30** in the Time Slider, then **RMB** and select
  Tangents → Spline to set the tangents of the selected keyframe.

- **Playback** the results.

  Now the bear's head is deviating from his original clip-based animation.

3 **Modify the lookAt**

- **Repeat** the last steps in order to correctly animate where the bear is looking throughout
  the animation.

The bear now looks at the SUV

> **Note:** *These keys are not altering the clips in any way. In fact, these keys can be deleted or moved around and the clip-based animation will remain intact. You could also create another clip from these new keyframes.*

4 **Create a clip**

- From the Trax Editor, select **Create** → **Animation Clip** → **◻**.

- Set the following options:

  Name to *animModifier*;

  Leave Keys in Timeline to **Off**;

  Clip to **Put Clip in Trax Editor and Visor**;

  Time Range to **Animation Curve**;

  Subcharacters to **Off**;

  Time Wrap to **Off**;

  Include Hierarchy to **On**.

- Click on the **Create Clip** button.

  A new clip is added to the Trax Editor. The keyframes of this new clip are added to the existing animation clip.

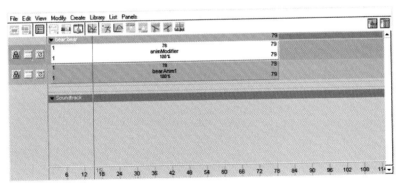

Animation modifier clip in Trax

5 **Save your work**

- **Save** the scene as *19-trax_02.ma*.

Adding sound to Trax

The Trax Editor offers you the ability to import and sync sound files to your animation.

You can import **.wav** or **.aiff** sound files into Trax to synchronize motion and audio. More than one audio clip can be imported into the soundtrack, but you will be able to hear only one file at a time upon playback. The audio file at the top of the soundtrack display will take precedence over those below.

You will now import some pre-created sound files into your scene.

1 **Set playback preferences**

- Select **Windows** → **Settings/ Preferences** → **Preferences...**

- In the **Timeline** category under the **Playback** section, make sure **Playback speed** is set to **Real-time [24 fps]**.

   If this option is not set to real-time, the sound might not be played.

2 **Add a sound file**

- From the Trax Editor, select **File** → **Import Audio...**

- From the *sound* directory, select *hop.wav*.

3 **See and hear the sound file**

- **RMB** in the Time Slider.

- From the pop-up menu, select **Sounds** → **Use Trax Sounds**.

   A green indicator bar will appear on the global timeline and the clips will display an audio waveform.

4 **Move the clip**

- Select the sound clip and **click+drag** it to frame **48**.

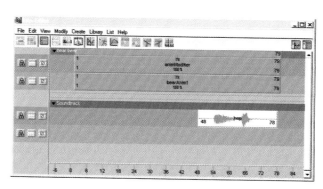

Sound clip in Trax

5 Import a second sound file

- Select **File** → **Import Audio...**

- From the *sound* directory, select *SUV_start.wav*.

6 Sync the sound to the animation

- **Play** the animation with the sound.

  Notice that the top-most audio clip takes precedence as the scene is playing.

- **Click+drag** the engine sound clip so that it syncs up to when Boog is seated.

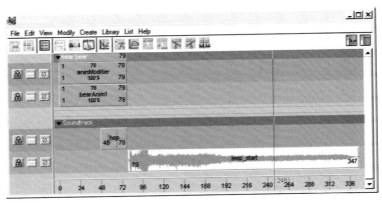

Two sound clips in Trax

> **Note:** *Don't worry if the engine sound is longer than your animation; you will be animating the SUV in the next project.*

Animating a camera

You will now add a new camera to the scene and animate it so that you can follow the bear as he walks.

A camera can be created on its own or with additional nodes that provide control over the *aim point* and *up direction*. Most cameras only need one node that lets you key the camera's position and rotation. You will create a camera to control both the *camera point* and the *view-point*. Both these nodes can be keyed individually.

1 Set-up your panel display

- Select a **Two Panes Stacked** view layout.

- In the Perspective view, make sure Show → **Cameras and Show** → Pivots are **On**.

  You will need to see these in order to work with the camera.

2 Create a two-node camera

- Select **Create** → **Cameras** → **Camera and Aim**.

- Instead of the *front* view, select **Panels** → **Perspective** → ❐.

- Press **6** to view the textures in the *camera1* view.

- In the *camera1* view, select **View** → **Camera Settings** → **Resolution Gate**.

- Still in the *camera1* view, select View → Camera Attribute Editor.

- Change **Fit Resolution Gate** to **Vertical**.

3 Frame the character

- Select the **Show Manipulator Tool**.

- In the *Perspective* view, position the *camera* and *camera1_aim* handles as follows:

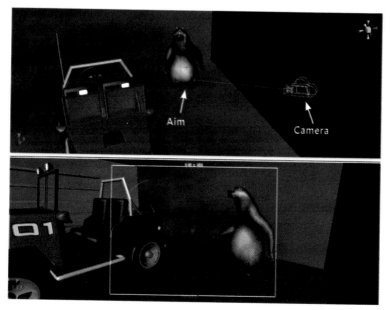

Camera manipulator handles

> **Note:** You can position the camera using either the Perspective or camera1 view.

4 Follow the action

You will now set keys on the camera point to follow the character from frames 1 to 60.

- Set the current character to **None**.
- Go to frame **1**.
- **Select** the *camera1* and *camera1_aim* nodes.
- Press **Shift+w** to keyframe the current position.

  Doing so sets a keyframe for the current camera position.

- Go to frame **65**.
- **Move** the *camera1_aim* node so that it is again looking at the character, framing both the bear and the SUV.
- **Select** the *camera1* and *camera1_aim* nodes.
- Press **Shift+w** to keyframe the new view position.

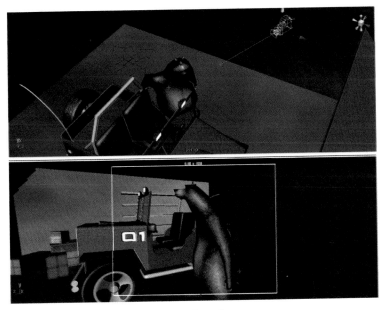

View at frame 65

5 Dolly around the SUV

The camera animation now frames the first portion of the animation correctly, but the second part of the animation could be better. You can set keys on the viewpoint node to fix this.

- Go to frame **140**.

- **Move** the *camera1* node from the *Perspective* view to the back of the SUV to frame the upcoming SUV leaving the garage.

- **Select** the *camera1* and *camera1_aim* nodes.

- Press **Shift+w** to keyframe the new view position.

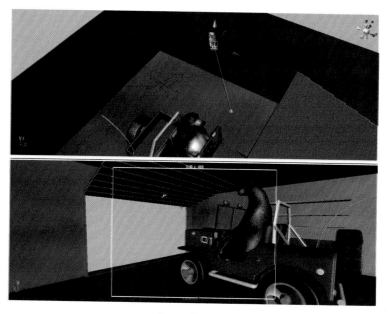

View at frame 140

- If you don't like the framing in the in-between frames, you can reposition the camera and set new keys. **Repeat** this until you get the camera movement you want.

6 Playblast the animation

You can now playblast the scene to test the motion. This will give you the chance to confirm the camera animation.

Tip: *Make sure you maximize the camera view by tapping the spacebar and displaying only NURBS surfaces and polygons. You can also set the bear's smoothness to be high resolution and set the NURBS smoothness to its finest setting.*

The high resolution model in playblast

7 **Save your work**

- **Save** the scene as *19-trax_03.ma.*

Conclusion

In this lesson, you completed your first non-linear animation using Trax. You used some features available to you in the Trax Editor and you also animated on top of clips using non-destructive keyframes.

In the next lesson, you will learn about lighting and effects which can greatly improve the quality of your scene once rendered.

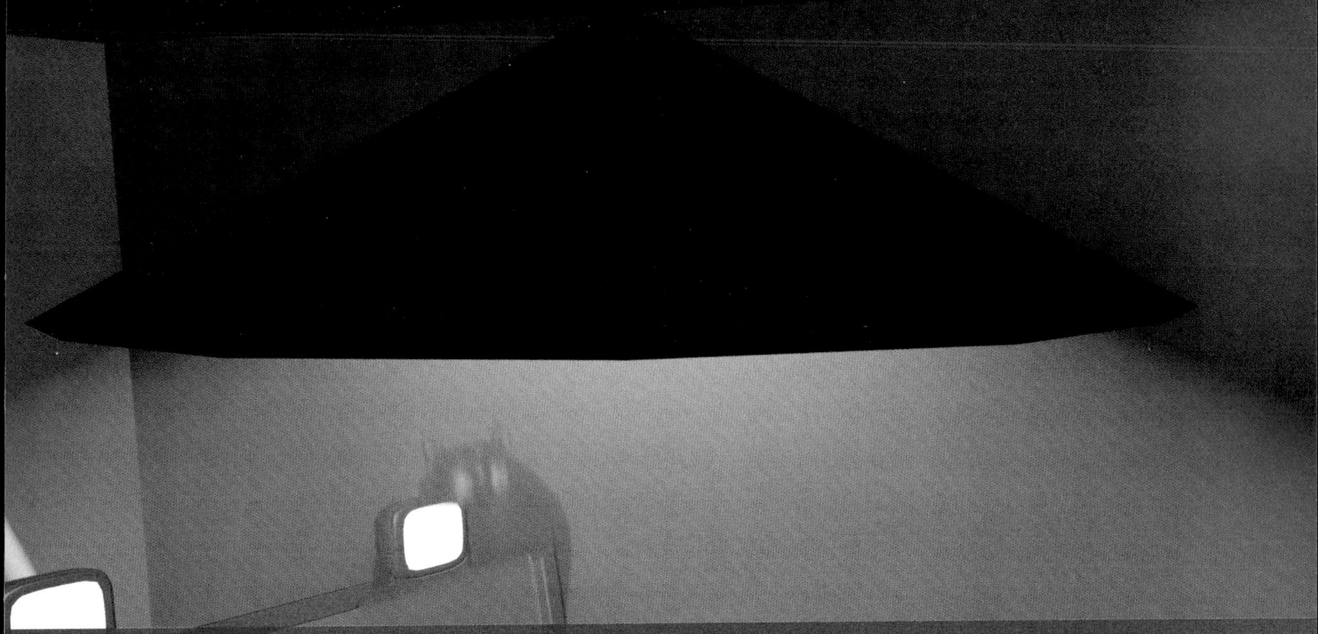

Lesson 20
Lights and effects

In the real world, it is light that allows us to see the surfaces and objects around us. In computer graphics, digital lights play the same role. They help define the space within a scene, and in many cases, help to set the mood or atmosphere. As well, several other effects besides lighting can be added to the final image in order to have it look more realistic. This lesson explores and explains some of the basic Maya effects.

In this lesson you will learn the following:

- How to add lighting to your scene;

- How to enable shadows;

- How to add light fog and lens flare;

- How to add shader glow;

- How to set-up motion blur;

- How to software render an animation;

- How to use fcheck.

Placing a point light

To create the primary light source in the scene, you will use a point light. This light type works exactly like a lightbulb, with attributes such as color and intensity.

1 Scene file

- Continue using the file saved in the previous lesson.

OR

- **Open** *19-trax_03.ma* from the support files.

2 Create a point light

- Select **Create → Lights → Point Light**.

  This places a point light at the origin.

- With the light still selected, **translate** the point light within the garage lightbulb.

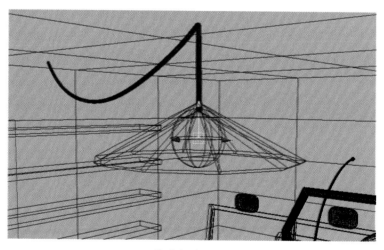

The light placement

3 Turn on hardware lighting (if possible)

One step beyond hardware texturing is *hardware lighting*. This lets you see how the light is affecting the surface that it is shining upon.

- Press the **6** hotkey to display textures in the viewport.

- Select **Lighting → Use All Lights** or press the **7** hotkey.

  You will see the scene being lit by the point light.

The hardware lighting enabled

4 **Test render the scene**

- Go to frame **90**.

- Make *camera1* the current camera by selecting **Panels → Perspective → camera1**.

- **Render** the scene.

Notice the rendered image is dark without much contrast.

The rendered scene

Placing a spot light

So far, you used a point light to fill the room with light, but it did not use any shadows to create depth in the scene. This kind of light can be thought of as ambient lighting, which comes from light bouncing off walls that fills the room.

As a second light source in the scene, you will use a *spot light*. This light type lets you define the same attributes as the point light, as well as others including the light's cone angle.

1   **Create a spot light**

  *   Select **Create → Lights → Spot Light**.

      This places a spot light at the origin.

2   **Edit the spot light's position**

The Show Manipulator Tool provides a manipulator for the light's *look at point* and *eye point*. You can edit these using the same method as you would with a typical transform manipulator.

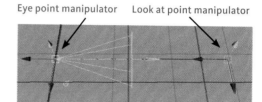

Eye point manipulator   Look at point manipulator

Show Manipulator Tool

  *   Press the **t** key to access the **Show Manipulator Tool**.

  *   **Click+drag** on the manipulator handles to reposition the light.

  *   **Move** the manipulator and **scale** the light up until it appears as shown to the right:

3   **Edit the spot light's cone angle**

You can now edit some of the light's attributes to control its effect. You will reveal other light manipulators to let you edit this attribute interactively.

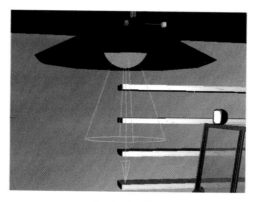

New light position

  *   With the spot light still selected, press **t** to select the **Show Manipulator Tool**.

      Next to the light is a small icon that displays a circle with a small line pointing up and to the right. This icon is the cycling index and is used to cycle between different types of light manipulators.

- Click two times on the manipulator's cycle index.

  The cycling index rotates to show that you are accessing new manipulators. The chosen manipulator consists of a little blue dot just outside of the light cone. The new manipulator lets you edit the cone angle of the spot light.

- **Click+drag** on the cone angle manipulator to fit the lamp cone shape.

  *In the Attribute Editor, you can watch the **Cone Angle** attribute update as you drag the manipulator.*

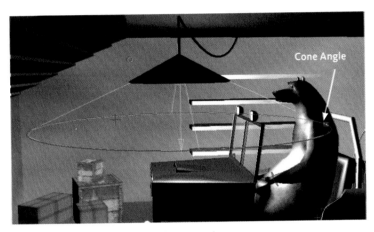

New cone angle

4 Adjust the penumbra angle

For softness at the edge of the spotlight, you can adjust the light's penumbra.

- In the Attribute Editor, set the **Penumbra Angle** to **20**.

- Click one more time on the manipulator's cycle index.

  You can now see a second circular line inside the cone angle icon that indicates the area where the light will be soft.

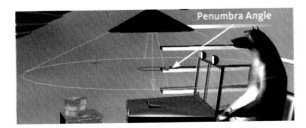

Penumbra manipulator

5 Change the light attributes

- In the Attribute Editor, expand the **Shadows** section for the spot light.

- **Enable** shadow casting by checking the **Use Depth Map Shadows** attribute.

- **Render** the scene.

  Notice that you don't see the effect of the spot light as it should be in the rendered image. This is because the spotlight is inside the bulb geometry which is casting shadows, so everything is in the shadow of the spot light. To correct this, you can disable shadow casting on the bulb surface.

- Select the *bulb* surface and open its Attribute Editor.

- Under the **Render Stats** section, set the following:

  Casts Shadows to **Off**;

  Receive Shadows to **Off**.

- **Render** the scene again.

Shadows section in the Attribute Editor

The properly lit scene

6 Refine the shadows

Right now, the shadow resolution is a little coarse. The following shows how to increase the depth map shadow resolution.

- Open the Attribute Editor for the *spotLight1*.

- In the **Depth Map Shadow Attributes** section, set **Resolution** to **1024** rather than **512**.

- **Render** the scene again to see how this makes the shadow smoother.

7 Adding light fog

To actually see the light beam when you render, you need to add *light fog*. Light fog mimics light bouncing off microscopic particles in the air. In the Attribute Editor, set the light's **Color** to a pale yellow.

- Set the light's **Decay Rate** to **Linear**.

  The decay rate controls how fast the light fades as it is traveling through space. A linear decay rate simply tells Maya to fade off the light faster so that it doesn't light up crisp shadows further than a certain distance.

- Since the decay reduced the strength of the light, increase its **Intensity** to 3.

- Open the **Light Effects** section of the light's attributes in the Attribute Editor.

- Set the **Fog Intensity** attribute to 5.

- Click on the map button on the right of the **Light Fog** attribute.

  Doing so will automatically create a lightFog node and it will also display a fog cone in the viewports. The lightFog node is automatically selected and displayed in the Attribute Editor.

- Set the *lightFog*'s color to yellow.

- **Render** your scene.

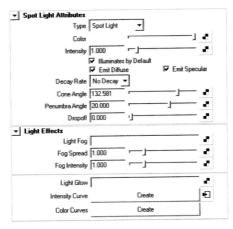

Light Effects section

Light Fog render

Refining the lightbulb

Your lightbulb looked a little dull in the latest render. You will remedy this by adding glow and lens flare so that your scene looks more realistic.

1 Adding shader glow

Most Maya surface shaders can foster the illusion that the object they are assigned to is glowing. This works especially well if an object has some kind of incandescence added to it. Here, you will enable glow on the *bulb* material.

- Select the *bulb* object.

- At the top of the Hypershade, click on the **Graph Materials on Selected Objects** button.

  This should display the bulbM material in the workspace area of the Hypershade.

Graph Materials on Selected Objects button

- Select the *bulbM* material.

- In the Attribute Editor, open the **Special Effects** section.

- Set **Glow Intensity** to 0.5.

- **Render** your scene.

  The Maya glow is rendered in a second pass. This means you will not see the glow until the render is completely finished.

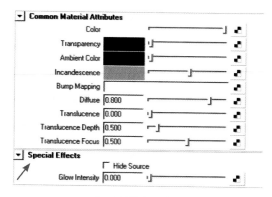

Special Effects section

2 Adding light glow

Since the rendered camera is looking directly at bright light, adding lens flare would add realism to your renders.

- Open the Attribute Editor for the *spotLightShape1*.

- Click on the **map** button next to the **Light Glow** attribute in the **Light Effects** section.

The glowing bulb render

Maya will automatically create, select and display an opticalFX node in the Attribute Editor.

- Set the *opticalFX1* attributes as follows:

  Lens flare to **Enabled**;

  Glow Type to **None**;

Halo Type to None.

- Under **Lens Flare Attributes,** set **Flare Intensity** to 5.

  Since the bulb material already has glow enabled, it would not be relevant to also have a light glow.

- **Render** your scene to see the lens flare.

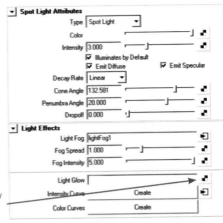

Map the Light Glow attribute

Sunlight on planets

Tip: *If you find it difficult to see, increase the Flare Intensity on the Optical F/X node some more.*

Bulb lens flare

Rendering animation

Now that you have defined the lighting in your scene and you are happy with your test rendering, it is time to render an animation. This is accomplished using Maya's *batch renderer*. In preparation, you will add motion blur to your scene to simulate the blur generated in live action film and video work.

1   Render Settings

Render Settings are a group of attributes that you can set to define how your scene will render. To set-up the quality of the rendering, you need to set the Render Settings.

- In the Render view window, click with your **RMB** and choose **Options** →
  Render Settings.

- Select the **Maya Software** tab.

- Open the **Anti-aliasing Quality** section if it is not already open.

- Set the **Quality** presets to **Intermediate Quality**.

  Anti-aliasing is a visual smoothing of edge lines in the final rendered image. Because bitmaps are made up of square pixels, a diagonal line would appear jagged unless it was anti-aliased.

2   Set the image output

To render an animation, you must set-up the scene's file extensions to indicate a rendered sequence. You must also set-up the start and end frames.

- Select the **Common** tab in the Render Settings window.

- From the **Image File Output** section, set the following:

  File Name Prefix to *garage*.

  This sets the name of the animated sequence.

  Frame/Animation Ext *to:*

  name.#.ext (for Windows, Mac);

  name.ext.# (for IRIX).

  This sets up Maya to render a numbered sequence of images.

  Start Frame to 1;

  End Frame to 140;

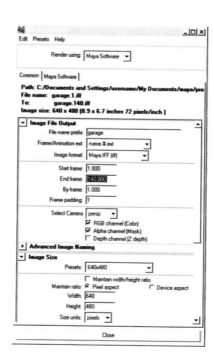

Render Settings

By Frame to 1.

This tells Maya to render every frame from 1 to 140.

3 Turn on motion blur

- Select the **Maya Software** tab.

- Under the **Motion Blur** section, click on the **Motion Blur** button to turn it **On**.

- Set the **Motion Blur Type** to be **2D**.

This type of motion blur renders the fastest.

Motion blur render

4 Save your work

- **Save** your scene as *20-lightsEffects.ma*.

5 Batch render the scene

- Press **F5** to change to the **Rendering** menu set.

- Select **Render** → **Batch Render**.

- If for any reason you want to cancel the current batch render, select **Render** → **Cancel Batch Render**.

6 Watch the render progress

- The sequence will be rendered as a series of frames. You can look in the Command Feedback line or through the **Window** → **General Editor** → **Script Editor** to see the status of the current rendering process.

7 View the resulting animation

After the rendering is complete, you can preview the results using the *fcheck* utility.

On Windows, Mac

- To open the *fcheck* utility on Windows, click on *Start* and select *Programs*. From there go to **Autodesk** → **Maya 8.0** → **FCheck.**

- Select **File** → **Open Animation.**

- Navigate to the *project3\images* folder.

- Select the file *garage.1.iff* and click **Open.**

  This is the first frame of your rendered animation.

On IRIX

- In a shell window, set your current directory to the *maya/projects/project3/images* directory.

- Type the following:

```
fcheck garage.iff.
```

Animation previewed with fcheck utility

By Frame to 1.

This tells Maya to render every frame from 1 to 140.

3 Turn on motion blur

- Select the **Maya Software** tab.

- Under the **Motion Blur** section, click on the **Motion Blur** button to turn it **On**.

- Set the **Motion Blur Type** to be **2D**.

This type of motion blur renders the fastest.

Motion blur render

4 Save your work

- **Save** your scene as *20-lightsEffects.ma*.

5 Batch render the scene

- Press **F5** to change to the **Rendering** menu set.

- Select **Render** → **Batch Render**.

- If for any reason you want to cancel the current batch render, select **Render** → **Cancel Batch Render**.

6 Watch the render progress

- The sequence will be rendered as a series of frames. You can look in the Command Feedback line or through the **Window** → **General Editor** → **Script Editor** to see the status of the current rendering process.

7 View the resulting animation

After the rendering is complete, you can preview the results using the *fcheck* utility.

On Windows, Mac

- To open the *fcheck* utility on Windows, click on *Start* and select *Programs*. From there go to **Autodesk** → **Maya 8.0** → **FCheck.**

- Select **File** → **Open Animation.**

- Navigate to the *project3\images* folder.

- Select the file *garage.1.iff* and click **Open.**

  This is the first frame of your rendered animation.

On IRIX

- In a shell window, set your current directory to the *maya/projects/project3/images* directory.

- Type the following:

```
fcheck garage.iff.
```

Animation previewed with fcheck utility

In both cases, the animation will load one frame at a time and playback more quickly once in memory.

Tip: *To learn more about the capabilities of fcheck for previewing your animations, enter* `fcheck -h` *in a shell window or select the Help menu.*

Conclusion

You are now familiar with the basic concepts of lighting and rendering a scene. You began by enabling various light options such as color, shadows, light fog and light glow. Then, you added material glow and 2D motion blur, just before launching your first animation batch render. Once your render was complete, you viewed it in the fcheck utility.

In the next lesson, you will add basic particle systems to your scene.

Lesson 21
Rendering

This lesson will make extensive use of the Maya Interactive Photorealistic Renderer (IPR). This tool allows you to create a rendering of the scene that can then be used to interactively update changes to the scene's lighting and texturing. You will see how fast and intuitive it is to texture in Maya IPR.

So far in this book, you have been using only the Maya software to render your scenes. In this lesson, you will also learn about three additional rendering types: Maya Hardware, Maya Vector and mental ray for Maya. Each has its own strengths and you should determine which rendering engine to use on a per project basis depending on the final application.

In this lesson you will learn the following:

- How to render a region and display snapshots;
- How to open and save images, and display an image's alpha channel;
- How to start the IPR;
- How to make connections in the Hypershade;
- How to enable high quality rendering in a viewport;
- How to render with mental ray, Maya Vector and Maya hardware.

Rendering features

You are now ready to refine the rendering of your scene. In this section, you will experiment with the Render view features, such as snapshots, image storage and region rendering.

1 Scene file

- Continue with the scene file you were using in the last lesson.

OR

- Open the scene *20-lightsEffects_01.ma*.

2 Panel set-up

- In the Perspective view, select **Panels** → **Saved Layouts** → **Hypershade/Render/Persp**.
- Frame one of the SUV's *headlights*.
- **RMB-click** in the Render view and select **Render** → **Render** → **Persp**.

Note: *You can change the size of the panels by* **click+dragging** *on their separators.*

3 Keep and remove image

When test rendering a scene, it is good to be able to keep previously rendered images for comparison with the changes you implement.

- To keep the current render for reference, select **File** → **Keep Image in Render View** or click the **Keep Image** button.

  Notice a slider bar appears at the bottom of the Render view.

- In the Perspective view, select the headlight geometry.
- In the Hypershade, click on the **Graph Material on Selection**.

Note: *Here, you will be modifying the SUV textures when the SUV is referenced. This way, your changes will only be in that scene file and not in the original SUV scene file.*

- In the Create Maya Node section, scroll down and set the **2D Textures** option to **As Projection** and click on the **File** node.

- **Scale** the projection manipulator to the headlight geometry you are currently framing.

Tip: *If you are keeping the projection in the scene rather than converting to a texture, make sure to parent or constrain the projection node to the headlight.*

- **Double-click** on the *file1* node to open the Graph Editor.

- Click the **Browse** button and select the *headlight.tif* texture from the *sourceimage* folder.

- In the Hypershade work area, **MMB+drag** the *projection1* node onto the *headlight* material.

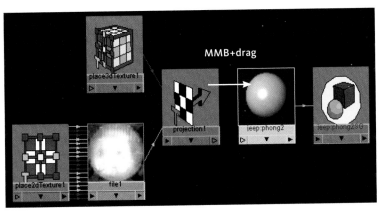

Dragging to create a connection

- Choose **Color** from the context menu to map the file in the color of the material.

- In the Render view, **render** the model again.

- Click the **Keep Image** button.

- **MMB+drag** the *projection1* node onto the *headlight* material again.

- Choose **Incandescence** from the context menu to map the file in the incandescence of the material.

  This will reuse that same texture file, but for incandescence. Incandescence will give the illusion that the light is emitting light.

- **Render** the model again.

- Once the rendering is done, scroll the image bar at the bottom of the Render view to compare the previous render results.

- Scroll the image bar to the right (the older image), and select **File → Remove Image from Render View** or click the **Remove Image** button.

This will remove the currently displayed image stored earlier.

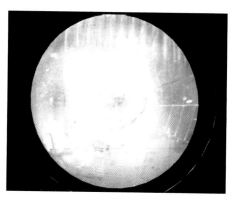

The headlight render

Note: *You can keep as many images as you want in the Render view. The images will be kept even if you close and reopen the Render view window.*

4 Region rendering

You might think it is a waste of time to render the entire image again just for the small portion of the image that changed. With the Render view, you can render only a region of the current image.

- Select a region of the current image by **click+dragging** a square straight on the rendered image.

- Click on the **Render Region** button to render the selected region.

- To automatically render a selected region, **RMB** and enable the **Options → Auto Render Region.**

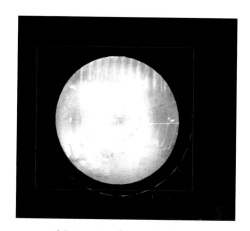

Select a region of the rendered image

With this option, every time you select a region on the rendered image, it will automatically be rendered.

Note: *You can still keep an image that has a region render into it.*

5 Snapshots

If your scene is long, you might not want to wait for a complete render before selecting a region to render. The Render view allows you to take a wireframe snapshot of the image to render so that you can easily select the region you want.

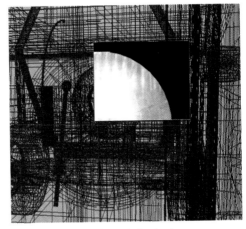

A snapshot in the Render view

- **RMB** in the Render view and select **Render → Snapshot → Perps**.

  A wireframe image is placed in the Render view for reference.

- Select the region you would like to render.

6 Open and save images

You can open renders or reference images directly in the Render view.

The SUV reference

- To open a reference image, select **File → Open Image**.

- Browse to the reference image *SUVReference.tif* located in the *images* folder of the current project.

Tip: *Keep reference images in the Render view to easily compare them with the render.*

You can also save your renders to disk from the Render view.

- To save your current Render view image, select **File → Save Image**.

7 Display the alpha channel

When rendering, you often want to display the image's alpha channel to see if it will composite well onto another image.

- Select the *bear* geometry group.

- Select **Display → Hide → Hide Unselected Objects.**

- Select **Display → Show → Lights.**

- Frame the bear and render your scene.

- Once the render is finished, click on the **Display Alpha Channel** button located at the top of the Render view.

- To go back to the colored images, click on the **Display RGB Channels** in the Render view.

The bear's alpha channel

Note: *In an alpha channel, black is totally transparent, white is completely opaque and grey tones are semi-transparent. The above image is slightly blurred because of motion blur.*

IPR

To give you access to interactive updating capabilities, you will set-up an IPR rendering. An IPR rendering creates a special image file that stores not only the pixel information about an image, but also data about the surface normals, materials and objects associated with each of these pixels. This information is then updated as you make changes to your scene's shading.

1 IPR set-up

- From the Render view panel, click on the **Render Settings** button.

- Click on the **Maya Software** tab.

- From the **Anti-aliasing Quality** section, set **Quality** to **Production Quality**.

  For IPR, you can use the best settings if desired. Your initial IPR rendering will be slower, but the interactive updates will still be fast.

- Close the Render Globals window.

2 IPR render

- Select **Display → Show → Lights.**

- From your Render view panel,
  select **IPR → IPR Render → persp.**

  *Now what seems to be a regular
  rendering of the scene appears.
  Notice the message at the bottom
  of the Render view saying:* Select a
  region to begin tuning.

- **Click+drag** to select an area of the
  IPR rendering that will cover the
  entire bear.

  *This is the area that will be updated
  as you make changes.*

Initial IPR rendering

Note: *You can still change the region by* **click+dragging** *again in the Render view.*

3 Tweak your materials

- In your Hypershade panel, graph the *bodyM* shading group.

- **Drag** the *bear file1* onto the *bodyM* material and **drop** it in the **specularColor** attribute.

- **Drag** the *bear file1* onto the *bodyM* material and **drop** it in the **bump map** attribute.

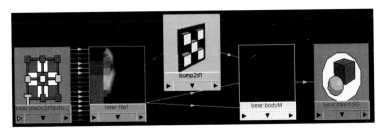

The updated shading group

Notice how the IPR updates every time you bring a change to the shading group.

- Select the *bump2D* node and change the **Bump Depth** to 0.3.

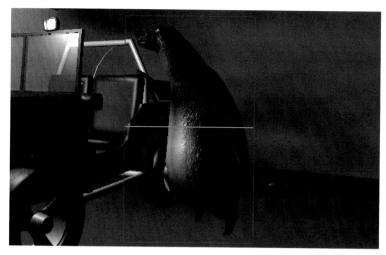

IPR update

4 Stop the IPR

- **Stop** the IPR by clicking on the button located at the top right of the Render view.

IPR functions

5 Drag and drop feature

- Select the headlight geometry and graph its shading network.

- In the Hypershade, select the headlight material.

- Select **Edit → Duplicate → Shading Network.**

  Doing so duplicates the entire selected shading network(s).

- Frame the lights on the top of the windshield in the *Perspective* view and launch another IPR.

- Select the render region surrounding the lights.

- With your **MMB**, drag the new phong in the Render view and drop it on the *tube*.

Note: *Dropping a material directly in the IPR has the same effect as dropping it on a model in a viewport.*

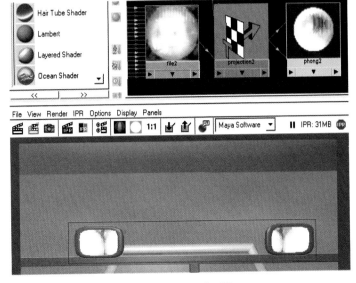

Dropping a material in IPR

- **Scale** and **place** the *projection* manipulator according to the top headlight.

6 IPR and the Attribute Editor

- Open the Attribute Editor.

- Click on an object in the IPR image and see the Attribute Editor update to show its shader.

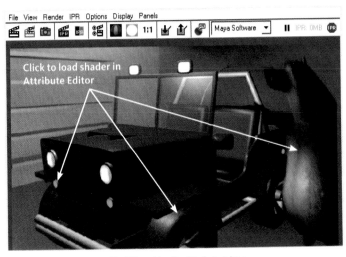

The IPR updates the Attribute Editor

7 Refresh the IPR image

When you have models outside the IPR region, you can refresh the entire image without losing your selected region.

- To refresh the entire image, click on the **Refresh the IPR Image** button.

  The entire image gets redrawn and your original region is maintained.

8 IPR lighting

You can also use the IPR window to explore different lighting scenarios. Changing the light direction or properties will cause the IPR to redraw accordingly.

> **Note:** *When you don't have any lights in your scene, the IPR creates a directional light for you by default. The defaultLight node gets deleted when you stop an IPR rendering.*

- Using the Outliner, select any light.
- Change the light intensity or color to see the IPR update with the new lighting.

New lighting color and intensity in IPR

9 IPR shadows

- Make sure the **Use Depth Map Shadows** is set to **On** on a light.

  You will notice the IPR did not render shadows.

- Select **IPR** → **Update Shadow Maps**.

  Now the IPR updates and the shadows are visible.

- **Stop** the IPR.

10 Save your work

- **Save** your scene as *21-rendering_01.ma*.

High quality rendering

When high quality rendering is turned on, the scene views are drawn in high quality by the hardware renderer. This lets you see a very good representation of the final render's look without having to software render the scene.

1 Enabling high quality rendering

- In the Perspective view, press **5**, **6** or **7**.

  High quality rendering is not available while in wireframe.

- Select **Renderer** → **High Quality Rendering**.

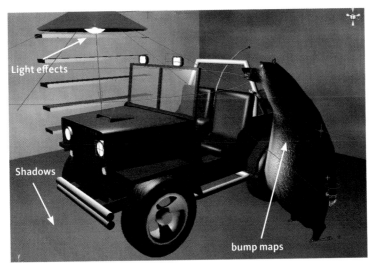

High quality rendering

Tip: *If you require faster playback or camera tumbling while using high quality rendering, turn on* **Shading → Interactive Shading**.

Note: *If the surfaces appear black even when you have lights in your scene, you might need to reverse the surface so the normals points outwards.*

mental ray

Perhaps the most complex and powerful rendering type available in Maya is mental ray. It offers many solutions for the creation of photorealistic renders, such as Global Illumination, caustic reflections and refractions, support for High Dynamic Range Imaging (HDRI), custom shaders and motion blurred reflections and shadows.

In this exercise, you will open an existing scene that includes the bear with animation, reflection and lighting. Using mental ray, the shadows will have motion blur and the motion blur on the bear will be reflected into a mirror.

1 Scene file

- Select **File → Open** and choose *21-rendering_02.ma*.

2 Open the Render Settings

- Select **Window → Render Editors → Render Settings...**
- In the **Render Settings** window, select **Render Using → mental ray**.

10 Set the rendering options

To render the animation, you must set-up the scene's file extensions to indicate a rendered sequence. You must also set-up the start and end frames.

- Click on the **Common** tab.
- From the **Image File Output** section, set the following:

  File Name Prefix to *mentalRay*.

  This sets the name of the animated sequence.

  Frame/Animation Ext *to:*

  name.#.ext (for Windows, Mac);

name.ext.# (for IRIX).

This sets up Maya to render a numbered sequence of images.

Start Frame to 60;

End Frame to 70;

By Frame to 1.

11 Set-up the mental ray Render Settings for motion blur

- Under the **mental ray** tab, select **Quality** → **ProductionMotionblur**.

This image quality preset automatically turns on high quality motion blur. It also sets up raytracing, as well as high quality anti-alias and texture sampling values for mental ray.

12 Set-up the depth map shadows for mental ray

- Select *pointLight1* from the *Light* tab in the Hypershade and open the Attribute Editor.

- Under the *spotLightShape1* tab, open the **mental ray** section.

- Enable the **Shadow Map** checkbox.

- Click on the **Take Setting From Maya** button.

The resolution, samples and softness will be automatically updated.

13 Perform a test render

- Go to frame **63**.

- Make the Perspective view active.

- Select **Render** → **Render Current Frame**...

14 Batch render

- Select **Render** → **Batch Render**.

mental ray rendering

> **Tip:** *If you have a multiple processors computer, it is recommended that you set Use all Available Processors to On in the batch render options, since the render can be time-consuming.*

- When the render is complete, select **Render → Show Batch Render...** This will invoke the fcheck utility to playback the animated sequence.

OR

- From the browser, select one of the frames of the animation, then click **Open**.

  Notice that the reflection and shadows in the scene have a motion blur.

Maya Vector

The Maya Vector renderer can output files in 2D vector format. It can also be used to create stylized flat renderings seen in illustrations and 2D animation.

Using the previous scene, you will set-up a Maya Vector render.

1 Set-up the depth map shadows

- Select *pointLight1* and open the Attribute Editor.

- Under the *spotLightShape1* tab, expand the **Shadows** section.

- Set **Use Depth Map Shadows** to **On**.

- Change the **Shadow Color** to a **dark grey**.

2 Open the Maya Vector Render Settings

- Select **Window → Rendering Editors → Render Settings** ...

- In the **Render Settings** window, select **Render Using → Maya Vector**.

3 Set-up the Maya Vector options

- Select the **mental ray** tab.

- In the **Fill Options** section, set the following:

    Fill objects to **On**;

    Fill style to **Single color**;

Show back faces to On;

Shadows to On;

Highlights to On;

Reflections to On.

- In the **Edge Options** section, select the following:

    Include Edges to On;

    Edge Weight Preset to 3.0 pt;

    Edge Style to Outlines.

4 Perform a test render

- Make the Perspective view active.

- Select Render → Render Current Frame...

Maya Vector rendering

5 Batch render

- **Repeat** step 7 from the previous exercise to render the sequence.

Maya Hardware

Not to be confused with the Hardware Render Buffer, which will be introduced in the next project, the Maya hardware renderer allows you to create broadcast resolution images faster than with the software renderer.

In many cases, the quality of the output will be high enough to go directly to broadcast, but some advanced shadows, reflections and post-process effects cannot be produced with the hardware renderer. The final image quality of the Maya hardware renderer is significantly higher than that of the viewport and Hardware Render Buffer.

1   **Set-up the depth map shadows**

- Make sure the **Use Depth Map Shadows** attribute for the *pointLight1* is still **On** from the previous exercise.

2   **Open the Maya Hardware Render Settings**

- Select **Window** → **Rendering Editors** → **Render Settings…**

- In the **Render Settings** window, select **Render Using** → **Maya Hardware**.

- Select the **Maya Hardware** tab.

- Under the **Quality** section, set **Presets** to **Production Quality.**

- Under the **Render Options** section, set **Motion Blur** to **On.**

3   **Perform a test render**

- Make the *Perspective* view active.

- Select **Render** → **Render Current Frame…**

  You cannot see a reflection in the mirror since the raytracing feature is unavailable with the hardware renderer. However, the renderer is otherwise capable of fast high quality rendering, including texture mapped reflections, depth map shadows and motion blur.

Note: *You might need to reverse some surfaces in order to render them correctly.*

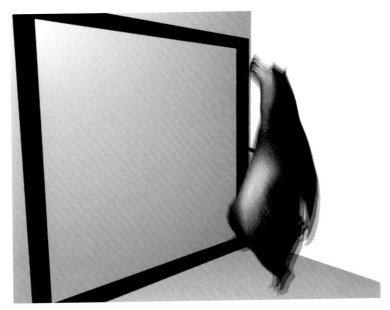

Maya hardware render

4 Batch render

- **Repeat** step **7** from the mental ray exercise to render the sequence.

Conclusion

You have now completed this short introduction to the rendering engines available in Maya. The Maya IPR helps speed up the creative process and allows you to explore fast shading, lighting and texturing possibilities. For more mental ray, Maya Vector, Maya hardware and Maya software rendering tutorials, see the Maya online documentation.

In the next project, you will model using the third surface type available in Maya, which is subdivision surfaces. You will also have fun with Paint Effects, rigid bodies and particles.

Project 04

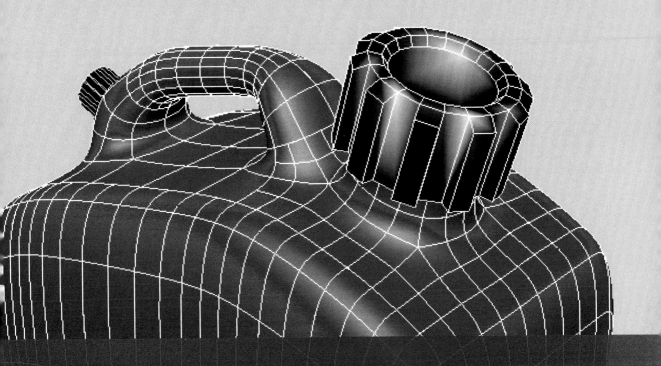

Lesson 22
Subdivision surfaces

In this lesson, you will work with subdivision surfaces (SubDs) to create organic-looking models. Subdivision surfaces exhibit characteristics of both polygon and NURBS surfaces, allowing you to model smooth forms using comparatively few control vertices. They will enable you to create finer levels of detail exactly where you want.

As a prerequisite to modeling with SubDs, it is essential to complete *Lesson 07 - Polygonal Modeling*, because when creating the geometry you will rely heavily on the polygonal modeling techniques taught in that lesson.

In this lesson, you will learn the following:

- How to convert a model from polygons to subdivision surfaces;
- How to model using subdivision surfaces' Poly Proxy and Standard modes;
- How to create finer levels of detail;
- How to work with creases;
- How to import shaders and scene files;
- How to clean the topology of subdivision surfaces.

Initial set-up

Start a new file within the *project4* directory copied onto your system.

1 Set the current project

- Select **File → Project → Set...**

- Select the *project4* directory.

> **Note:** *If project4 cannot be found, copy it from the support files.*

2 Create a new scene

- Select **File → New Scene**.

Modeling a gas tank

In order to learn about subdivision surfaces, you will model a simple gas tank to be placed on the SUV's tail gate. You will start with a polygonal cube primitive. You will then convert the cube to a subdivision surface. The basic form will be constructed using the *subdivision surfaces' Poly Proxy mode*.

Poly Proxy mode creates an unshaded polygonal cage around the subdivision surface, similar to the one used by the Smooth Proxy polygonal tool. This cage can be edited using the same set of tools as a regular polygon. The subdivision surface will remain smooth and maintain the history of edits made on the proxy object.

1 Primitive cube

- Select **Create → Polygon Primitives → Cube**.

- Set each modeling view to **Shading → Smooth Shade All**.

- Change the construction history of the cube as follows:

  Width to 4.5;

  Height to 5;

  Depth to 3;

  Subdivisions Width to 6;

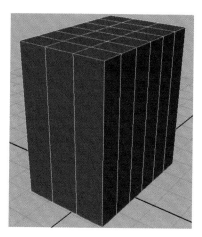

The start cube

Subdivisions **Height** to 1;

Subdivisions **Depth** to 3.

- **Translate** the cube above the grid.

2 Convert to subdivision surface

- With the cube selected, select **Modify → Convert → Polygons to Subdiv**.

- Press the **3** hotkey for a smooth display of the surface.

- **Rename** the surface *tank*.

3 Poly Proxy mode

- Press **F4** to enable the **Surfaces** menu set.

- Select **Subdiv Surfaces → Polygon Proxy Mode**.

- In the **Outliner**, set **Display → Shapes** to **On**.

- Click the **+** sign next to *tank* to display the shape nodes beneath.

  A new node called tankShapeHistPoly has been created and grouped underneath the tank node. This is the proxy node that you will edit using the polygon toolset.

4 Tweak the vertices

The Marking Menu of subdivision surfaces allows quick selection of subdivision tools and will be used extensively throughout this lesson.

- **RMB** over the *tank* node.

- Select **Vertex** from the Marking Menu.

- From the *front* view, select the vertical row of vertices and tweak the shape as follows:

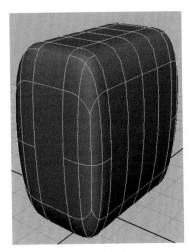

Smooth shaded subdivision surface

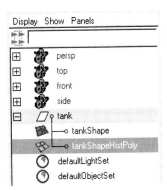

Outliner with the proxy object selected

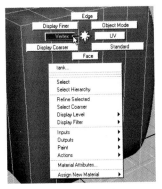

Marking Menu display

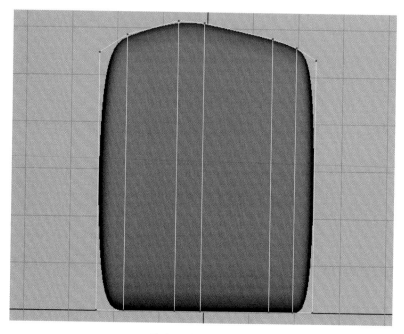

The basic shape of the tank

5 Extrude polygonal faces

- **RMB** on the *tank* and select **Face**.

- Select the top central face where the gas tank spout should be.

- Press **F3** to enable the **Polygons** menu set.

- Select **Edit Mesh → Extrude** .

- **Click+drag** to extrude the face upwards.

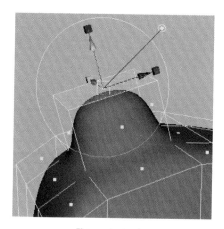

The spout extrusion

Note: At this time, the geometry doesn't look exactly like it should, but this will be fixed later in the lesson.

6 Extrude the handle

- **Extrude** the handle as shown to the right:

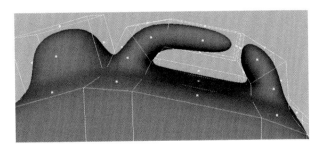

The handle extrusion

7 Merge the handle

- Select the two polygonal faces facing each other in the above handle extrusion and **delete** them.

- **RMB** on the model and select **Vertex**.

- Select one vertex on one side of the handle.

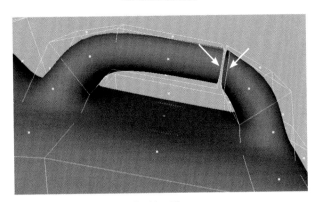

The deleted faces

- With the **Move Tool** enabled, hold down **v** to **Snap to Point**.

- **Click+drag** the center of the manipulator towards the corresponding vertices on the other side of the handle.

- **Repeat** for the three other vertices to close the handle opening.

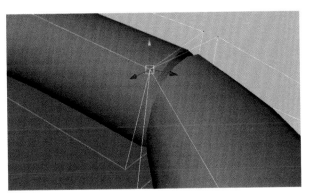

Snapped vertex

- Go back in **Object** mode.

- With the *tank* selected, select **Edit Mesh → Merge**.

  The hole in the handle is now closed.

8 Extrude the air valve

- Select the face at the back of the handle.

- Do a first **extrusion** and scale the face down.

- Do a second **extrusion** to extrude the valve itself.

- **Refine** the shape of the valve.

9 Tank holes

- Using **extrusions**, create the holes in both the spout and the air valve.

- Once the holes are made, make sure to **delete** the bottom face to create the openings.

10 Save your work

- **Save** your scene as *22-tank_01.ma*.

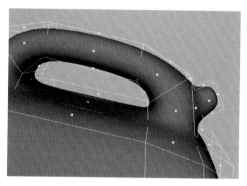

The air valve

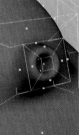

The tank holes

Standard mode

So far, you have been using Poly Proxy mode to create a smooth subdivision surface by editing a few faces and edges on a simple polygon mesh. The polygonal cage surrounding the subdivision surface has provided enough detail to this point.

Now, you will leave Poly Proxy mode and edit the model using Standard mode. You will see in the rest of the lesson that in Standard mode you can edit vertices, faces and edges, plus you can adjust edge or vertex creases and achieve a greater level of detail using the hierarchical levels of refinement available with subdivision surfaces.

Creases

When defining an edge or a vertex to be creased, the underlying subdivision surface is changed in order to get the geometry closer to the defined edge or vertex.

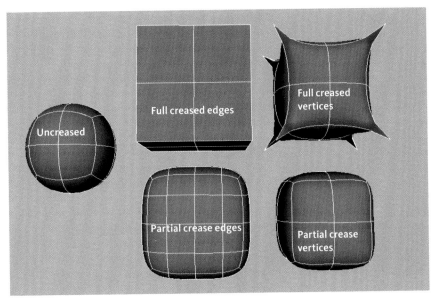

Different crease examples

1 **Leave Poly Proxy mode**

- Select the *tank*.

- Select **Subdiv Surfaces** → **Standard Mode** from the **Surfaces** menu set.

  This eliminates the Poly Proxy mode geometry. The proxy can be regenerated and edited by invoking **Subdiv Surfaces** → **Poly Proxy Mode** *again if necessary, but the construction history will not be rebuilt.*

2 **Display subdivision surface edges**

- **RMB** over the subdivision surface and select **Edges** from the Marking Menu.

  This displays edges at the same coordinates as the proxy vertices and refers to the roughest level of subdivision surface refinement. Edges of subdivision surfaces look similar to NURBS hulls and can help realize the shape defining the surface. They can also be selected individually, just like polygonal edges.

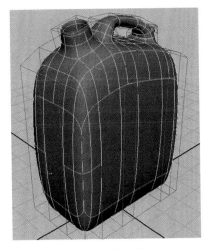

Subdivision surface edges

3 Partial creases

- Select the main edges defining the gas tank.

Tip: *Those are the same edges from the original polygonal cube.*

- Select **Subdiv Surfaces → Partial Crease Edge/Vertex**.

  A partial crease will define and sharpen the surface outlined by the selected edges or vertices. Notice the creased edges are displayed with hashed lines.

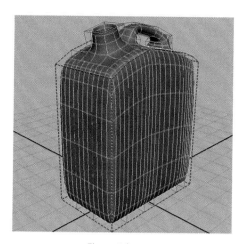

The partial creases

Note: *Note how the subdivision surface's topology was increased in order to reflect the changes.*

4 Full creases

- Select the outer and inner edges of the spout and air valve.

- Select **Subdiv Surfaces → Full Crease Edge/ Vertex** to get the following results:

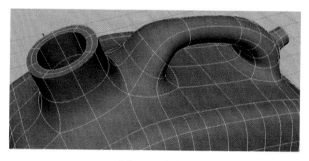

Fully creased edges

- Make the handle and base of the spout and air valve partially creased.

5 **Save your work**

- **Save** your scene as *22-tank_02.ma*.

The final tank

Texture the gas tank

Texturing subdivision surfaces is very similar to polygon UV mapping techniques learned in Lesson 8. To map the gas tank, you will import a pre-created procedural texture to the model and convert this procedural texture to a file. This is one way to stop a 3D texture from sliding on a deformed surface.

1 **Import the procedural shader**

- Switch to the **Hypershade/Persp** layout from the **Tool Box**.

- Inside the Hypershade window, select **File → Import** and choose the file *tankShader.ma* from the *renderData/ shaders* folder.

  This shader is simply a pre-made red plastic shader with a file texture used for the bump. For more info on this shader, simply select it on the Hypershade and graph its connections.

- **MMB+drag** the shader onto the *tank*.

- **Render** the scene to see the effect of the shader and bump map on the tank.

The rendered gas tank

Note: *It is possible that the texture doesn't perfectly fit your gas tank model. If so, you can tweak the UVs of your model through the UV Texture Editor, just like you would do with polygons. Or, you can use the 3D Paint Tool to paint the bump channel accordingly.*

2 Finish modeling the tank

- Spend some time modeling caps for both the spout and air valve out of your favorite geometry type.

3 Clean up the scene

- **Freeze** the transformations on the objects.

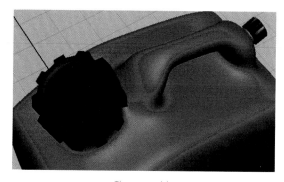

The cap models

- **Group** the objects all together.

- **Delete** all the history.

- **Optimize** the scene size.

- **Rename** everything correctly.

4 Save your work

- **Save** your scene as *22-tank_03.ma*.

5 Import the tank in the SUV scene

You will now import the tank in the SUV scene from the last project.

- **Open** the scene *17-SUVRig_03.ma* from Project 3.

- Select **File → Import → ❒**.

- Turn **Off** the **Use Namespaces** options.

- **Set Resolve Clashing nodes** with this string: *tank*.

- Click the **Import** button.

- **Browse** the *scenes* directory of Project 4 and select the *22-tank_03.ma* file.

  The gas tank is now in the SUV scene.

6 **Place the tank correctly**

- **Unlock** and **unhide** the *spareWheel* group **translateX** attribute from the Channel Control, if locked and hidden.

- **Move** the *spareWheel* aside to leave some room for the gas tank.

- **Lock** back the *spareWheel* group **translateX** attribute.

- **Move** the gas tank and scale it appropriately to fit the bumper.

7 **Gas tank support**

- **Model** a simple gas tank support as follows:

The tank support

- **Delete** the new model's construction history.

8 **Parent the models**

- **Parent** the gas tank and the gas tank support in the SUV hierarchy.

- **Freeze** their transformations.

- **Lock and Hide** their attributes accordingly.

9 **Save your work**

Save that scene normally. When you reopen any scene with a reference to the SUV file, it will be updated with the gas tank automatically.

Model a cliff side

In order to experiment more with the subdivision surfaces tools, you will now model a terrain so Boog can drive away. Doing so will allow you to model with a finer level of detail on the SubD model.

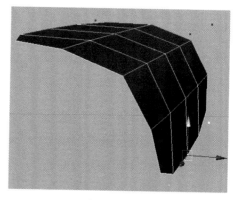

The starting plane

1 SubD plane

- In a new scene, select **Create → Subdiv Primitives → Plane.**

- **Scale** the plane to **100** in all axes.

- **RMB** on the plane and select **Vertex.**

- Select a row of vertices on the edge of the plane and bring them down under the central row of vertices.

2 Display finer levels of detail

- **RMB** on the plane and select **Display Level → 1.**

  Doing so changes the displayed level of components. You were previously on the base display level (0), and now the second level of refined components is displayed (1).

- **Select** the finer vertices and **move** them forward to produce cliff edge definition, as indicated in the following image:

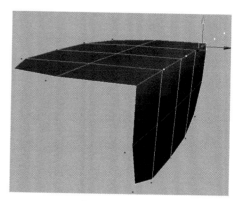

Finer vertices moved

3 Create more detail in the area by refining selected vertices

- Keep the same vertices selected.

- Select **Subdiv Surfaces → Refine Selected Components.**

  This will refine the area and display new vertices.

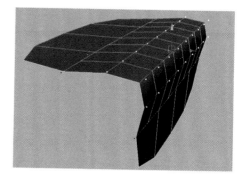

Refined vertices

4 Refine the cliff edge

- **RMB** and select **Edges** from the Marking Menu.

- Select and **move** edges forward to create a refined cliff edge.

  Notice that when you move edges or vertices, the subdivision surface topology is automatically updated to reflect those changes.

Note: *Even when undoing refinement actions, the subdivision surface will keep its refined resolution. You will see how to clean up the model later in this lesson.*

5 Keep on refining

- **Refine** the selected edges and keep on increasing the cliff edge.

- **Move** some vertices down underneath the cliff edge and set them to **Full Crease**.

Note: *It is possible that you have created gaps when editing subdivision surfaces. This is a normal viewport display and will not show up in renders.*

- Get the cliff side to look as shown to the right:

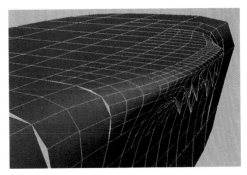

Vertices and edges edited to create cliff edge

Note: *Notice that every time you refine the components, only the components available in that display level are shown.*

6 **Lower display level**

• **RMB** and select **Vertex** from the Marking Menu.

• **RMB** on the plane and select **Display Level** → 1.

Doing so brings you back to the second level of refinement. You now have access to all the vertices on the surface.

• Try to move vertices from the cliff edge.

Notice how the vertices in finer levels are updating accordingly, and are totally dependent on the lower level components.

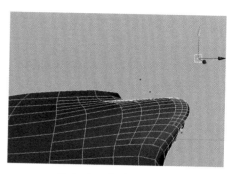

Moving lower level components

7 **Refine the landscape**

• **Refine** the landscape to create mountains, hills and valleys.

• Try to hide the exterior edges of the surface by moving them down.

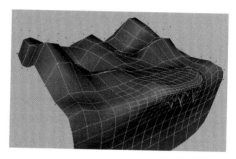

The refined terrain

8 **Test render**

• **Render** the scene to see how your geometry looks.

9 **Texture the terrain**

• Using what you have already learned in Lesson 8 with the **3D Paint Tool**, texture the landscape using colors and Paint Effects brushes on a new lambert material.

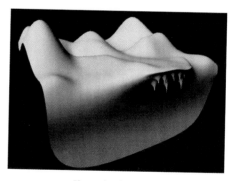

The rendered geometry

Tip: *Create a texture for the landscape that is large enough, such as* **1024 x 1024** *or even* **2048 x 2048**.

- Define a place for the garage and also a road leading into the mountains.

The textured landscape

10 Clean up the model

When modeling with subdivision surfaces, geometry will be automatically added to your model and sometimes this geometry will not be necessary. In order to remove the extra information, you can clean the surface's topology.

- Select the model, and then select **Subdiv Surfaces → Clean Topology**.

  Unused geometry is automatically removed from the surface.

11 Save your work

- **Save** your scene as *22-cliff_01.ma*.

Conclusion

You have now gone through the process of modeling organic forms with subdivision surfaces and texturing them. You learned how to refine components and how to crease edges and vertices. In the process, you also imported scenes and shaders.

In the next lesson, you will learn how to fill your environment with one of the most powerful tools found in Maya: Paint Effects.

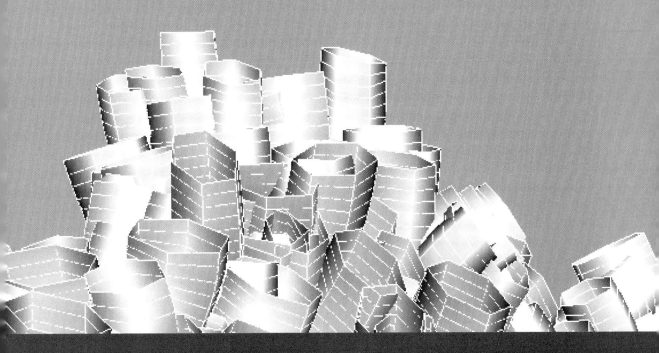

Lesson 23
Paint Effects

For this next stage, you need to generate content for your environment from the last lesson.
The *Paint Effects Tool* gives you access to lots of preset brushes, ranging from grasses to
trees or buildings to lightning bolts, but they can also be customized for your own scenarios.

In this lesson, you will use several Paint Effects brushes and render your scene.

In this lesson, you will learn the following:

- How to paint on canvas;
- How to set an image plane;
- How to share, blend and customize brushes;
- How to save brush presets;
- How to auto paint a surface;
- How to convert Paint Effects to polygons.

Paint on canvas

In order to test various Paint Effects brushes, you will create a nature scene with trees and grass. First, you will need a background night sky image to establish the mood for the rest of the lesson.

1 Open a new scene

2 Paint in the Paint Effects window

- Press **8** to display the Maya Paint Effects preview window.

- Select **Paint → Paint Canvas**.

  This will set the canvas to a 2D paint mode.

- In the Paint Effects window, select **Brush → Get Brush**.

  The Visor will open, letting you browse through the various template Paint Effects brushes.

- Open any brush folder, select a brush and paint on the canvas.

  You can now experiment with different brushes.

- Select **Canvas → Clear.**

3 Change the background color

- Select **Canvas → Clear → □**.

- Set the **Clear Color** to **black**, then press the **Clear** button.

> **Note:**   You can also import an image as a starting point by selecting **Canvas → Open Image.**

4 Paint your image

- In the Visor window, open the *galactic* folder.

- Select the *galaxy.mel* brush and paint some space onto your image.

> **Note:**   Hold down *b* and LMB+drag to change the size of the current brush.

- Continue painting space elements to your image using the different preset brushes.

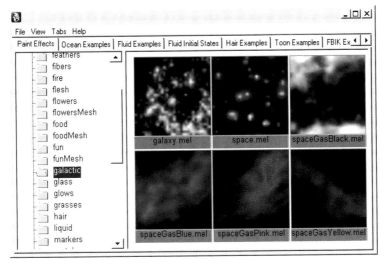

The Visor

- If you make a mistake, you can **undo** the last brush stroke by selecting **Canvas** → **Canvas Undo**.

Background image

5 Save the image

- When you are finished with your image, select **Canvas** → **Save As** → ❑.

- In the Option window, make sure that **Save Alpha** is turned **Off**.

- Click on **Save Image** and name your image as *background*.

- Tap the **spacebar** to return to the original view layout.

Setting up the image plane

You are now going to import the background image and set it as a camera image plane. This plane will be used behind the rest of the scene to help compose the final shot.

1 Scene file

- **Open** the scene file *21-rendering_01.ma* from the last project.

- **Reference** the terrain scene *22-cliff_01.ma* from the last lesson.

  Doing so will add the terrain to your animated scene.

2 Modify the terrain

- **Scale** and place the terrain appropriately.

Note: Since you will only be seeing the garage from the inside, just the portion visible through the garage door needs to be worked on.

- Fix the ground underneath the garage so that it is a level plane.

Tip: Refine the components under the garage and use the scale manipulator to flatten all the vertices on their Y-axes.

The garage and terrain

3 Create a new camera

You will now create a new camera with an image plane attached to it.

- **Open the Outliner and delete** the old *camera1_group* that was used earlier.

- Select **Create → Cameras → Camera**.

  This places one node camera at the origin.

- Make *camera1* the current camera in the view by selecting **Panels → Perspective → camera1**.

- In the Attribute Editor for the *camera1* shape node, set the camera **Focal Length** to **25**.

- Select **View → Camera Settings → Resolution Gate**.

- **Frame** the scene as shown on the right:

Camera framing

4 Add the image plane

- From the *camera1* view panel, select **View → Image Plane → Import Image**.

- Choose the *background.iff* image file from the *sourceimages* directory.

  Your background image is loaded as the image plane of camera1. By default, the image is probably too close to the garage, so you will need to change it so that it is away from the camera.

- Select **View → Image Plane → Image Plane Attributes → imagePlane1**.

  Doing so brings up the Attribute Editor.

- Scroll down in the Attribute Editor and set **Depth** to **1000** or more.

  The image plane is now in the background as intended.

Image plane seen from the Perspective view

> **Note:** *Notice that if you move the camera, the image plane moves with it. This is because it is attached to the camera for which it was created.*

5 Set-up the image plane

- Still in the Attribute Editor for the *imagePlane1*, scroll down to the **Placement** section.

- Set the **Fit** attribute to **Horizontal**, then click the **Fit to Resolution Gate** button.

  This will place the image to horizontally fit the resolution gate.

- Select the *camera1* and scroll down to the **Display Options** section in the Attribute Editor.

- Set the **Overscan** attribute to **1.1**.

  This will reduce the gap around the resolution gate.

6 Save your work

- **Save** your scene as *23-pfx_01.ma*.

Paint Effects strokes

You will now learn how to paint strokes on geometry and how strokes can share the same brush. As well, you will learn how to scale Paint Effects.

1 Convert the geometry

Paint Effects can only be painted onto either NURBS or polygonal surfaces. Since the terrain you modeled in the last lesson is made out of a subdivision surface, you wil need to convert it to polygons.

- Make the *Perspective* the current camera.

Tip: *You might want to set the Far Clip Plane of the Perspective camera to a higher value in the Attribute Editor if you see the geometry getting clipped when zooming out to see the entire scene.*

- Select **File → Reference Editor**.

- Highlight the cliff referenced file, then select **File → Import Objects from Reference**.

  The reference is now imported in the scene and can be modified as needed.

- Select the terrain geometry.

- Select **Modify → Convert → Subdiv to Polygons → ❐**.

- In the option window, set the following:

    Tessellation method to **Adaptive**;

Divisions per face to 2;

Original object to Replace.

- Click the **Convert** button.

The surface is converted with more faces, since polygons will not render as smoothly as the subdivision surface. The options also made the command replace the original surface with the converted one.

Note: *Since you will be painting trees on top of the terrain, you do not require a lot of polygons to define smooth edges at render time.*

- **Rename** the converted surface to *terrain*.

2 Paint trees

- Press **F6** to select the **Rendering** menu set.

- With the *terrain* selected, select **Paint Effects → Make Paintable**.

Doing so will allow you to paint directly on the surface.

- Select **Paint Effects → Get Brush...**

- In the Visor, select the **trees** directory, then click on the **pineForest.mel** brush preset.

Clicking on a brush preset in the Visor automatically invokes the Paint Effects Tool.

- Make *camera1* the current camera.

- Hold down **b** and **click+drag** to increase the size of the brush.

- **Paint** directly on the *terrain* to create a forest.

The forest in the viewport

Tip: *Since you will be seeing the forest only from the garage door opening, you should concentrate on painting the visible area.*

3 Test render the planet

- Add a **directional light** to your scene with an **Intensity** of **0.2**.

- Select **Render** → **Render Current Frame**.

The rendered forest

4 Share one brush

It would be good to scale the brush up to minimize the need for a lot of trees.

- Open the Outliner.

  You should see all the different strokes you have drawn on the terrain.

At the moment, all of these strokes are using a different brush, letting you customize each one individually. The method for scaling down the trees simultaneously is to tell all the similar strokes to share the same brush.

- Select all the *strokePineForest* strokes.

- Select **Paint Effects** → **Share One Brush**.

  Now all the strokes use the same brush. Modifying this brush will change all the trees at the same time.

5 Scale up the trees

- Press **Ctrl+a** to open the Attribute Editor for any of the selected strokes.

- Select the *pineForest* tab.

  This is the brush shared among all the strokes.

- Set the **Global Scale** attribute roughly two times bigger.

6 Test render the scene

7 Save your work

- **Save** your scene as *23-pfx_02.ma*.

Bigger trees

Customize brushes

In this exercise, you will blend brushes together and customize your own brushes. You will also save your custom brush presets on your shelf for later use.

1 Blending brushes

- Select **Paint Effects → Get Brush...**

- In the Visor, select the **grasses** directory, then click on the **astroturf.mel** brush preset.

- Still in the Visor, **RMB** on the *grassBermuda.mel* brush preset.

  This will display a menu letting you blend the current brush with the new one.

- Select **Blend Brush 50%**.

  This will blend part of the second brush onto the first brush, giving a little bit of profile from both brushes. **RMB** *again on the* **grassBermuda.mel** *brush preset and select* **Blend Shading 5%**.

  This will blend the shading of the two brushes together.

2 Paint the new brush

- Select **Paint Effects → Paint Effects Tool → ❑**.

- **In the option window, turn Off the Draw as Mesh option.**

  Rather than displaying meshes when painting the Paint Effects, only reference lines will be used. This drastically reduces the display refresh of the viewport.

- **Paint** one stroke of the new brush on the bottom of the garage entrance.

- Set the **Global Scale** of the Paint Effect brush as wanted.

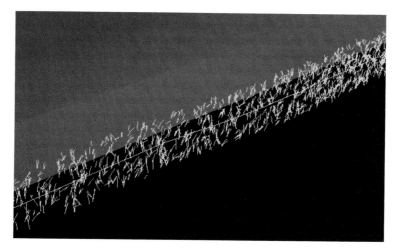

The painted grass

Tip: *To reduce the viewport refresh rate even more , you can also set the stroke's Display Density to a lower value. This attribute specifies how many of the Paint Effects you want to see interactively in the viewport.*

3   Customizing brushes

- In the Attribute Editor, select the *grassBermuda1* tab.

  Doing so will display all the Paint Effectsattributes for the current brush and the current stroke.

- Try changing some of the values to see their results on the current stroke. Following are some examples:

  Tubes → Creation → Tubes Per Step;

  Tubes → Creation → Length Min;

  Tubes → Creation → Length Max;

  Tubes → Creation → Width1;

  Tubes → Creation → Width2;

  Tubes → Creation → Tubes Width1;

  Tubes → Creation → Tubes Width2;

  Behavior → Forces→ Gravity;

Tip: *You may have to render the stroke in order to see changes.*

- **Reduce** the quality of the brush to speed up rendering time:

  Brush Profile → **Brush Width** to 3;

  Brush Profile → **Flatness1** to 1;

  Brush Profile → **Flatness2** to 1;

  Tubes → **Creation** → **Tube per Step** to 25;

  Tubes → **Creation** → **Segments** to 1;

  Tubes → **Creation** → **Segments** to 1;

  Tubes → **Growth** to **Branches** only.

4 Get brush settings from stroke

In order to draw more customized grass, you need to update the current template brush with the settings of the stroke you just modified.

- With the stroke selected, select **Paint Effects** → **Get Settings from Selected Stroke**.

  This will set the customized grass brush as the current template brush.

5 Save custom brushes

You can save the current template brush for later use. The brush can be saved either to your shelf or the Visor.

- Select **Paint Effects** → **Save Brush Preset...**

- Set the following in the Save Brush Preset window to save to current shelf:

  Label to **Custom Grass**;

  Overlay Label to **grass**;

  Save Preset to **To Shelf**.

Note: *The preset will be saved to the currently selected shelf, so make sure you select the appropriate shelf before executing these steps.*

OR

• Set the following in the Save Brush Preset window to a Visor directory:

> **Label** to *Custom Grass*;
>
> **Overlay Label** to *grass*;
>
> **Save Preset** to **To Visor**;
>
> **Visor Directory** to *brushes* from your *prefs* directory.

• Click the **Save Brush Preset** button.

Note: *You can obtain an image for your new brush only through the Paint Effects Canvas panel.*

6 Automatically paint a surface

If you do not need to paint strokes by hand, you can use the **Paint Effects** → **Auto Paint** command. This will automatically paint onto a surface according to the options set.

7 Scene set-up

• Open the Outliner.

• **Group** the strokes together and **rename** the group to *pfxGroup*.

• **Create** a new layer called *pfxLayer* and add *pfxGroup* to it.

Tip: *To speed up the rest of the lesson, you can hide the pfxLayer.*

8 Save your work

• **Save** your scene as *23-pfx_03.ma*.

Conclusion

You have now experienced one of Maya's greatest tools, but you have only scratched the surface of the power available in Paint Effects. Learning how to use the Paint Effects Canvas, how to paint on objects and how to customize your brushes will serve you well as you become more and more familiar with the tool. There are so many ways to use Paint Effects to generate scene content that there should be no reason for your future scenes to look dull and empty.

In the next lesson, you will learn how to convert Paint Effects and how to use deformers.

Lesson 24
Deformers

Deformers can be used for numerous reasons; examples include being used and to be animated within character set-up, for facial expressions, for modeling, etc. In this lesson, you will be introduced to various Maya deformers to experiment using a Paint Effects tree converter to polygons. These deformers will help to tweak the tree's shape while still keeping an organic feel to your geometry.

In this lesson, you will learn the following:

- How to use wire deformers;
- How to use point on curve deformers;
- How to use clusters;
- How to use the Soft Modification Tool;
- How to use non-linear deformers;
- How to change the deformation order.

Convert Paint Effects

To begin, you will need geometry to deform. In this lesson, you will be using a polygonal tree originally from Paint Effects. Most Paint Effects strokes can be converted to geometry and even animated dynamically.

For the sake of this lesson, you will only be using the output geometry of the conversion as a surface to deform.

1 Open a new scene

2 Paint a tree

- From the **Rendering** menu set, select **Paint Effects** → **Get Brush**.

- Under the **Trees** directory, click on the **treeBare.mel** brush preset.

- **Paint** a single tree at the origin.

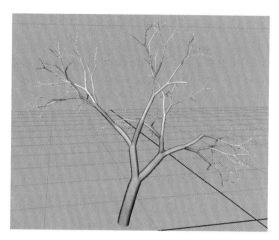

Paint Effects tree

3 Convert to polygons

- With the stroke selected, select **Modify** → **Convert** → **Paint Effects to Polygons** → ❒.

- In the options, turn **On** the **Quad output** option.

- Click on the **Convert** button.

4 Delete history

Some Paint Effects brushes are animated by default, and when you convert the Paint Effects to polygons, the construction history keeps the ability to animate the mesh automatically. In this lesson, you will not require construction history.

- Select **Edit** → **Delete All by Type** → **History**.

5 Center the tree

- Select the tree mesh and **move** it so it grows straight up from the origin.

- **Freeze** its transformations.

- **Rename** it to *tree*.

6 Save your work

• **Save** the scene as *24-deformer_01.ma*.

Wire deformer

You will now modify the tree using a wire deformer. A *wire deformer is* used to deform a surface based on a NURBS curve. You will use that type of deformer for one of the tree branches.

1 Draw a curve

• Select **Create** → **EP Curve Tool**.

• From a *side* view, **draw** a curve along a main branch, then press **Enter**.

• **Tweak** the curve to follow the branch in other views.

The curve to be used as a deformer

2 Create the wire deformer

• From the Animation menu set, select **Deform** → **Wire Tool**.

The Wire Tool requires two steps. First, you must select the deformable surfaces, then you must select the NURBS curve to be the deformer.

• Select the tree geometry and press **Enter**.

• Select the NURBS curve and press **Enter**.

The wire deformer is created.

3 Edit the shape of the curve

• With the *curve* selected, press **F8** to go in Component mode.

• Select some CVs and **move** them to see their effect on the geometry.

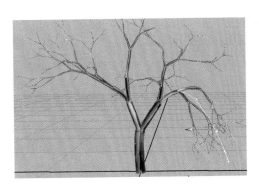

The default wire deformer effect

4 Edit the deformer attribute

Just like any other deformers, the attributes of the wire deformer can be changed through the Channel Box.

- In the Channel Box, select the *wire1* history node.

- Highlight the **Dropoff Distance** attribute in the Channel Box.

- Hold down **Ctrl**, then **MMB+drag** in the viewport to see its effect.

   The effect of the wire deformer changes across the geometry.

Note: *Holding down the **Ctrl** key makes the virtual slider change with smaller increments.*

5 Edit the deformer membership

The dropoff has a nice effect, but the deformer is affecting other branches of the tree. You can correct that by defining the membership of the geometry to the deformer.

- Select **Deform** → **Edit Membership Tool**.

- Select the *curve* to define the vertices affected by it.

   All the vertices of the tree geometry will be highlighted yellow.

- Hold the **Ctrl** key and **deselect** the vertices of neighboring branches.

   All the vertices that are no longer deformed will move back to their original positions.

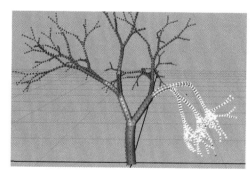

The deformer's membership

Tip: *You can also use **Deform** → **Paint Set Membership Tool** to define the membership of the tree's vertices.*

6 Finalize the deformer's effect

Now that the deformer no longer affects the other branch, you can set its dropoff to a higher value.

- Go back to **Object** mode.

- Press **q** to exit the **Edit Membership Tool** and enable the **Pick Tool**.

- Select the *curve* and set the **Dropoff Distance** to **10** in the Channel Box.

- Experiment with moving the *curve*'s CVs to see the effect of the deformer.

Point on curve and cluster deformer

The wire deformer is working well to deform the tree, but it is not practical to deform the curve for animation. Several other types of deformers can be used to deform the curve itself. Here you will experiment with the *point on curve* deformer and the *cluster* deformer.

1 Point on curve deformer

The point on curve deformer will create a locator linked to a curve edit point.

- **RMB** on the *NURBS curve* and select **Edit Point**.

  Unlike CVs, edit points are located directly on the curve.

- Select the edit point located at the tip of the branch.

- Select **Deform → Point on Curve**.

  A locator is created at the edit point's position.

- Select **Modify → Center Pivot** to center the pivot of the *locator*.

- **Move** the locator to see its effect on the curve.

The point on curve deformer

Note: *Rotating a point on curve deformer has no effect on the curve.*

2 Cluster deformer

The point on curve works well, but has its limitations. For instance, it can only control one edit point at a time, and it cannot be used for rotation. The cluster deformer will create a handle that controls one or more vertices. When a cluster has multiple vertices in it, it can also be rotated.

- **RMB** on the *NURBS curve* and select **Control Vertex**.
- Select the two CVs next to the point on curve deformer.

Tip: It might be easier to locate the CVs by also displaying hulls.

- Select **Deform** →
  Create Cluster.

  A cluster handle is displayed with a **C** *in the viewport.*

- **Move** and **rotate** the *cluster handle* to see its effect on the curve and branch.

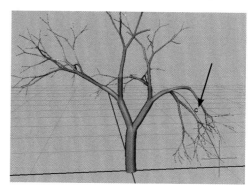

The cluster handle

Note: Both the point on curve locator and cluster handle can be animated.

Soft Modification Tool

The *Soft Modification Tool* lets you push and pull geometry as a sculptor would push and pull a piece of clay. By default, the amount of deformation is greatest at the center of the deformer, and gradually falls off moving outward. However, you can control the falloff of the deformation to create various types of effects.

1 **Create the deformer**

- **RMB** on the *tree* surface and select **Vertex**.

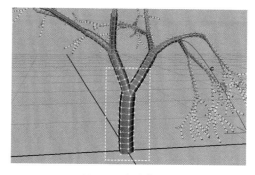

Vertices to be deformed

- Select some vertices at the base of the tree.

- Click on the **Soft Modification Tool** in the toolbox, or select **Deform → Soft Modification**.

*An **S** handle similar to the cluster handle will be created. The tool's manipulator will also be displayed and the influence of the deformer is shown. Yellow stands for fully deformed, while black is not deformed at all.*

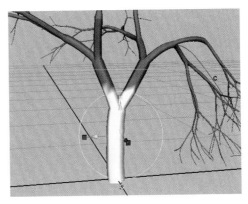

The influence of the deformer

2 Edit the deformer

- **Move**, **rotate** and **scale** the deformer to see its effect on the geometry.

- Press **Ctrl+a** to open the Attribute Editor for the deformer.

The various deformer options can be edited here.

- Set the **Falloff Radius** to **0.4**.

- Click on the button next to the **Falloff Curve** graph.

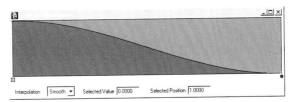

Falloff curve

- See the effect of the deformer on the geometry.

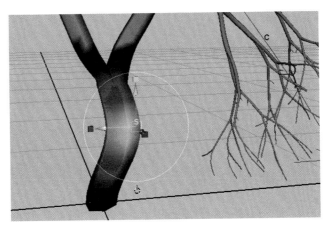

The new influence

3 **Modeling with Soft Modification Tool**

When modeling a high resolution model, such as a character's face, you can create multiple Soft Modification deformers to achieve a final shape. The deformers can even overlap.

4 **Delete Soft Modification deformers**

If you want to delete the deformer, simply select its **S** handle and **delete** it. If you want to keep the shape of the geometry but remove the deformers, you must delete the model's history.

Non-linear deformers

Maya has several *non-linear deformers*. Non-linear deformers can affect one surface, multiple surfaces or parts of a surface, and are very simple to use. In this exercise, you will experiment with all the non-linear deformers.

1 **Scene file**

• **Open** the scene as *24-deformer_01.ma* without saving your changes.

2 **Bend deformer**

• Select the *tree* geometry, then select **Deform → Create Nonlinear → Bend**.

The Bend handle is created and selected.

• In the Attribute Editor, highlight the *bend1* input.

All the attributes for this deformer type are listed.

• Experiment and combine the different attributes to see their effect on the geometry.

Tip: Most of the attributes have visual feedback on the deformer's handle in the viewport. You can also use the Show Manipulator Tool to interact with the deformer in the viewport.

• **Moving**, **rotating** and **scaling** the handle will also affect the location of the deformation.

• When you finish experimenting, select the deformer and delete it.

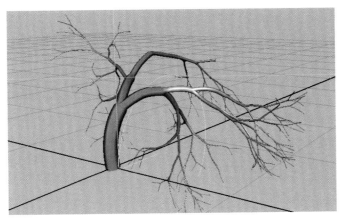

Bend deformer

3 Flare deformer

- Select the *tree* geometry, then select **Deform → Create Nonlinear → Flare**.

  The Flare handle is created and selected.

- In the Attribute Editor, highlight the *flare1* input.

- Experiment by moving, rotating, scaling and combining the different attributes to see their effect on the geometry.

- When you finish experimenting, select the deformer and delete it.

Flare deformer

4 Sine deformer

- Select the *tree* geometry, then select **Deform → Create Nonlinear → Sine**.

  The Sine handle is created and selected.

- In the Attribute Editor, highlight the *sine1* input.

- Experiment by moving, rotating, scaling and combining the different attributes to see their effect on the geometry.

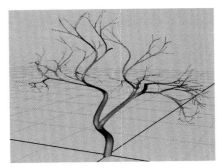

Sine deformer

- When you finish experimenting, select the deformer and delete it.

5 Squash deformer

- Select the *tree* geometry, then select
  Deform → Create Nonlinear → Squash.

  The Squash handle is created and selected.

- In the Attribute Editor, highlight
  the *squash1* input.

- Experiment by moving, rotating, scaling
  and combining the different attributes to
  see their effect on the geometry.

- When you finish experimenting, select the
  deformer and delete it.

Squash deformer

6 Twist deformer

- Select the *tree* geometry, then select
  Deform → Create Nonlinear → Twist.

  The Twist handle is created and selected.

- In the Attribute Editor, highlight
  the *twist1* input.

- Experiment by moving, rotating, scaling
  and combining the different attributes
  to see their effect on the geometry.

- When you finish experimenting,
  select the deformer and delete it.

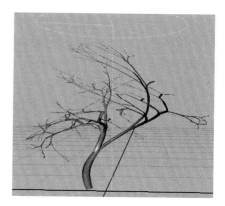

Twist deformer

7 Wave deformer

- Select the *tree* geometry, then select
  Deform → Create Nonlinear → Wave.

  The Wave handle is created and selected.

- In the Attribute Editor, highlight the
  wave1 input.

- Experiment by moving, rotating, scaling
  and combining the different attributes
  to see their effect on the geometry.

- When you finish experimenting, select
  the deformer and delete it.

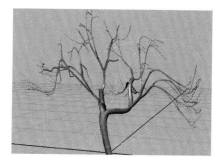

Wave deformer

8 **Finalize the tree**

Spend some time deforming the tree as you would like. To animate the scene later in this project, consider keeping the deformers in the scene.

Once you are finished, add the deformer handles to a new layer for easy access.

9 **Save your work**

Deformation order

The deformation order of a surface is very important to take into consideration. For instance, if you apply a *sine* deformer and then a *bend* deformer, the results are different than if you apply a *bend* deformer and then a *sine* deformer.

But, the deformation order does not only apply to non-linear deformers. For instance, a rigid binding and a polygonal smooth will have a different effect than a polygonal smooth and a rigid bind.

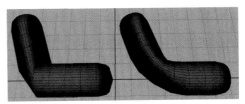

Smooth/Rigid bind vs Rigid bind/Smooth

Note: *In the previous statement, a rigid bind followed by a smooth would evaluate much faster and give better results than a smooth followed by a rigid bind, since the rigid binding would have to skin a higher resolution model.*

1 **New Scene**

- Select **File → New**.

2 **Create a cylinder**

- Select **Create → Polygon Primitives → Cylinder**.

- Edit the *cylinder* as follows:

3 **Apply deformers**

- Select the *cylinder*, then select **Deform → Create Nonlinear → Bend**.

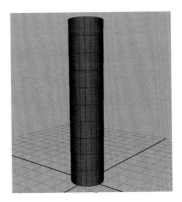

Example cylinder

- Select the *cylinder*, then
  select **Deform** → **Create
  Nonlinear** → **Sine**.

4 Edit the bend deformer

- Select the *cylinder*.

- In the Channel Box, highlight
  the *bend1* deformer.

- Set the **Curvature** attribute to 2.

5 Edit the sine deformer

- Select the *cylinder*.

- In the Channel Box, highlight the
  sine1 deformer.

- Set the **Amplitude** attribute to 0.1.

- Set the **Wavelength** attribute to 0.35.

6 List input for the cylinder

- **RMB** on the *cylinder*.

- Select **Inputs** → **All Inputs...**

  *Doing so will display a window
  with all the history nodes
  affecting the cylinder.*

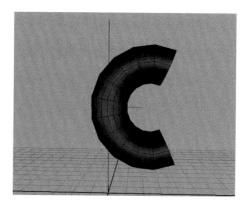

Bend deformer effect

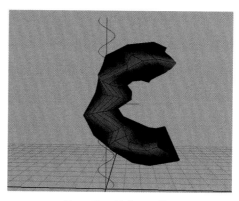

Sine and bend deformer effect

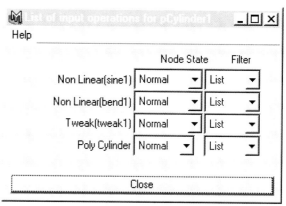

List of input for cylinder

7 **Change the order of deformation**

- In the Input window, MMB+drag the *Non Linear(sine1)* item over the *Non Linear(bend1)* item to change their order.

8 **Result of the new order of deformation**

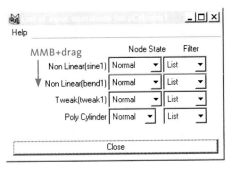

List of input for cylinder

New deformation order effect

Conclusion

You should now be comfortable using basic deformers. Being aware of the results created by the deformation order will allow you to reorder them if needed.

In the next lesson, you will animate Boog and his SUV to leave the garage and drive away into the forest.

Lesson 25
Motion path

In this lesson, you will drive Boog and the SUV out of the garage. To do so, you will use a *motion path* to determine the trajectory of the SUV, then keyframe some secondary animation to refine the motion.

In this lesson you will learn the following:

- How to make a surface live;

- How to define a motion path;

- How to shape the path to edit the animation;

- How to update the path markers;

- How to constrain the SUV to the normals of the terrain;

- How to constrain the character to the SUV;

- How to keyframe secondary animation.

Path animation

Path animations are created by assigning an object or series of objects to a path. This creates a special *motionPath* node that allows you to key its motion along the path.

1 Scene file

- **Open** the scene file *23-pfx_03.ma*.

2 Make live

- Select the *terrain* surface.

- Select **Modify → Make Live**.

  When making a surface live, it is displayed in green wireframe. You can then draw a curve directly on the surface, which will create a curve that follows the hills of the terrain.

3 Draw a path animation curve

- Change the viewport for the top view.

- Make sure the Paint Effects layer is visible in the scene so you can draw around it.

- Select **Create → EP Curve Tool → □**.

- Make sure to reset the options of the tool.

- **Draw** a curve leaving the garage and leading out into the forest as follows:

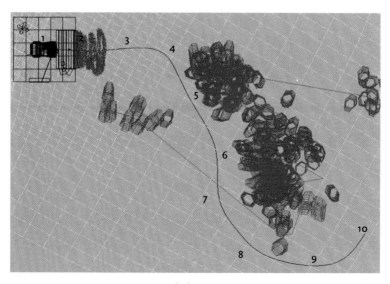

Path curve

Tip: *Try to keep the the curve points evenly spaced.*

- When you are done, hit **Enter** to complete the curve.
- Select **Modify** → **Make Not Live** again to remove the live state of the terrain surface.

4   **Attach the SUV to the path**

- Change the **Time Slider** range to go from 1 to 300 frames.
- Select the *SUV:master* node using the Outliner, then hold down **Ctrl** and select the path you have just drawn.

Note: *In order to create a path animation, the path must be picked last. The last object picked is indicated in green.*

- Go to the **Animation** menu set.
- Select **Animate** → **Motion Paths** → **Attach to Motion Path** → ❑.
- Set the **Time Range** to **Time Slider**.
- Click the **Attach** button and playback the results.

5   **Edit the motion path input node**

The SUV is moving down the path, but it is not aimed in the correct direction. You can change this using the *motionPath* input node.

- With the *SUV:master* selected, open the Attribute Editor.
- Click the tab for *motionPath1* and set the following:

   Follow to **On**;

   Front Axis to Z;

   Up Axis to Y.

Tip: *If the SUV does not face the right direction while moving down the path, change the Front Axis or turn **On** the Inverse Front checkbox.*

- **Playback** the results and see how the SUV now points in the direction it is traveling.

SUV attached to path

Note: *You can also use the Bank option to have the object automatically roll when following the path. In this example, you will use another technique involving constraints to have the SUV follow the surface's angle.*

6 Edit the path's shape

Edit the shape of the path using the curve's control vertices and the object will follow the path.

- Select the path curve.

- **RMB** on the path curve and select **Control Vertices** from the context menu.

- **Move** the CVs along the **Y-axis** in order to minimize how the SUV interpenetrates with the ground.

- **Playback** the results.

Tip: *You can change the view in the Perspective window as the animation is playing back. This lets you preview the animation from different angles.*

7 Change the path's start time

Notice the start and end markers on the path. They tell you the start and end frame of the animation along the path.

- Go to frame **85**.

- Select the *SUV:master* using its selection handle.

- In the Channel Box, click on the *motionPath1* input node.

- Still in the Channel Box, click on the **U Value** channel name to highlight it.

Notice the two keyframes in the Time Slider at the first and last frame. Those keyframes are defining the animation of the motion path from start to end.

Updated start marker

- Select the first keyframe in either the Time Slider or from the Graph Editor.

- **Move** the first keyframe at frame **85**.

This specifies that the SUV should only start moving once Boog is seated in the SUV.

8 Key a path value

You can also set a key on the *motionPath's* U value to add more markers to the path. You will use this to slow down the SUV as it exits the garage and then to speed up once outside.

- Go to frame **130**.

- Ensure that the **Auto Key** button is turned **On**.

- Select the path curve, and then highlight the *motionPath* node in the Channel Box.

- Select the **Show Manipulator Tool** by pressing **t**.

A manipulator appears with handles for positioning the object along the path. You will use the handle on the path to move the SUV back to slow it down.

- **Click+drag** on the path manipulator handle to drag the SUV back a little.

- Another path marker is placed on the curve.

A new marker is placed where the new key is set. You are setting a key on the position of the SUV along the U direction of the curve. The value represents the parameter of the curve.

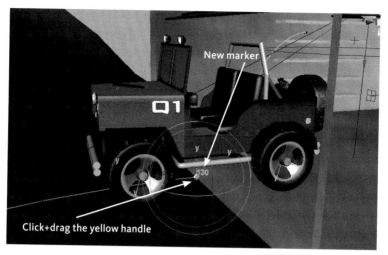

New path marker

Tip: *It is always good to remember that input nodes may have manipulators that you can access using the Show Manipulator Tool.*

9 Edit the path marker's position

The position of the markers can be moved to edit the animation of the ship.

- Click on the **Auto Key** button to turn it **Off**.

- Select the **Move Tool**.

- To select the path marker that is labeled as **130**, click on the number without touching the curve to select the marker on its own.

    When selected, the marker is yellow.

- **Click+drag** the marker to change the position of the SUV.

    The marker is constrained to the curve as you move it.

- **Playback** the results.

10 Edit the timing

Since the marker points are simply keys set on the U Value of the *motionPath* node, you can edit the timing of the keys in the Graph Editor.

- Select the *SUV:master* using its selection handle, and then click on the *motionPath* input node in the Channel Box.

- Open the Graph Editor.

- Press **a** to frame all into the window.

  The position of the attached object in the U direction of the curve is mapped against time. You can see that a key has been set for each of the path markers.

- Select the key at frame **130**.

- In the Graph Editor's **Stats** area, change the time from **130** to **140**.

- In the Graph Editor, select **Tangents → Spline**.

  You can edit the effect of the path keys' in-between frames using the same techniques as for set keys.

- Select the last keyframe, then **Tangents → Linear**.

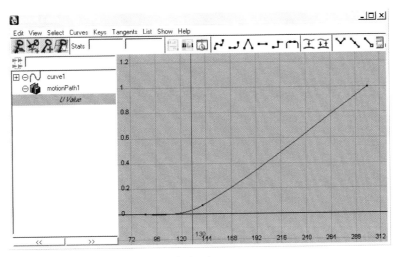

Edited path curve

You can see that the path marker is now labeled as **140** in the view panel.

Note: *You can also select the marker in the viewport and delete it by pressing the Delete key.*

Secondary animation

Now that you have a basic animation for your SUV, you can keyframe *secondary animation* on top of what you already have. Secondary animation usually adds life to an animation, making the scene more natural. For the SUV, you will create a normal constraint so it follows the terrain, and then keyframe some drifting. You will also animate the *wheelOverride* in order to get the wheels to spin upon gaining speed.

1   Normal constraint

The normal constraint is a constraint that takes the normal from a surface and applies the associated rotation to a constrained object. Here, you will constrain the normal of the terrain to the rotation of the SUV rotation override.

- Select the *terrain*, then **Shift-select** the *SUV:rotOverride*.

- Select **Constrain → Normal → ❑**.

- **Set the options as follows:**

    Aim Vector to **0, 1, 0**;

    Up Vector to **1, 0, 0**;

    World Up Type to **Object Up**;

    World Up Object to *SUV:master*.

    You are setting the up object to be the SUV master since it already defines proper path rotation.

- Click the **Add** button.

- **Playback** the animation.

    Notice how the SUV rolls sideways when on the hillside.

The normal constraint effect

2 **Drifting**

- Make sure **Auto Key** is turned **On**.

- Go to frame **180**.

- With the *SUV:SUV* node selected, press **Shift+w** and **Shift+e** to set a keyframe on translation and rotation.

- Go to frame **195**.

- **Translate** the SUV towards the outside of the curve and **rotate** it towards the path.

- Go to frame **210**.

- Bring the translation and rotation of the SUV back to **0** in all directions.

Drifting offset

3 **Spinning wheels**

Using the wheel overrides, set keyframes to get the wheels to spin when the SUV is starting its motion.

- Set a keyframe on all four wheels at frame **80**.

- Set a keyframe on all four wheels at frame **100** with some forward rotation.

Doing so will cause the wheels to spin on top of the wheel automation created previously.

4 **Constrain Boog**

You must set-up Boog and the SUV to be perfectly synchronized. The easiest way of doing this is to constrain Boog's master to the SUV node.

- Go to frame **85**.

  This is the frame just before the SUV starts moving. Thus, Boog must be in a good position at that frame before constraining.

- Select Boog's *OffsetTranslateControl1* node.

  This was the node used to place Boog's animation correctly with the Trax clips.

- **Translate** the node to place Boog correctly in the driver's seat.

- Select the *SUV:SUV* node, then **Shift-select** the *Boog's master* node.

- Select **Constrain** → **Parent** → ❑.

- In the options, make sure that **Maintain Offset** is set to **On**.

- Click the **Add** button.

- **Delete** the *OffsetTranslateControl1* node as it is no longer required.

- **Playback** the animation.

  Boog should now be following the SUV perfectly.

5 **Other animation**

- Spend some time animating Boog's reaction to his driving.

  Doing so will add lots of realism to the actions, rather than having just a stiff character following the SUV.

6 **Save your work**

- **Save** your scene as *25-motionpath_01.ma*.

7 **Playblast the animation**

Boog driving away

Conclusion

You are now more familiar with animating using motion paths, constraining and keyframing secondary animation. As a result of your work, the SUV and Boog are now driving out of the garage and into the forest.

In the next lesson, you will implement a dynamic simulation so that the SUV and boxes collide and crumble to the floor.

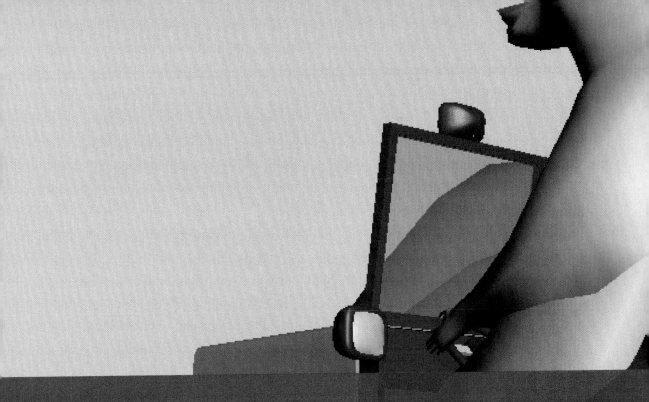

Lesson 26
Rigid bodies

In animation, sometimes there are scenarios that just aren't worth spending the time to keyframe. Collisions between objects, for example, would look too complex to animate by hand. In that case, it is better to use dynamic simulations.

In this lesson, you will experiment with the basics of *rigid bodies*, an example of dynamic simulations. Rigid bodies are polygonal or NURBS surfaces converted to unyielding shapes. Unlike conventional surfaces, rigid bodies collide rather than pass through each other during animation. To animate rigid body motion, you use fields, keys, expressions, rigid body constraints, or collisions with other rigid bodies or particles. In our case, the SUV will be colliding with the boxes and the floor, all affected by a gravity field.

In this lesson you will learn the following:

- How to create a passive rigid body and an active rigid body;
- How to add a gravity field to rigid bodies;
- How to set rigid body attributes and rigid body keyframes
- How to simulate your dynamics and how to cache a dynamic simulation.

Active and passive

Maya has two kinds of rigid bodies—active and passive. An *active rigid body* reacts to dynamics—fields, collisions, and springs—not to keys. A *passive rigid body* can have active rigid bodies collide with it. You can key its translation and rotation attributes, but dynamics has no effect on it.

1 Test scene

- Select **File → New**.

- **Create** one polygonal cube and **scale** it so that it looks like a floor.

- **Rename** the cube *floor*.

- **Create** a polygonal sphere and another polygonal cube and place them side by side above the floor.

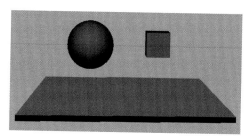

The test scene

2 Active rigid body

- Select the sphere.

- Press **F5** to display the **Dynamics** menu set.

- Select **Soft/Rigid Bodies → Create Active Rigid Body**.

- **Playback** the animation.

   Nothing is happening because there are no forces in the scene.

3 Playback the simulation

- Click the **Animation preferences** button found at the right side of the Range Slider.

- In the **Timeline** section, set the following:

   Playback Speed to **Play every frame**.

   When working with rigid bodies or particles, it is very important that the playback speed is set to play every frame. Otherwise, your simulations may act unpredictably.

- Click the **Save** button.

4 Gravity field

- Select the sphere.

- Select **Fields → Gravity**.

- In the Attribute Editor, make sure the **Magnitude** is set to 9.8.

A magnitude of 9.8 mimics the earth's gravity.

- **Playback** the animation.

  The sphere falls straight down.

Note: *You may want to increase your playback range in the Time Slider.*

5 Passive rigid body

- Select the *floor*.
- Select **Soft/Rigid Bodies** → **Create Passive Rigid Body**.
- **Playback** the animation.

  The sphere falls and collides with the floor.

6 Rotate the floor

- Select the *floor* and **rotate** it sideways.
- **Playback** the animation.

  The sphere collides and rolls off the floor.

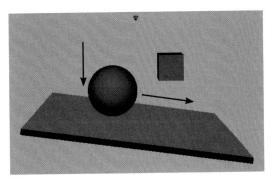

Rotate the floor

Note: *It is very important to rewind to frame 1 before playing a dynamic simulation to see accurate results. Also, you should not scrub in the timeline.*

7 Set the cube as active

- Select the *cube*.

- Select **Soft/Rigid Bodies** →
  Create Active Rigid Body.

- **Playback** the animation.

  The cube does not fall with gravity since it was not connected.

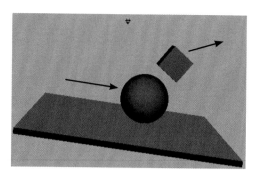

The cube collides without gravity

8 Assign gravity

- Select the *cube* and **Shift-select** the gravity field.

- Select **Fields** → **Affect Selected Object(s).**

- **Playback** the animation.

  The cube falls on the floor like the sphere.

9 Change dynamic attributes

- Select the *cube.*

- In the Channel Box, highlight the *rigidBody* input connection.

- Set the following:

  Mass to 2;

  Bounciness to 0.1;

  Static Friction to 0.5;

  Dynamic Friction to 0.5.

  Setting those attributes specifies that the cube is heavier and will react differently against other rigid bodies, that it doesn't bounce much and that it has more friction against other rigid bodies.

- **Playback** the animation.

  The cube falls and stops on the floor. This is because you have reduced attributes like bounciness and increased friction.

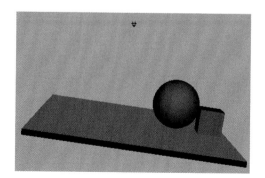

The cube stops the sphere

10 **Center of mass**

If you look closely at the rigid bodies, you will notice a small **x** that defines the rigid bodies' center of mass.

Rigid body center of mass

Not all objects have their center of mass exactly at their centers. For example, a clown's inflatable boxing bag stays straight even when it is pushed over.

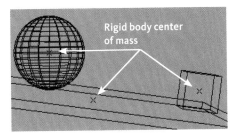

Rigid body center of mass

The center of mass

- Select the sphere to change its center of mass.

- In the Channel Box, highlight the *rigidBody* input connection.

- Set the **Center Of Mass Y** to **-1**;

The center of mass icon moved to the bottom of the sphere.

- **Playback** the animation.

The sphere falls and stops on the floor, bobbing from side to side.

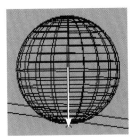

The new center of mass

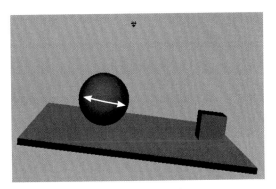

The sphere is bobbing in place

Box simulation

With your knowledge, you can now add a rigid body simulation to the SUV scene. You will first set the active and passive rigid bodies. You will then keyframe the orb rigid body from passive to active, which will allow it to maintain the path animation until the malfunction. Once the orb becomes an active rigid body, it will crash into the box stack.

1   **Scene file**

- **Open** the file *25-motionPath_01.ma*.

2   **Create rigid bodies**

- Select the *garage* geometry and **Shift-select** the *terrain* surface.

- Press **F5** to select the **Dynamics** menu set.

- Select **Soft/Rigid Bodies** → **Create Passive Rigid Body**.

3   **Box stack**

- Select all the *boxes* from the box stack.

- **Move** them in front of the SUV.

    Doing so will force the SUV to collide with the boxes.

Note: *Make sure that none of the boxes interpenetrate with each other or the floor. If this happens, translate them to produce a small gap between the boxes.*

- With all the boxes still selected, select **Soft/Rigid Bodies** → **Create Active Rigid Body**.

The active box stack

4 Make a simplified SUV

The SUV geometry is quite complex to calculate dynamics for. A simple way to avoid this unnecessary calculation is to place a large box over the entire SUV and use that bounding box as a passive rigid body.

SUV bounding box

- **Create** a primitive polygonal cube.

- **Scale** and **move** the cube to be as big as the SUV itself.

- **Rename** the cube to *simpleSUV*.

- **Group** the new box to itself and **rename** it *simpleGroup*.

    You need to group the simplified box because both a parent constraint and a rigid body want to control the translation and rotation attributes of an object.

- **Parent constrain** the *simpleGroup* with the *SUV:SUV* node.

5 Create the SUV rigid bodies

- Go to frame **1**.

    It is important to be at frame 1 when creating a passive rigid body on an animated object, or the dynamics might not simulate as expected.

- Select the *simpleSUV* box.

- Select **Soft/Rigid Bodies →
  Create Passive Rigid Body**.

- Press **Ctrl+h** to **hide** the *simpleSUV*.

- **Playblast** the animation.

The passive SUV collides with the boxes

Note: *During a dynamic simulation, if two objects intersect, a warning is displayed in the Command Feedback line and the objects are automatically selected.*

6 Assign gravity

- Select **Edit** → **Select All by Type** → **Rigid Bodies**.

- Select **Fields** → **Gravity**.

  A new gravity field with the default earth-like gravity appears at the origin.

- **Playblast** the animation.

  Now all the rigid bodies bounce off the floor.

7 Initial state

When you playback the animation, you can notice the boxes falling on the floor because their were all slightly floating in the air. A dynamic initial state tells Maya the position of all the dynamics on the first animation frame.

- **Playback** the animation up to frame **40** where the boxes are settled on the floor.

- Select **Solvers** → **Initial State** → **Set for All Dynamic**.

- **Playback** the animation.

  Notice how the boxes no longer fall on the ground at the start of the animation.

The boxes with gravity and proper initial state

Note: *You can also set keys onto the rigid bodies to go from passive rigid bodies to active rigid bodies by selecting* **Soft/Rigid Bodies → Set Active Key.** *This could, in this case, eliminate the need for setting the intial state because you could turn the boxes into active rigid bodies just before the collision with the SUV.*

8 Fine-tune the simulation

For a better simulation, the rigid bodies' attributes should be tweaked to give more realism to the scene. Following are some general steps that you should do, but it may vary from scene to scene.

For the *boxes*, **change the following:**
- Move down the **Center Of Mass Y** of the bigger boxes.
- Change the **Mass** attributes between **0.2** and **1.5**, depending on the size of the boxes;
- Lower their **Bounciness** attributes to **0.2**;
- Increase their **Static Friction** and **Dynamic Friction** attributes to **0.5**.

For the *garage*, **change the following:**
- Lower the **Bounciness** attribute to **0.2**;
- Increase the **Static Friction** and **Dynamic Friction** attributes to **0.5**.

For the *terrain*, **change the following:**
- Lower the **Bounciness** attribute to **0.1**;
- Increase the **Static Friction** and **Dynamic Friction** attributes to **0.8**.

For the *simpleSUV*, **change the following:**
- Lower its **Bounciness** attribute to **0.2**.

9 Save your work

- Save your scene as *26-rigidbodies_01.ma*.

The final simulation

Simulation cache

When you simulate rigid body dynamics, the rigid body solver recalculates the simulation every time you play through the Time Slider. You can speed up the playback of your scene by saving a rigid body cache in memory. A cache stores the positions of all the rigid bodies at every frame, letting you quickly preview the results without having to create a playblast. This offers many benefits, including scrubbing back and forth in the Time Slider.

If you want to tweak the objects' attributes to alter the simulation, you will not see the results until you delete the cache so that the solver can recalculate a new simulation.

1 Enable the cache

- Select **Solvers → Rigid Body Solver...**

  This will open the Attribute Editor for the rigid body solver in the scene.

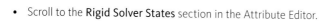

> **Note:** *It is possible to have multiple rigid body solvers in a scene. This is useful when you have distinct systems that don't interact together.*

- Scroll to the **Rigid Solver States** section in the Attribute Editor.
- Turn **On** the **Cache Data** checkbox.
- **Rewind** and **playback** the entire scene so that the solver can create the cache.

  When it finishes playing the scene and writing the cache to memory, you should see a difference in the playback speed since it does not recalculate the simulation.

> **Note:** *The rigid body cache is saved in Maya's memory and is not written to disk.*

2 Tweak the simulation

- Select the boxes and change some of their rigid body attributes.

  You should not see any difference when you playback your scene since no recalculation is done.

- Select **Solvers → Rigid Body Solver...**

- In the **Rigid Solver States** section, click the **Delete Cache** button.

  This will force the solver to recalculate the cache.

- **Rewind** your scene and **play** it so that the solver can create a new cache.

- If you want to disable the solver's cache, simply turn **Off** the **Cache Data** checkbox.

Conclusion

You have experienced the basics of the powerful dynamics tools in Maya. You learned how to create active and passive rigid bodies, as well as gravity fields. You also tweaked their attributes to add realism to your simulation.

You are now ready to delve into more advanced topics. In the next lesson, you will use dynamics along with particles.

Lesson 27
Particles

Particles are small object types that can be animated using dynamic forces in place of traditional keyframes. These effects are, in essence, *simulations* of physical effects such as water, smoke and fire.

To experiment with particle effects, you will add fire to your scene. The flames will be generated using the Maya default particle fire effect. You will then create sparks that will collide against the boxes and floor.

In this lesson you will learn the following:

- How to add a fire effect to an object;
- How to set the particles initial state;
- How to add an emitter;
- How to define a particle attribute using a ramp;
- How to collide particles against geometry;
- How to add gravity fields;
- How to software and hardware render a particle animation.

Start a fire

Using one of the Maya preset particle effects, you will add fire to your scene. This preset creates everything needed to make the particles act and look like fire.

1 Scene file

- **Open** the scene file from the last lesson, which is *26-rigidbodies_01.ma.*

2 Adding the fire effect

- Press **F5** or hold down **h** and click in the viewport to select the **Dynamics** menu set.

- Select the highest *box* from the box stack.

- Select **Effects → Create Fire**.

  The fire effect is the result of a particle object that is controlled by several dynamic fields, such as gravity and turbulence. The fire preset added these elements to your scene and lets you easily control them.

- **Rewind** to frame **1** and **playback** the simulation.

Default fire particles

Note: When working with dynamics, it's important that you always use the rewind button to move to the beginning of your simulation and to ensure that the scene playback is set to **Play every frame** in the general preferences. Never scrub through a scene that has dynamics in it unless you cache the particles to disk. Otherwise, you might get unpredictable results.

3 Editing the fire attributes

To control various parts of the fire effect, you can simply edit attributes that are designed specifically for this effect.

- **Playback** the simulation to a point where some particles are visible, then stop.

- Select the fire particles.

- In the Attribute Editor, make sure that the *particle1* tab is selected.

- **Rename** the particles to *flame*.

> **Note:** *When renaming the transform node, the shape node automatically gets renamed.*

- Change tab to the *flameShape*.

- Scroll down to the bottom and open the **Extra Attributes** section.

- Set the following attributes:

  Fire Scale to 1.6;

  Fire Turbulence to 200;

  Fire Density to 10;

  Fire Intensity to 0.2;

  Fire Lifespan to 0.5.

- **Rewind** to frame 1 and **playback** the simulation.

4 Setting the initial state

One thing you may notice with the simulation is that there are no particles when the animation starts. If you want the fire to be visible right from the beginning, you must set the particle's initial state.

- **Playback** the scene until around frame 30, then **stop** playback.

- Select the particles.

- From the **Solvers** menu, select **Initial State → Set for Selected**.

- Go back to frame 1 and **playback** the simulation.

  By setting the initial state for the particles, you can see that at frame 1, the particles are already created.

5 Test render the particles

- Press **F6** to go to the **Rendering** menu set.

- From the **Render** menu, select **Render current frame...**

The scene is now rendered with the fire particles included. Some particles can be rendered using the software renderer, which allows them to be automatically integrated into the scene.

Software rendering

Note: *If you can see the flame's shadows, you will notice they don't look very convincing because the depth map shadows don't work well with the fire's volumetric shader. Also, there might be a strange halo around the fire if you used 2D motion blur.*

Tip: *For a faster rendering, lower the anti-aliasing setting to Preview and turn off the motion blur option in the Render Settings. Do this from the Render view window, by selecting the clipboard icon beside the IPR button to open the Render Settings window.*

Sparks

As an added effect, you will set-up more particles that will represent emitted sparks from the blaze. To create particles that look like sparks, you need to adjust various particle attributes. In this case, you will create streaks particles that will die fairly quickly after being emitted. Their color will start out yellow, and then turn to red and finally black. You will also set-up those sparks to collide on the surrounding geometry.

1 Add an emitter

In order to have new particles in your scene, you must first create a particle emitter.

- Select the fire particles and press **Ctrl+h** to hide them.

- Press **F5** to go back to the **Dynamics** menu set, then from the **Particles** menu, select **Create Emitter**.

An emitter will appear at the origin.

- Select the new emitter, then **Shift-select** the *box*.

- Press **p** to **parent** the emitter to the *box*.

- Place the emitter in the center of the box.

- Press **4** to set the display to wireframe.

- **Playback** your scene to see the new default particles being emitted.

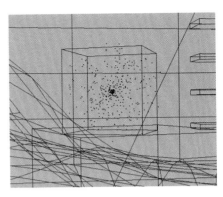

Default particles

2 Change render type to streak

Particles can have their render type set from a list of possible looks. You can switch between the different types until you get one that suits your needs.

- Select the new particles.

- **Rename** them *sparks*.

- In the Attribute Editor, go to the **Render Attributes** section of the *sparksShape* node.

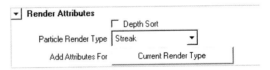

Render Attributes

- Set **Particle Render Type** to **Streak**.

This render type is designed to work with hardware rendering. This means that later, you will have to composite the final hardware rendered particles with software rendered scenes.

3 Add and edit render attributes

- Click on the **Current Render Type** button.

- Set the **Render Attributes** as follows:

    Line Width to 4;

    Tail Fade to 0;

    Tail Size to 5.

This gives the sparks a much stronger presence. The higher tail size value lengthens the sparks.

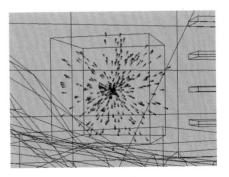

Streak particles

4 Add color per particle

The particle node has the ability to have new attributes added to it as needed. This lets you add complexity to a particle node when necessary.

You can use this technique to add color to the particles individually (per particle or PP), instead of as an entire group.

- In the **Add Dynamic Attributes** section of the Attribute Editor, click on the **Color** button.

- From the Particle color window, select **Add Per Particle Attribute,** then click the **Add Attribute** button.

  This adds an rgbPP line to the **Per Particle (Array) Attributes** *section.*

- Click on the *rgbPP* field with your **RMB** and select **Create Ramp.**

- Click again on the *rgbPP* field with your **RMB** and select **<-arrayMapper.outColorPP → Edit Ramp.**

  In the Ramp window, you will find three markers, each with a square and a circular icon.

- Click on the circle icon at the bottom of the ramp, then click on the color swatch next to **Selected Color.**

- Change the color to **yellow.**

- Complete the same steps to change the middle marker to **red** and the top marker to **black.**

- **Click+drag** the circle to change its position in the ramp as follows:

- Press **6** to go in hardware texturing mode.

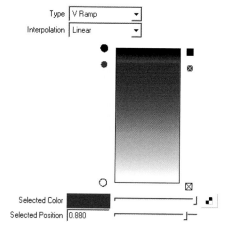

Particle color ramp

5 Particle lifespan and randomness

The **Lifespan** attribute lets you determine how long the particle will remain in the scene before it disappears or dies. You will add a slight randomness to the lifespan of the particles.

- With *sparks* selected, go to the **Lifespan Attributes** section in the Attribute Editor.

- Change **Lifespan Mode** to **Random range.**

- Change the **Lifespan** to 1.5.

- Change the **Lifespan Random** to **0.5.**

  The lifespan is uniformly distributed with **Lifespan** *as the mean and* **Lifespan Random** *as the width of the distribution.*

  The particles in this case have a lifespan between 1 and 2. This gives the sparks a more random look.

6 Change the settings of the emitter

Some attributes on the emitter should be changed to get a better sparks simulation. The rate at which the emitter creates particles should be decreased and the emitting speed should be increased.

- From the Outliner, select *emitter2.*

- Go to the **Basic Emitter Attributes** section in the Attribute Editor.

- Set the **Rate (Particles/Sec)** attribute to **10.**

- Go to the **Basic Emission Speed Attributes** section that is lower in the Attribute Editor.

- Set the **Speed** attribute to **10.**

- Set the **Speed Random** attribute to **2.**

- **Playback** the simulation.

Fine-tuning the sparks

The current particles don't quite move like real sparks. They should react to gravity and collide with the surrounding surfaces.

1 Add gravity to the particles

- Select *sparks.*

- From the **Fields** menu, select **Gravity**.

  A gravity field appears at the origin.

- **Playback** the simulation.

  Now the particles drop straight to the ground without collisions. The gravity field is pulling them down.

2 Set-up particle collisions

To make the particles collide against the boxes and the floor, you must define them as colliding objects.

- Select the *sparks* particles.

- Press the **Shift** key and **select** the *garage*.

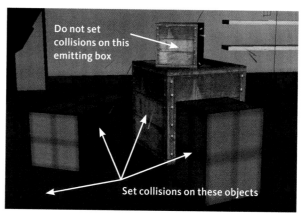

Note: *The garage should be selected last.*

- From the **Particles** menu, select **Make Collide**.

- **Repeat** these steps for all the surrounding objects in the range of your particles.

  Do not set collisions on the box emitting the sparks; the sparks would collide and stay inside the box.

Do not set collisions on this emitting box

Set collisions on these objects

Particle collision

3   Adding friction

As you playback the scene, the sparks seem to bounce too much off the colliding objects. To fix this, you must change the resilience and friction attributes for each surface.

- Select the *sparks* particles on their own.

- At the top of the Attribute Editor, click on the first *geoConnector* tab.

- Set the following attributes:

    Resilience to 0.1;

    Friction to 0.6.

- **Repeat** for all the remaining *geoConnector* tabs.

  The geoConnector objects have been created for the collision objects specified.

- **Playback** the simulation.

  Now the sparks react more realistically when colliding with the objects. Resilience is used to calculate the bounciness of a surface and friction is used to slow down the particles when they touch a surface.

4 Create a particle event

Use the **Collision Event Tool** to emit a new smoke particle upon collision.

- Select the *sparks*.

- From the **Particles** menu, select **Particle Collision Event Editor**.

- In the **Particle Collision Event Editor**, go to the **Event Type** section and set the following:

  Type to **Emit** enabled;

  Num particles to 5;

  Spread to 1;

  Inherit Velocity to 1.

- Click **Create Event** and close the window.

- **Playback** the simulation.

Particle collision event

Several small particles are emitted after the sparks collide. These particles float around based on the momentum they gained from the collision. Now you will adjust how they react and look.

- Stop at a frame where the new particles are visible.

5 Set the new particles as smoke

- Select the new particles.

- **Rename** them *smoke*.

- In the Attribute Editor, set the **Particle Render Type** to **Cloud**.

Tip: *The (s/w) beside the Cloud particle type means it is a software particle type.*

- Click on the **Current Render Type** button.

- Set the **Radius** attribute to 0.6.

- In the **Lifespan Attributes** section, set a **Constant Lifespan** of 1.

- In the **Add Dynamic Attributes** section, click on the **Opacity** button and select **Add Per Particle Attribute**.

- In the **Per Particle Attributes** section, **RMB** on the **OpacityPP** field and select **Create Ramp**.

  The default opacity ramp should turn from white (opaque) to black (transparent).

6 Smoke goes up

- Select the *smoke* particles.

- Click on **Fields** → **Gravity**.

- Change the **Magnitude** of the new gravity field to **-1**.

  Reversing the gravity's magnitude will push the particles up instead of pulling them down.

Smoke particles

- Select **Display** → **Show** → **Show Last Hidden** to show back the flame particles.

7 Save your work

- **Save** the scene as *27-particles_01.ma*.

Rendering particles

It was mentioned earlier that the sparks used a particle type that could only be rendered using hardware rendering, while the fire and smoke used software rendering. The question, therefore, is: how do you bring hardware rendered particles together with a software rendered scene?

The answer is to render them separately, and then bring them together using a compositing package such as *Combustion*.

To composite the spark particles with the rest of the scene, you will need to render the top layer (in this case, the sparks), with a matte, or *mask*.

The mask is a grayscale channel that defines which areas of the color image are going to be transparent when brought into a compositing package. In this scene, the background contains all the scene's geometry.

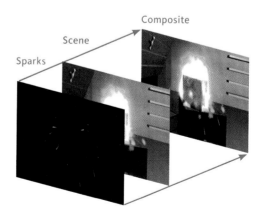

Diagram of compositing layers

Software rendering

The flames created using the fire effect and the smoke can be rendered using software rendering. This means creating another batch rendering of your scene. This will represent the first render pass that can be later composited together with the sparks.

1   Change your motion blur type

Since the 2D motion blur used so far doesn't render well with the flame particles, you will switch to the 3D motion blur type.

- Select **Window** → **Rendering Editors** → **Render Settings...**

- Open the **Motion Blur** section and change the **Motion Blur Type** to 3D.

    This type of motion blur renders more slowly, but is more accurate and works better with software rendered particles.

2   Fix the flame and smoke shadows

Earlier it was noted that the shadows generated from the particles didn't look correct. The depth map shadows cannot recognize the subtleties of the volumetric shader used by the particles. Raytrace shadows are needed.

- Select the spot light that is illuminating and casting shadows in the scene.

- In the Attribute Editor, open the **Shadows** section, scroll down to **Raytrace Shadow Attributes** and set **Use Ray Trace Shadows** to **On**.

- Set the **Ray Depth Limit** to 2.

    This sets up the light, but to use raytraced shadows you will need to turn on raytracing itself.

- Open the **Render Settings**.

- Open the **Raytracing Quality** section and turn **Raytracing** to **On**.

Note: *Maya uses a selective raytracer and only objects that require reflections, refractions or raytraced shadows will use this technique.*

3   Limiting the reflections

When raytracing is turned on, any shader that has a reflectivity value will render with reflections. If the object is not required to be reflective, then it's a good idea to turn Reflectivity off.

- Go into the material node and set its **Reflectivity** to o.

- **Repeat** for each material in the scene that has a shader with unwanted **Reflectivity**.

OR

- Select the geometry that you don't want to be involved in raytracing.

- Under its **Render Stats** section, turn **Visible in Reflections Off**.

  When you do this, the object will not reflect and won't be calculated in the raytrace.

- **Repeat** for each object in the scene that has a shader with the **Reflectivity** attribute.

Note: *Lambert shaders do not have a reflectivity attribute.*

4   **Batch render the scene**

- Select **File** → **Save Scene as...**

- Enter the file name *27-background_01.ma* and click **Save**.

- Press **F6** to change to the **Rendering** menu set and select **Render** → **Batch Render**.

  This will create a render pass that includes the geometry and software particles. You will now render the sparks using hardware rendering.

Tip: *From now until the end of this lesson, do not move the rendered camera, or the software and hardware renders won't match. You can use the [and] keys to undo and redo camera moves.*

Hardware rendering

You have been using hardware rendering in the Perspective view panel to help preview the scene. You can also use hardware rendering to render the spark particles so that they match the rendered scene.

1   **Hide the software particles**

Since you only want the sparks to appear in the hardware rendering, you will need to hide the flame and smoke particles.

- Select the *flame* particles and **Shift-select** the *smoke* particles.

- Press **Ctrl+h** to hide them.

  Now the particles will not be visible in the hardware rendering.

2 Set the hardware render attributes

- Select **Window** → **Rendering Editors** → **Hardware Render Buffer**.

- Select **Render** → **Attributes**.

- In the Attribute Editor, set the following attributes:

  Filename Prefix to *sparks*;

- To match the extension setting you chose for your software rendering set:

  Extension to **name.1.ext** (Windows, Mac);

  OR

  Extension to **name.ext.1** (IRIX).

- To match the render setting of your software rendering set:

  Start Frame to **1**;

  End Frame to **300**;

  Resolution to **640x480**.

- Go to the **Render Mode** section and set:

  Geometry Mask to **On**.

  This will use the geometry as mask objects to hide particles falling behind them. An alpha channel, also known as a matte channel, is important for layering images in a compositing package.

- Go to the **Multi-Pass Render Options** section and set:

  Set **Multi-Pass Rendering** to **On** and leave **Render Passes** to **3**.

> **Note:** *These attributes only affect hardware rendering.*

- Close the Attribute Editor.

3 Test a frame

- **Playback** the simulation until you hit a frame where some of the sparks appear.

- Click on the **Test** button in the middle of the Render Buffer's time controls.

4 Render a sequence

You can now render an entire animation using this window. Compared to software rendering, it lets you use the speed of hardware rendering to generate animations quickly.

- Select **Render** → **Render Sequence**.

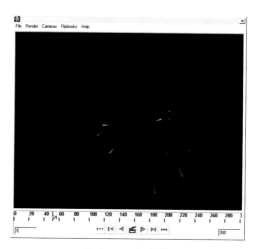

Hardware render buffer

5 Preview the resulting animation

- Once the rendering is done, select **Flipbooks** → **sparks.1-300**.

  Doing so opens the fcheck utility and plays the animation for you.

6 Composite rendered animations

You currently have a software rendered animation of fire and smoke, and a hardware rendered sequence of sparks with an embedded alpha channel. You can now use your compositing software to layer all these elements together.

There are several advantages to compositing your layers instead of rendering all of them into one scene:

- By separating background and foreground elements and rendering them individually, rendering times can be greatly reduced;

Animation flipbook in fcheck

Final composite

- By rendering different elements on different layers, it is easier to make revisions later to one layer without having to re-render the whole scene;

- By compositing hardware and software rendered particles, you can achieve interesting effects;

AND

- By using different layers, your compositing software can adjust the color for one particular layer without affecting other layers.

Conclusion

You now have a better understanding of Maya hardware and software particles. You created and modified the preset fire effect and added your own effect by customizing emitter and particle attributes. The lesson also covered some of the most important aspects of particle simulations, including per particle attributes, gravity, collisions and collision events.

In the next lesson you will experiment with MEL scripting.

File Edit History Command Help

setAttr "blendShapel.browDown" (
// Undo:
setAttr "blendShapel.sad" 1;
// Undo:
setAttr "blendShapel.browUp" 1;
// Undo:
setAttr "blendShapel.browDown"

Lesson 28
MEL scripting

In this lesson, you will set keys on the Blink attribute that you created on the *lookAt* node in the Boog rig. To help with this task, you will create a MEL™ (Maya Embedded Language) script that will help you animate the blink.

MEL is a powerful scripting language that can be used by both technical directors and animators to add to Maya's capability. Animators can take advantage of simple *macro-like* scripts to enhance their workflows, while technical directors can use more advanced MEL commands to rig up characters, add special visual effects or set-up customized controls.

If you know nothing about programming and scripts, this lesson will, at first, seem foreign to your world of graphics and animation. While you can certainly be successful with Maya without relying on the use of MEL, this lesson offers a good chance to get your feet wet and see the possibilities. If you do learn how to use MEL, you might be quite surprised how a simple script can be used to enhance your work.

In this lesson you will learn the following:

- How to recognize and enter MEL commands;
- How to create a MEL script procedure;
- How to use this procedure within Maya's existing UI;
- How to build a custom UI element for the procedure;
- How to animate the creature's blinking using the procedure.

Starting a new file

Rather than working in the character scene file, you will practice using MEL in a new file. Once your scripts have been written and saved, you will return to the creature scene and use the custom UI tools in context.

1 Start a new file

- Select **File** → **New Scene**.

- Set-up a single *Perspective* view panel.

- Make sure the Command line, the Help line and the Channel Box are all visible. If not, you can make them visible in the **Display** → **UI Elements** menu.

WHAT IS MEL?

MEL stands for Maya Embedded Language. It is built on top of Maya's base architecture and is used to execute commands used to build scenes and create user interface elements. In fact, every time you click on a tool, you are executing one or more MEL commands.

Typing commands

A MEL command is a text string that tells Maya to complete a particular action. As a user, it is possible to skip the graphical user interface and use these commands directly. Generally, animators will choose the user interface instead – but it is still a good idea to know what MEL can do at a command level.

The Command line

You will now use Maya's Command line to create and edit some primitive objects. The goal at this point is to explore how simple commands work.

1 Create a cone using the Command line

- Click in the Command line to make it active.

  The Command line can be found at the bottom left, just above the Help line.

- Enter the following:

Entering a MEL command

- After you finish, press the **Enter** key on the numeric keypad section of your keyboard.

Tip: *The keyboard has two Enter keys that each work a little differently with the Command line. The Enter key associated with the numeric keypad keeps your focus on the Command line, while the Enter key associated with the alpha-numeric keyboard switches your focus back to the view panels.*

---

2   Rotate and move the cone with commands

The next step is to transform the cone using MEL commands.

- Enter the following:

```
rotate 0 0 90 < Enter >

move 5 0 0 < Enter >
```

You now have a cone sitting on the ground surface, five units along the X-axis. You first entered the command, then you have added the desired values.

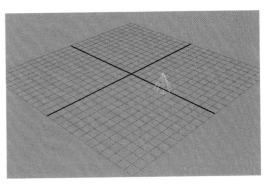

Perspective view of cone

3   Rename the cone

You can also rename objects from the Command line.

- Enter the following:

```
rename nurbsCone1 myCone < Enter >
```

Look in the Channel Box to confirm that the object has been renamed.

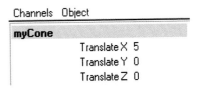

Channel Box with cone's name

4   Execute two commands at once

If you want to quickly enter more than one command without pressing the Enter key along the way, you can place a semicolon between the commands.

- Enter the following:

```
sphere; move 0 0 6;
scale 4 1 1 < Enter >
```

Using the semicolon(;), you executed three commands in a row. First, you created a sphere, then you moved it, then you scaled it. The semicolon will become more important later when you write scripts.

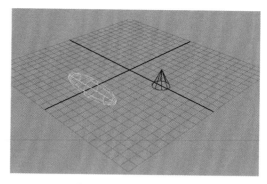

Perspective view of new sphere

5 Execute a command on an unselected object

If you want to execute a command on an object that is not selected, you simply add the name of the node that you want to affect. The node will follow the command without requiring the cone to be selected.

- Enter the following:

```
move -5 0 0 mycone < Enter >
```

Oops! You got an error message saying that Maya cannot find the mycone object. This is because the object name has a capital C for the word 'Cone'. MEL is case sensitive, which means you should be especially aware of how you spell and capitalize any names or commands.

- Enter the following:

```
move -5 0 0 myCone < Enter >

scale 5 1 1 myCone < Enter >
```

Always remember the importance of spelling commands correctly. Just like the semicolon, correct spelling will be essential later when you write scripts.

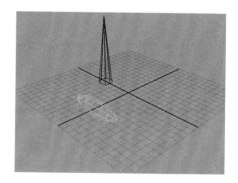

Perspective view of edited cone

6 Use command flags

Another important MEL capability is the command flag. You can use these flags to be more specific about how you want the commands to be executed. The command flags can have short or long names. Flags are indicated with a hyphen in your script. Shown below are examples of both kinds of flags.

- Enter the following using long names for flags:

```
cylinder -name bar -axis 0
1 0 -pivot 0 0 -3 < Enter >
```

- Enter the following using short names for flags:

```
cylinder -n bar2 -ax 0 1 0
-p 0 0 -6 -hr 10 < Enter >
```

The short flag names represent the following:

`-n`	name
`-ax`	axis
`-p`	pivot
`-hr`	height ratio

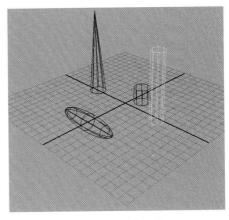

Perspective view of cylinders

> **Tip:** *You will notice that long flag names can create a command that is easy to read but hard to type in –short names are harder to decipher but easy to type. Generally, the Command line is a good place for entering short flags, while long flags should be used in scripts to aid in readability.*

7 Delete all objects

- Enter the following:

```
select -all; delete < Enter >
```

The Script Editor window

You may have noticed that the Command line is a small space to work in and only one line of feedback. The Script Editor is a special user interface element that will make entering commands easier.

Up until now, you have been entering random commands in order to learn about their syntax and how they work. You will now use the Script Editor to build a sphere and a locator that will mimic the *eyeballs/lookAt* relationship that you set in Boog's rig. The ultimate goal is to set-up a Blink attribute that will control the blinking of Boog's eyes.

1 Open the Script Editor window

- Click on the Script Editor button in the lower right of the workspace, or select **Window** →
  General Editors → **Script Editor**.

  The window opens to show all of the commands you just entered.

  The upper part of this window contains the commands already executed (the history), while the bottom portion is the input section where you enter commands.

- From the Script Editor, select **Edit** → **Clear History**.

2 Create a primitive sphere

- Select **Create** → **Polygon Primitives** → **Sphere**.

  In the Script Editor, you can see the MEL command that was used to create the sphere. Also included are the flags with default settings presented in their short form.

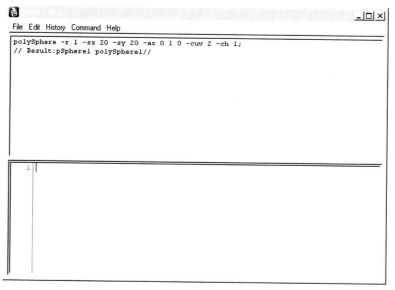

Script Editor

- In the lower portion of the Script Editor, type the following:

  ```
  delete
  ```

- Press the numeric keypad **Enter** key to execute the command.

Tip: *In the Script Editor, the numeric keypad's Enter key executes an action while the alpha-numeric keypad's Enter key returns to the next line.*

3 Copy and edit the sphere commands

Now that the sphere command is in the Script Editor's history, you can use this command as a start point to write your own command.

- In the Script Editor, select the part of the command with the `-r 1` flag.

- **Copy** the text into the lower portion of the Script Editor.

  You can do this by highlighting the text and selecting **Edit → Copy** *from the Script Editor window, or by pressing* **Ctrl+c**. *Then, click in the input section and select* **Edit → Paste**, *or press* **Ctrl+v**.

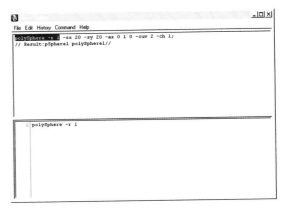

Dragged script in the Script Editor

- Edit the first part of the command to read as follows:

  ```
  polySphere -r 2 -ax 1 0 0
      -name eyeball
  ```

- Press the **Enter** key on your numeric keypad.

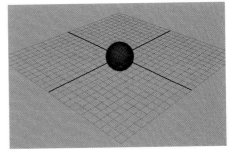

The eyeball

4 Create a locator

- Select **Create → Locator**.

  In the Script Editor, you will see a corresponding MEL command.

- Enter `undo` to go back one step.

5 Echo all commands

• In the Script Editor, select **Script** → **Echo All Commands**.

• Select **Create** → **Locator**.

In the Script Editor, you can now see a MEL command that you can use to create a locator:

```
createPrimitive nullObject;
```

> **Note:** *This command is surrounded by other commands that belong to Maya. You only need to focus on the locator command.*

• In the Script Editor, select **Script** → **Echo All Commands** to turn this option **Off**.

6 Rename and move the locator

You will now name the locator as *lookAt*. This object will be used as a substitute for the control node you built earlier in the creature scene.

• Enter the following:

```
rename locator1 lookAt;

move 10 0 0 lookAt < Enter >
```

7 Add an attribute to the locator

You will now add a Blink attribute. This command is the same as using **Modify** → **Add Attribute** from the UI.

• Enter the following:

```
addAttr -ln blink -at "float" -min 0.1 -max 1 -dv 1 lookAt  < Enter >
```

The short flag names represent the following:

-ln	long name of the new attribute
-at	attribute type
-min/max	minimum/maximum values for the attribute
-dv	default value for the attribute

8 **Make the attribute keyable on the Blink attribute**

At this time, the attribute has been added to the node, but is visible only in the Attribute Editor and not in the Channel Box until you set it to keyable. The following will solve this issue.

- Enter the following:

```
setAttr -keyable true lookAt.blink < Enter >
```

9 **Set-up your Perspective view panel**

- Set-up your view panel to see the eyeball object and locator.

- Press **5** to turn on hardware shading.

- Select **Display** → **Grid** to turn **Off** the grid.

- Select **Shading** → **Wireframe on Shaded**.

Eyeball and locator

Learning more about commands

You now know how to use a few of the many Maya commands. To learn more about the commands, refer to the online documentation where you will find a complete list of all the commands available in MEL. Each command is listed with descriptions of the various flags.

Expressions

When you write an expression in the Expression Editor, it can be written as a MEL script. You can also use MEL to create the expressions from within the Script Editor.

You will create an expression to control the *scale Y* of the *eyeball* node. In Boog's rig, you used a different setup involving connections, but for the sake of this lesson, it will be simpler to mimic the blink by animating the scaling of the sphere. You can thus compare the use of expressions and connections.

1 **Add an expression to the eyeball**

This expression will ensure that the Blink attribute scales the eyeball on the **Y-axis**.

- Enter the following:

```
expression -n blinkExpression -s "eyeball.sy = lookAt.blink"< Enter >
```

2 Test the Blink attribute

- Enter the following:

```
setAttr "lookAt.blink" 0.1 < Enter >
```

3 Set keys on the Blink attribute

- Enter the following:

```
setKeyframe -at blink -t 1 -v 1 lookAt;

setKeyframe -at blink -t 5 -v 0.1 lookAt;

setKeyframe -at blink -t 10 -v 1 lookAt < Enter >
```

The short flag names represent the following:

-at	attribute that is being keyed
-t	time at which you want the key set
-v	value of the attribute you want to key

- **Playback** the results.

Keys have been set on three frames so the eye is closing and opening.

Building a blink procedure

You are now going to create a blink procedure that you will save as a MEL script. The next few steps outline every part of the MEL script with some tips on how to enter and execute it. At the end of this lesson, you will find the script without descriptive text. You can enter the script later, in case you want to read over this section first.

Writing the script

You will write the blink procedure, not in the Script Editor, but in a Text Editor. A *Text Editor* is an application that lets you work quickly with text and then save in a generic text format.

1 Open a Text Editor

- Open a Text Editor such as *WordPad* or *TextEdit*.

2 Type comments to create header information

Every script should start with a header that contains important information for other people who might read your script later. Below is an example header. The // placed in front of these lines indicates that they are comments and therefore will be ignored when you later execute the script.

- Type the following:

```
//

//      Creation Date:                      Today's date

//      Author:                             Your name here

//

//      Description:


//                          Learning Maya tutorial script

//                          This script builds a procedure for animating

//                          the creature's lookAt.blink attribute

//
```

Tip: Don't underestimate the importance of commenting on your scripts. Down the line, someone will need to read what you have done and the comments are much easier to follow than the actual script.

3 Declare the procedure

The first thing you enter is designed to declare the procedure. This line loads the procedure into Maya's memory so that it can be executed later.

- Type the following:

```
global proc blink (float $blinkDelay){
```

This line defines a procedure named *blink*. The required argument resides within the round brackets. This tells Maya what the script requires to execute. In this case, the length of the blink action is required. This is defined as a floating value called **$blinkDelay.** Because this value is not yet determined, it is known as a variable. The **$** sign defines it as a variable. The open bracket – the **{** symbol – is added to the end of the declaration to let you start inputting MEL statements.

4   Set-up variables

Within your script, you will use variables to represent values that may need to change later. At the beginning of the script, you need to set-up the variables and set their value. In some cases, you may set their value with an actual number. But, for this script, you will use attribute names and values instead.

- Type the following:

```
//      Set up variables that will be used in the script
string $blink = "lookAt.blink";
float $time = `currentTime -query`;
float $blinkCurrent = `getAttr $blink`;
```

The first variable set defines *$blink* as the Blink attribute found on the *lookAt* node. The second variable queries Maya for the current time. The third attribute gets the actual value of the *lookAt.blink* at the queried time.

Note: *To generate the quotation marks for the float $time and float $blinkCurrent in the above lines, use the ` quotation mark located to the left of the number 1 key on most keyboards.*

5   Set keys on the blinking

Next, you want to set keys on the Blink attribute at the beginning, middle and end of the blink. The length of the blink will be defined by the *blinkDelay* variable that was set as the main argument of the procedure. Notice that while other variables were set at the beginning of the script, the *blinkDelay* is used as an argument so that you can set it when the script is executed later. As you enter the keyframe commands, notice how you use the normal setup of command/flag/node name.

- Type the following:

```
// set key for the blink attribute at the current time

  setKeyframe  -value $blinkCurrent

                           -time $time

                           -attribute $blink

                           $blink;


// set key for a blink of 0 half way through the blink

  setKeyframe  -value 0

                           -time ($time + $blinkDelay/2)

                           -attribute $blink

                           $blink;


// set key for the original blink value at the end of the blink

  setKeyframe  -value $blinkCurrent

                           -time ($time + $blinkDelay)

                           -attribute $blink

                           $blink;

  }
```

In this part of the script, you have set keys using the *setKeyframe* command. The keys set at the beginning and end of the blink use the queried value of the Blink attribute, while the key set in the middle uses a value of zero. At the end, a closed bracket – the **}** symbol – is used to declare the statement complete.

6 Save your script

You can now save your script into your Maya scripts directory. This will ensure that the procedure is easily available within Maya any time you need it.

- In your Text Editor, save the script using the following path:

    ```
    \[drive]:\maya\scripts\blink.mel
    ```

Note: Because the procedure is named blink, it is important to save the file as blink.mel. This makes it easier for Maya to find the function.

7   **Loading the script**

Because you named the file *blink.mel* and placed it in your *maya/scripts* directory, the script will be loaded automatically the next time you launch Maya. For now, you need to load the script manually.

• In the Script Editor, select **File → Source Script...**

• Browse for the script you saved in the last step.

The script is loaded and you now have access to it.

8   **Testing the script**

If you enter `blink` with a value for the blink delay, Maya will look in the scripts directory for a procedure called *blink.mel*.

• Set the Time Slider to frame **40**.

• Enter the following:

```
blink 10 < Enter >
```

• Scrub in the Time Slider to test the results.

If this works, you can congratulate yourself on completing your first MEL script and move on to the next section. Nice work!

If it doesn't, you must have typed something incorrectly. Open the Script Editor to review its feedback to find your mistake.

9   **Debugging your script**

To debug your script, you need to find out which line is causing the error, and then go back and check your spelling and syntax. Did you use the correct symbols? Did you name your nodes correctly? Is your capitalization correct?

• To display line numbers in the Script Editor, select **Script → Show Line Numbers**.

Adding the function to the UI

Now that you have created your own function, you will want to have easy access to it. Below are three methods for adding your function to the default UI, which you can easily set-up using interactive methods.

1   **Creating a shelf button**

• In the Script Editor, select the text `blink 10`.

• Click on the selected text with the **MMB** and drag it up to the shelf.

It is placed on the shelf with a MEL icon. You can now move the Time Slider to a new position and test it. You could also drag up different blinkDelay settings to offer different blink settings. Or, you could set-up a Marking Menu as outlined below.

2   Creating a blink Marking Menu set

- Select **Window** → **Settings/Preferences** → **Marking Menus...**

- Click on the **Create Marking Menu** button.

- Click on the top middle square with your right mouse button and select **Edit Menu item...** from the pop-up menu.

- In the Edit North window, type *Blink 10* in the **Label** field.

- In the **Command(s)**: field, type `blink 10.`

- Click **Save** and **Close**.

- **Repeat** for the other quadrants to set-up blink commands that use a *blinkDelay* of 20, 30, and 40.

- In the **Menu Name** field, enter: `blinking`.

- Click the **Save** button, then **Close**.

3   Prepare the blink Marking Menu for a hotkey

The blink Marking Menu now needs to be set-up.

- In the Marking Menu customize window, set the following:

    Use Marking Menu in to **Hotkey Editor**.

    Now the Marking Menu can be set-up in the Hotkey Editor so that it can be evoked using a hotkey.

- Click the **Apply Settings** button, then **Close**.

4   Assign the blink Marking Menu to a hotkey

- Select **Window** → **Settings/Preferences** → **Hotkeys...**

- Scroll to the bottom of the **Categories** list and click on the **User Marking Menus**.

- In the **Commands** window, click on the **blinking_Press** listing.

- In the **Assign New HotKey** section, set the following;

    Key to **9**;

    Direction to **Press**.

A message will appear stating whether or not a particular key has been assigned or not. In this case, 9 is not assigned.

- Press the **Assign** key.

A message should appear stating that the hotkey will not work properly unless the release is also set. Maya will ask if you want the release key set for you.

- Click **Yes**.

- Click on **Save** in the Hotkey Editor window and then **Close**.

5 Use the new Marking Menu

- Go to frame **80**.

- Press and hold **F7**, **LMB+click**, then pick one of the blinking options from the Marking Menu.

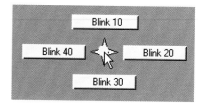

Blink Marking Menu

Building a custom UI script

In the next section, you will write a second script that will build a custom user interface window that includes a slider for the *blinkDelay* variable and a button that executes the blink procedure you scripted earlier. In Maya, you have the ability to use MEL to build custom user interface elements.

Custom user interface window

1 Start a new text file

2 Adding the opening comments

Start the script with a commented header that helps others read your work. While this was mentioned earlier, it should be emphasized again.

- Type the following:

```
//
//      Creation Date:              Today's date
//      Author:                     Your name here
//
//      Description:
```

```
//                      Learning Maya tutorial script
//                      This script builds a custom user interface
//                      for executing the blink procedure
//                      and for setting the blink delay
//
```

3 Declare a get info procedure

You are now going to create a procedure called *blinkGetInfo* that will be used to get the *blinkDelay* value from a slider, which you will build later in the script. Since the value set in the slider is meant to be the chosen value for the blink, this procedure queries the slider to set the *blinkDelay*, and then adds that value next to the blink command.

- Type the following:

```
global proc blinkGetInfo() {
  // get necessary information from Maya
  float $blinkDelay = 'intSliderGrp
  -query -value blinkWindow|columnLayout|delaySlider';
  blink $blinkDelay;
}
```

4 Declare a second user interface procedure

You are now going to declare a procedure that will build a floating window. This window will look and act like any other window in Maya, but will be designed to help you put a blink to the creature's eye.

- Type the following:

```
global proc blinkWindow() {
```

5 Remove any existing blink windows

As you start a user interface script, it is a good idea to check if the same UI element already exists in the scene and, if so, to delete it. This ensures that your new element is the only one recognized by Maya at any one time.

- Type the following:

```
// clean up any existing blinkWindows
if ( `window -ex blinkWindow` ) == true ) deleteUI blinkWindow;
```

6 Build the window called blinkWindow

The next part of the script is designed to build a window that is 400 pixels wide and 75 pixels tall. You will call it Blink Control in its title bar, but Maya will know of it as *blinkWindow*.

- Type the following:

```
window
        -width 400
        -height 100
        -title "Blink Control"
blinkWindow;
```

7 Form a column layout

Within the window, you need to organize your user interface elements. One method of organization is a *columnLayout*. This sets up a column with a particular spacing in relation to the window.

- Type the following:

```
columnLayout
        -columnAttach "right" 5
        -rowSpacing 10
        -columnWidth 375
columnLayout;
```

8 Create a slider group

Within the layout, you want to build a slider that lets you set the *blinkDelay* value. MEL offers you preset *kits* using special group commands that build several UI types in one go. The *intSliderGrp* builds a slider along with a field for seeing the resulting value and for entering the value yourself. This slider is set to integer values, since frames are generally set in whole numbers. The flags let you set the various values for the minimum and maximum settings of the slider.

- Type the following:

```
intSliderGrp
        -label "Blink Delay"
        -field true
        -minValue 2
        -maxValue 30
```

```
        -fieldMinValue 0
        -fieldMaxValue 100
        -value 10
    delaySlider;
```

9 **Create a button**

The next part of the script builds a button that you will be using to execute the *blinkGetInfo* procedure, which in turn uses the *blinkDelay* value from the slider to execute the *blink* command. At the end, you will enter *setparent* to link the button to the *columnlayout*.

- Type the following:

```
    button
        -label "Blink"
        -width 70
        -command "blinkGetInfo"
    button;
        setParent ..;
```

10 **Show the window**

You are almost finished! Now you must tell Maya to show the window.

- Type the following:

```
    showWindow blinkWindow;1
```

11 **Finish the script**

Finally, you must complete the procedure and make one final declaration of the *blinkWindow* procedure name.

- Type the following:

```
    }
    blinkWindow;
```

12 **Saving the script**

You can now save your script into your Maya scripts directory.

- In your Text Editor, save the script using the following path:

```
    \[drive]:\maya\scripts\blinkWindow.mel
```

13 **Test your script**

- In the Script Editor, select **File → Source Script** and browse to the script you just saved.

- In the Command line or the Script Editor, type the following:

  ```
  blinkWindow < Enter >
  ```

  The window should open. You can now set the Time Slider to a new time, and then set the blink delay using the slider; pressing the button will key the blink.

Keyframing Boog's blink

Congratulations! You now have your own custom user interface element built and ready to go. You can open your character file, such as *13-boogRig_05.ma,* and use this script to make it blink.

This will only work if you named your *lookAt* node correctly and created a **Blink** attribute as outlined.

> **Note:** *If your character has been referenced, chances are that it has been prefixed with a certain string. You might have to change your scripts to reflect this name in order to have your script work.*

THE SCRIPTS

Here are the two scripts listed in their entirety for you to review:

> **Tip:** *These scripts can be found in the mel folder of the project4 support files.*

blink.mel

```
//
// Creation Date:      Today's date
// Author:             Your name here
//
// Description:
```

```
//    Learning Maya tutorial script

//    This script builds a procedure for animating

//    the creature's lookAt.blink attribute

//

global proc blink (float $blinkDelay){


// Set up variables that will be used in the script

   string $blink = "lookAt.blink";

   float $time = `currentTime -query`;

   float $blinkCurrent = `getAttr $blink`;

// set key for the blink attribute at the current time

   setKeyframe  -value $blinkCurrent

      -time $time

      -attribute $blink

      $blink;


// set key for a blink of 0 half way through the blink

   setKeyframe  -value 0

      -time ($time + $blinkDelay/2)

      -attribute $blink

      $blink;


// set key for the original blink value at the end of the blink

   setKeyframe  -value $blinkCurrent

      -time ($time + $blinkDelay)

      -attribute $blink

      $blink;

   }
```

blinkWindow.mel

```
//

// Creation Date:      Today's date
```

```
// Author:             Your name here
//
// Description:
//    Learning Maya tutorial script
//    This script builds a custom user interface
//    for executing the blink procedure
//    and for setting the blink delay
//
global proc blinkGetInfo() {
   // get necessary information from Maya
   float $blinkDelay = `intSliderGrp -query -value blinkWindow|columnLayout|
delaySlider`;
   blink $blinkDelay;
}
global proc blinkWindow() {
   // clean up any existing blinkWindows
   if ( (`window -ex blinkWindow`) == true ) deleteUI blinkWindow;
   window
      -width 400
      -height 100
      -title "Blink Control"
   blinkWindow;
   columnLayout
      -columnAttach "right" 5
      -rowSpacing 10
      -columnWidth 375
   columnLayout;
   intSliderGrp
      -label "Blink Delay"
      -field true
      -minValue 2
      -maxValue 30
      -fieldMinValue 0
```

```
    -fieldMaxValue 100

    -value 10

  delaySlider;

  button

    -label "Blink"

    -width 70

    -command "blinkGetInfo"

  button;

    setParent ..;

  showWindow blinkWindow;

}

blinkWindow;
```

Conclusion

By setting keys on the Blink attribute and using MEL to animate the blink, you learned the next stage of advancing your workflow. Understanding MEL scripts and commands and how they fit into your current user interface will allow you to build custom UI elements.

In the next project, you will build on this knowledge as you learn about Autodesk® Combustion® and Render Layers.

Project 05

In this project, you will use Autodesk® Combustion®, an Autodesk® compositing software. You will first learn how to render using Render Layers. Once that is done, you will learn the basics of the Combustion interface and from there you will jump into compositing frames from the support files. After this project, you should feel comfortable rendering and compositing your creations.

Lesson 29
Render Layers

Compositing is the process of merging layers of image information into one image to create a final look. In order to create layers to composite together, you can use Render Layers, which allows you to separate different objects and Render Settings within the same scene. In this lesson, you will learn about Render Layers and render passes.

In this lesson you will learn the following:

- About different rendering considerations;
- How to create Render Layers;
- How to specify render settings on a layer;
- How to test render a layer;
- How to use surface shaders for compositing;
- How to batch render your scene.

Rendering considerations

Before rendering, you should consider choosing a proper renderer for your needs, as well as setting attributes on the surfaces themselves and in the Render Settings. Listed below is a checklist of some of the considerations you should keep in mind when rendering.

OBJECT ISSUES

Some render attributes need to be set for your objects' *shape* nodes. You can set these attributes in the Rendering Flags window, in the *shape* node's Render section in the Attribute Editor, or in the Attribute Spread Sheet window. Below are some of the attributes you should consider when you render:

Surface tessellation

Set a NURBS surface tessellation that is appropriate to the scene. Larger and more prominent objects will require a larger tessellation than background elements.

It is important that you do not over-tessellate, otherwise you would slow down your renders.

You can also use the default tessellation settings, or choose **Explicit Tessellation** and refine even further.

Motion blur

When you turn on motion blur in the Render Settings, you can decide which objects will or will not use motion blur. If you have objects that are motionless or barely moving, turn motion blur off to speed up rendering.

You must also choose between 2D and 3D motion blur. The 2D motion blur is faster.

Lights and shadows

Limit the number of lights casting shadows in your scene. If possible, use depth map shadows, which are a little faster. If you want to add a lot of lights to a scene, consider linking some of the lights to only those objects that need the illumination.

RENDER ISSUES

Frame range

If you want to render an animation, you must choose a **Frame/Animation Ext.** in the **Render Settings** that supports animation. It is very easy to forget this and send off what you think is a long night of rendering frames, only to come in the next day to see just a single frame.

Renderable camera

Do you have the right camera set-up for rendering? By default, only the Perspective camera will be used when rendering. Do not leave the default *persp* camera as *renderable* when you want to render another camera.

Masks and depth masks

If you plan to composite your renderings later, you may want to use these settings to create a matte layer (mask) or a Z-depth layer (depth mask) to assist in the compositing process.

Render resolution

What is the render size that you want? Be sure that if you change the pixel size, you use the *resolution gate* in your view panel to make sure that the framing of your scene is preserved.

Raytracing

Do you want to raytrace some of your objects? Remember that Maya has a selective raytracer and only objects that require reflections, refractions, or raytraced shadows will be raytraced.

Therefore, if you limit your reflective and refractive materials to key objects, you can raytrace them knowing that other objects in the scene are using the A-buffer.

If you are raytracing, try to limit the number of reflections set in the globals. A setting of **1** will look good in most animations unless, for example, you have a chrome character looking into a mirror.

Render quality

You may want the *Anti-aliasing Quality presets* pop-up to suggest render quality options until you are familiar with the individual settings.

OTHER RENDERING CONSIDERATIONS

Test render, test render, test render

Do not start a major rendering unless you have test rendered at various levels. You should consider rendering the entire animation at a low resolution with low quality settings and frame steps to test your scene. Render random full-size single frames to confirm that materials, lights, and objects are rendering properly.

The more you test render, the less time you spend redoing renderings that didn't work out the way you wanted.

Command line rendering

You have learned how to batch render from within Maya. You can also render from a command prompt. Here is the basic workflow for a Maya software command line render for Windows:

- Set up your Render Settings.

- Save your scene file.

- Select **Start** → **Run**.

- In the Run prompt, type *cmd* and press **Enter**.

- Type Render -help for a list of all the command line options.

- Type chdir or cd into the directory with your file.

- Enter the Render command along with any flags, followed by the file name, such as the start and end frames for the rendering as shown in the following:

  Render -s 1 -e 150 –b 1 walkTest.mb

Compositing advantages

A common misconception is that compositing is for large productions with many artists. However, smaller production facilities and individual artists can also benefit from the opportunities and advantages offered by compositing. For example, with compositing you can:

- Have the flexibility to re-render or color correct individual elements without having to re-render the whole scene;

- Increase creative potential and achieve effects with a 2D compositing package that are not possible with the renderer;

- Take advantage of effects that are faster and more flexible in 2D, such as depth of field and glow, rather than rendering them in 3D;

- Combine different looks from different renderers, such as hardware and software particle effects;

- Combine 3D rendered elements with 2D live action footage;

- Save time when rendering scenes where the camera does not move; you only need to render one frame of the background to be used behind the whole animation sequence;

- Successfully render large complex scenes in layers so that you don't exceed your hardware and software memory capabilities.

Render for compositing

Rendering in layers refers to the process of separating scene elements so that different objects or sets of objects can be rendered as separate images. The first step is to determine how to divide the scene into layers. This may be very simple or incredibly complex, depending entirely on your needs for any given project. Once you have decided how you want to separate your scene elements, you can set-up Render Layers to suit your needs.

Render Layers

A typical approach to separating your scene elements is to use *Render Layers*. You can assign objects to Render Layers using the same workflow as you would when working with display layers.

Render Layers allow you to organize the objects in your scene specifically to meet your rendering needs. The most basic approach would be to separate objects into foreground, mid-ground and background layers. Or, you may decide to divide the scene elements by specific objects or sets of objects.

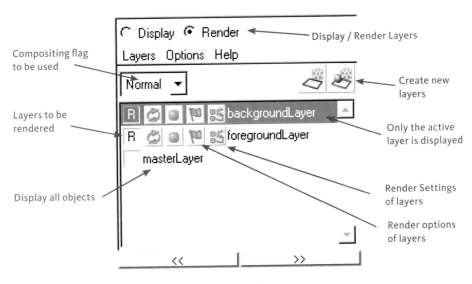

Render Layer Editor

Render passes

If you need to have very precise control over the color of your rendered objects separate from the shadows on them, you can further breakdown your scene by rendering separate passes within any Render Layer. The term *render passes* generally refers to the process of rendering various attributes separately such as: beauty, shadow, specular, color and diffuse. The Render Layer Editor allows you to set this up.

The following image shows Boog rendered with different render passes: specular highlights and diffuse. The image to the right shows the resulting composite image.

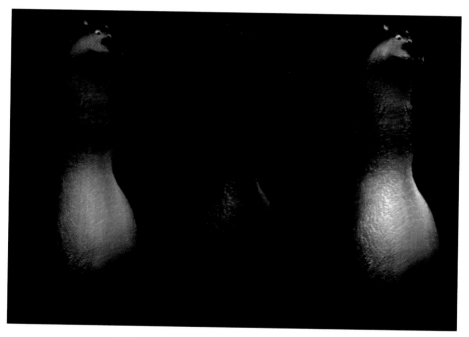

Diffuse and specular render passes along with composite image

Fire example

In order to experience the Render Layers, you will render the fire that was created in *Lesson 27: Particles* in four distinct passes. The first layer will be for geometry, the second for the flame software particles, the third for the smoke particles and the fourth for the sparks hardware particles.

1   **Scene file**

   • Set your current project to the *project5* folder.

- **Open** the scene file *29-fireRender_01.ma*.

  This scene is the same scene as the particle scene from the last project.

2   Render Layers

- In the Layer Editor located at the bottom of the Channel Box, select the **Render** radio button.

- Select **Layers → Create Empty Layer**.

  A new layer is created along with a masterLayer.

- Click on the new *layer1* to highlight it.

  Notice that all objects in your scene disappear. This is because this Render Layer is empty.

- Click on the *masterLayer* to highlight it.

  The masterLayer contains all objects in your scene, so everything in the scene is displayed.

3   Assign objects

- **Double-click** on the *layer1* and **rename** it to *geometryLayer*.

- Click on the *masterLayer* in order to see the content of your scene.

- Select **Edit → Select All by Type → Polygon Geometry**.

- **RMB** on the *geometryLayer* and select **Add Selected Objects**.

- **Repeat** the last two steps to add all **NURBS Surfaces** to the *geometryLayer*.

- **Repeat** again the last steps to add all **Subdiv Geometry** to the *geometryLayer*.

4   Assign lights

By default, the renderer will render a scene with no lights using default lighting. The same behavior is used when rendering Render Layers. In order to get your scene to render properly, you must add your lights to the Render Layer.

The geometry layer content

- Select **Edit → Select All by Type → Lights**.

- **RMB** on the *geometryLayer* and select **Add Selected Objects**.

Note: *You should also make the image plane part of the Render Layer.*

5 Render Layer settings

By default, all layers use the same Render Settings, so if you change something in the Render Settings window, all the layers will be updated accordingly. Fortunately, you can create layer overrides that are layer dependent. Each Render Layer can then have its own Render Settings. You will now specify specific Render Settings for the geometry layer.

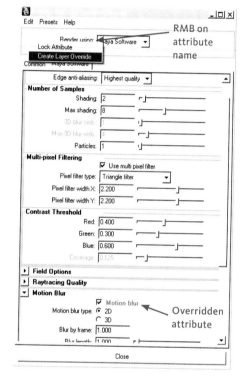

Overridden attributes in the Render Settings

- Click on the **Render Settings** button located to the right in the *geometryLayer* item in the Layer Editor.

  Doing so brings up the Render Settings specific to this Render Layer.

- Set **Render Using** to **Maya software**.

- **RMB** on the attribute's name in the Render Settings window to pop a contextual menu.

- Select **Create Layer Override** to override this attribute for the selected layer.

  Notice the overriden attribute's name is now displayed in orange.

- Set the different attributes to your liking, with motion blur, high anti-aliasing, etc., making sure to always **Create Layer Override** for each modified attribute.

- **Create** a layer override on the Output Name from the Common tab and set the render sequence's name to *geometry*.

> **Note:** *By clicking the Render button at the top of the Maya interface or when selecting*
> Render → **Render Current Frame**, *only the selected Render Layer will be rendered.*

6 Flame Render Layer

- Select the *masterLayer*.

- Select the *flame* particles.

- To create the new Render Layer, click on
  the **Create new layer and assign selected
  objects** button in the Layer Editor.

- **Rename** the layer to *flameLayer*.

- Set the proper rendering attributes to
  your liking for this layer.

- **Create** a layer override on the Output
  Name and name the sequence to *flame*.

The flame layer content

7 Smoke Render Layer

For the smoke particles, you will need to hide the particles emitted behind the boxes. To do
this, you must assign a different material onto the surrounding geometry. Fortunately, Render
Layers can allow you to do this in a few mouse clicks for only that particular layer.

- Select the *masterLayer*.

- Select the *smoke* particles.

- To create the new Render Layer, click on the **Create new layer and assign selected
  objects** button in the Layer Editor.

- **Rename** the layer to *smokeLayer*.

- **RMB** on the *geometryLayer* and select **Select Objects**.

- **RMB** on the *smokeLayer* and select **Add Selected Objects**.

- With the *smokeLayer* still highlighted and the geometry objects still selected, go to
  the Rendering menu set and select **Lighting/Shading** → **Assign New Material** →
  Surface Shader.

*This assigns a black surface shader material to the selected objects only for the selected Render
Layer. The Attribute Editor is shown to let you customize the new material.*

Note: *Make sure all the visible objects in the layer are properly assigned to the new surface shader. If some objects are not properly assigned, simply select them and assign the new material again from the Hypershade.*

- Set the **Out Matte Opacity** of the *surfaceShader* to be completely black.

  Doing so ensures that the surface objects render with a black alpha channel, leaving only the front particles with a proper alpha channel to be composited later on.

- Set the proper rendering attributes to your liking for this layer.

- **Create** a layer override on the Output Name and name the sequence to *smoke*.

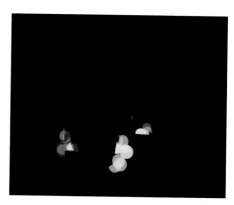

The smoke layer content

8 Sparks Render Layer

The sparks layer is different than the *smokeLayer* only because it will be using the hardware renderer rather than the software renderer.

- Highlight the *smokeLayer.*

- From the Layer Editor, select **Layers → Copy Layer → ❏**.

- In the option window, make sure to select the **Copy layer mode: With membership and overrides.**

- Click the **Apply and Close** button.

- **Rename the new layer** to *sparksLayer.*

- Select the *smoke* particles, then **RMB** on the *sparksLayer* and select **Remove Selected Objects.**

- Select the *sparks* particles from the *masterLayer*, and then add them to the *sparksLayer.*

  You now have a similar layer to the smokeLayer, but with only the sparks visible.

- Click the **Render Settings** button for the *sparksLayer.*

- Change **Render Using** to **Maya Hardware**.

- Under the **Render Options** tab in the **Maya Hardware** tab, turn **On** the **Enable Geometry Mask** option.

- **Create** a layer override on the Output Name and name the sequence to *sparks*.

The sparks layer content

Batch render

You now have four Render Layers in place, ready to be rendered. You will now launch the renders with a single command once the final touches are brought to the scene.

1   **Renderable camera**

It is important to define the proper camera to render your scene from. By default, only the Perspective camera's **Renderable** option is turned **on**. If you keep more than one camera renderable, Maya will be rendering all of them when batch rendering.

- Open the Hypershade and select the **Cameras** tab.

- In the Attribute Editor for each camera, make sure only the desired camera, such as the Perspective, is made **Renderable** under the **Output Settings** section.

2   **Place the camera properly**

- Make sure to frame the fire particles properly.

Tip: *Display the camera's Resolution Gate if you want to clearly see what will be rendered.*

3   **Common Render Settings**

It is also very important to set the proper frames to render in the Common tab of the Render Settings.

- Select the *masterLayer* in the Render Editor.

- Click on the **Render Settings** button at the top of the Maya interface.

- Under the **Common** tab, make sure to set the following:

  Start Frame to 1;

  End Frame to 200;

  By Frame to 1.

Tip: *For testing purposes, you might want to set a much smaller frame range.*

4   Test render the layers

- In the Layer Editor, select **Options** → **Render All Layers** → □.

  When **Render All Layers** *is enabled, this option window allows you to choose from three basic options for previewing your composite image in the Render view. The first one,* **Composite layers**, *will render all the layers and then composite the frames together. The second option,* **Composite and keep layers**, *will allow you to display any layers plus the composite images in the Render view. The third option,* **Keep layers**, *will only show you the individual layers.*

Note: *The order of the layers will determine the order of compositing. The bottom layer is furthest from camera and the top layer is closest to the camera.*

When **Render All Layers** *is disabled, only the current layer will be previewed in the Render view.*

Tip: *You can specify for each Render Layer how you would like to blend the layers together by selecting a Blend Mode from the dropdown menu at the top of the Layer Editor.*

- If you do not want to render a specific layer, simply toggle the **R** located on the left of the Render Layer item in the Layer Editor.

5 Save your work

- **Save** your scene as *29-fireRender_02.ma*.

6 Batch render

The time has come to launch a batch render and take a well-earned coffee break. The following shows how to launch a batch render.

- From the **Rendering** menu set, select **Render** → **Batch Render** → ❒.

- If your computer has multiple processors, you may profit from the **Use all available** processors option.

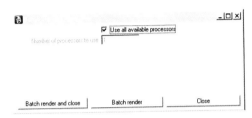

The batch render options

- Click the **Batch Render** and close button.

The batch render will launch and you can read the feedback messages in the Command Feedback line at the bottom of the interface.

Note: *Once the batch render is started, you can close Maya and the batch render will still be executed.*

7 Look at rendered images

- You can look in the current project's *images* folder for the output images that are placed in a folder named after each Render Layer.

The rendered images will be composited together in **Lesson 31**.

Conclusion

In this lesson, you have learned the basics of Render Layers. You should now have several rendered images ready to be composited together.

In the next lesson, you will learn about Combustion, an Autodesk compositing software. With your knowledge of Combustion, you will be able to finalize your scene render and even implement additional effects.

Lesson 30
Combustion

This lesson is intended to provide a basic understanding of how to operate the Combustion software. Combustion is the Autodesk stand-alone powerful desktop solution for creating stunning visual effects. It is a resolution-independent, vector paint, animation, editing and 2D/3D compositing software application for multi-platform work, from the Web to video and HDTV to feature film.

Whether you are a motion graphics designer, animator, visual effects artist, or Web designer, Combustion empowers you with the tools you need to create outstanding visual effects for your projects. You will now learn the basics of this compositing package.

In this lesson you will learn the following:

- About the Combustion terminology and Combustion interface;
- How to build a workspace;
- How to navigate into the workspace;
- How to use operators;
- How to create particles.

Terminology

With Combustion, you create workspaces that contain composites, paint projects and other effects' projects. Each of these contains footage items (movie clips or images) that you process to achieve results you want to render.

Interface

The interface is defined by multiple viewports that allow you to simultaneously see results of different operators. The workspace can be configured to support up to four independent monitors.

Operators

Operators define the different actions taken in your compositing tasks in order to get to the final resulting composite image.

Branch

When an operator is applied to the output of another operator, it creates a flow of image data. Each separate image flow (or stream), is called a branch.

Process tree

The process tree is the collection of all the branches in the workspace. There is only one process tree in each workspace file.

Workspace

A *workspace* contains all the work you have done within the same process tree. You can save your work as a workspace file (a file with the *.cws* file extension).

Clips

Sequence of consecutive images that are part of the same animation.

Composite

A *composite* is made up of layers. Layers are 2D objects that you can move in 2D or 3D space. Combustion offers powerful 3D compositing and optimized 2D compositing when the Z-axis, camera and lights are not needed. The engine also supports OpenGL hardware, so a composite can be modified, played and rendered quickly.

Particles

The software contains powerful 2D *particle systems* along with a library of predefined emitters. Those particles and emitters give you full control over their properties so that you can customize their look for your needs.

Create a workspace

You will learn how to build a workspace in Combustion. Since this lesson is only about experiencing the various sections of the software, you will open single images and manipulate them throughout this lesson.

1 Install Combustion

A demo of the Combustion software can be found along with the DVD accompanying this book. Before going on with this project, you will need to install this package.

2 Launch Combustion

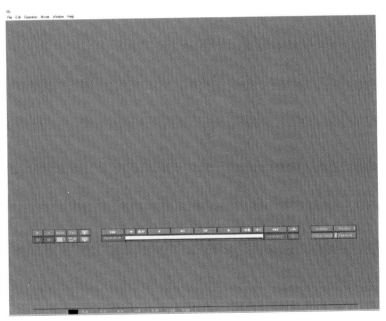

Combustion interface without workspace

3 Import footage

As you can see, when you launch Combustion, the viewport is empty because a workspace has not been created yet. All you see is the viewport options, the playback controls, and the animation and display quality options.

To start a workspace, you either create a workspace and then import footage into the workspace, or import footage and then choose the type of workspace you want to import the footage in.

- Select **File** → **Open** or press **Ctrl+o**.

  Doing so brings up the Open dialog in which you can select the footage you want to import.

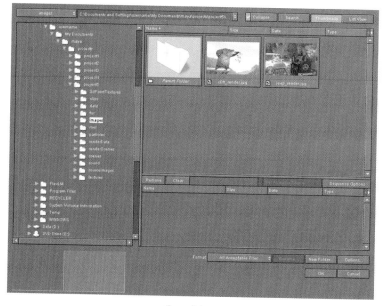

Open dialog

- You can see the files as **Thumbnails** or in **List View** by clicking on the button in the upper-right corner of the dialog. You can also choose to collapse image sequences with consecutive frame numbers.

- From the support files, select *cliff_render.jpg* and *SUV_render.jpg* from the *project5/image* directory.

Tip: *You can select more than one file in the same folder by holding down* **Ctrl** *or* **Shift**.

- Click the **OK** button.

  The **Open Footage** *dialog appears. This is where you choose what you are going to do with the selected footage. For this lesson you are going to create a* **2D Composite** *branch.*

- Select **2D Composite**, then click on the **OK** button.

A 2D composite branch containing the footage you just imported is created. The cliff_render image appears in the viewport since it is the footage you selected to import first, before the suv_render image.

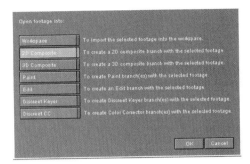

The Open Footage window

Tip: You can customize the appearance of the interface by selecting **File → Preferences**.

- Select **Window → Fit in Window**.

  Doing so will enable you to see the entire image in the viewport.

The current workspace

4 Save the workspace

In order to be able to close Combustion and later come back to the workspace you just created, you will need to save your work.

- Select **File → Save Workspace**.

  A browser is displayed, allowing you to save your workspace on your drive.

- Give the workspace a proper name, such as *myFirstWorkspace*, and then click the **OK** button.

  A file called myFirstWorkspace.cws will be saved at the chosen location.

Note: *When using a trial version of Combustion, the Save Workspace option is disabled.*

Interface overview

You are now going to review the Combustion interface. Once you have gone through this, you should be able to navigate the interface and locate the various key components.

Viewport

Animation and
Display Quality
Options

Viewport
Options

Toolbar &
Workspace
Panel

Timeline,
Operators &
Operators
Controls Panel

Info Palette

Playback controls

Combustion workspace

Viewport

The *viewport* shows the current composite at any point in the process tree. It also provides preview playback as you work on projects and updates dynamically as you make changes to your work. You can also use the viewport to select, transform and animate objects and layers.

> **Tip:** You can toggle On and Off the Show Viewports Only by pressing **F11**.

Viewport options

The *viewport* options enable you to organize the viewport layout and to zoom and pan. You can switch between five multiple-viewport layouts or use the single-viewport layout. It also gives you the ability to switch to a schematic view.

The viewport options

Playback controls

Combustion provides real-time playback for your composites. Use the Playback Controls to preview your work by playing or scrubbing through the clip.

The playback controls

Display Quality options

The *Display Quality* options enable you to control the amount of detail and image is displayed in the viewport(s). The higher the image quality setting, the more time is required to update the viewport(s). Enable the Feedback option to redraw objects in the viewport(s) as you modify them.

The Display Quality options

Toolbar

The *toolbar* shows the tools that you use as you work with operators.

> **Note:** The toolbar is context sensitive. It shows the tools for the current operator.

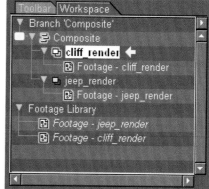

The toolbar

The Workspace panel

Workspace panel

The *Workspace panel* is shown as a hierarchy tree view. Use it to select layers, access operator controls and choose what is displayed in the viewport. You can also use it to organize the operators, the order of operator branches, or the layers to control your final output.

Note: *You will learn more about operators in the section "Working with operators" later in this lesson.*

Tip: *To expand the Workspace panel, you can press* **Shift-F10** *to dock it on the left side of the interface.*

Timeline

The *timeline* provides an overall view of all animated objects and channels in the workspace. Use it to view and edit the keyframes, or to create and modify expressions. The timeline can be viewed in two different modes:

- The **Overview** mode displays the duration of a layer, an object, or an operator in the composite.

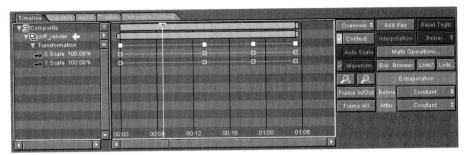

The timeline in Overview mode

- The **Graph** mode shows the value of a category's channel over time.

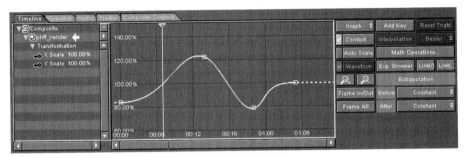

The timeline in Graph mode

Tip: *To increase your timeline's view, press* **Shift-F11** *to expand as a toggle mode.*

Operators panel

Use the *Operators* panel to quickly add operators to the process tree. The Operator panel includes a list of operator categories on the left, and a list of operator buttons in the selected category on the right.

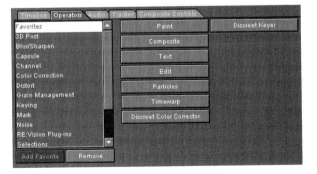

The Operators panel

Operator Controls panel

The *Operator Controls* panel is context sensitive. Only the controls that apply to the selected operator are displayed. When you select an operator in the Workspace panel, its controls appear and the name of the panel changes to that of the selected operator.

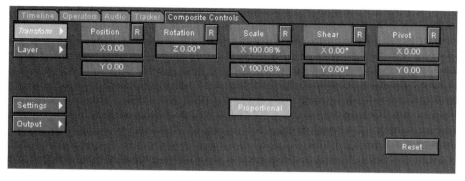

The Composite Controls panel

Info Palette

The *Info Palette* is located across the bottom of the Combustion interface and displays information about the cursor position, current tool, workspace name, cache and memory.

The Info Palette

Note: *You can choose which elements to display on the Info Palette by* **right-clicking** *on it.*

Customization

You can hide or show each one of the interface panels by accessing the **Window → Palettes** menu. You will be able to customize your Combustion interface as you like it.

Navigating the workspace

Perhaps the most useful panel to work with is the Workspace panel. You use the Workspace panel to select layers, access operator controls and choose what is displayed in the viewport. More importantly, you can use it to organize the order of operator branches, operators or layers to control your final composited image.

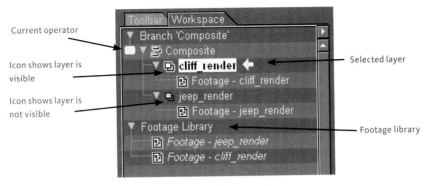

Current operator

Icon shows layer is visible

Icon shows layer is not visible

Selected layer

Footage library

The Workspace panel

Current operator

To display an operator in the viewport, double-click the operator's name in the Workspace panel. The viewport icon shown next to the operator indicates it is the current operator.

Selected operator

To select an operator in the Workspace panel, simply click on its name. An arrow will appear to the right and the information in the timeline and Operator Controls panel is updated.

Active and inactive layers and operators

To activate or deactivate a layer or operator in the Workspace panel, simply click the layer's or operator's icon. The icon is highlighted when activated.

Layer and operator order

You can use the Workspace panel to organize the order of the layers and operators in your composite by **click+dragging** on the layer or operator to another location in the Workspace panel.

Nested layers and operators

Nesting means taking selected layers or operators and grouping them. The following shows how to nest layers:

- Click a layer then **Ctrl-click** the layer(s) you want to nest.

- **RMB** on any of the selected layers and select **Nesting...** from the context menu or select **Object → Nest.**

- Click **Selected Layers** from the Nesting Options window.

- Click the **OK** button.

  *The layers you selected
  are now nested.*

Footage Library

The list of all footage used
in the workspace appears in
the Footage Library, located
at the bottom of the
Workspace panel.

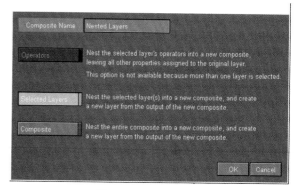

The Nesting Option window

Renaming layers

To quickly recognize each element that is part of your workspace, it is recommended that you
rename the elements. You can rename layers, operators and any operator objects. Do so by **right-clicking** on the element in the Workspace panel and choosing Rename from the context menu.

Working with operators

An *operator* is an operation that modifies a layer or a composite. It can be as simple as a blur, or
as complex as painted animation. Operators are processed one after another in the process tree.
The result of one operator serves as the input for the next. You can apply an operator to a single
layer or to an entire branch.

You will now work with operators with basic examples.

1 Workspace

- Open your last saved
  workspace name:
  myFirstWorkspace.cws.

- Select the *cliff_render* layer in
  the Workspace panel and go
  to the **Operators** panel.

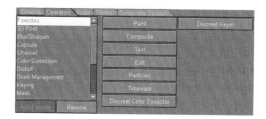

The Operators panel

2 Apply new operator

You will now experiment with the *Discreet Color Corrector* operator.

- Select the **Color Correction** category on the left side of the **Operators** panel.

  The list of **Color Correction** *operators is displayed.*

- Ctrl-click the Discreet Color Corrector operator.

  *The Discreet Color Corrector is added to the cliff_render layer in the Workspace panel and the **Color Correction Controls** panel is displayed.*

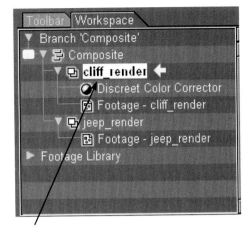

Operator added to a layer

3 Modifying operators

- **Adjust** the operator's properties in the Color Correction Controls panel and watch the results as the viewport gets updated.

The Color Correction Controls panel

Tip: *For a faster preview of the operator, you can temporarily decrease the viewport display quality by changing the Display Quality options located to the right under the viewport.*

4 Storing operator settings

You can use the storage buttons to store up to five versions of your operator setting and then quickly switch between the different settings to compare the results.

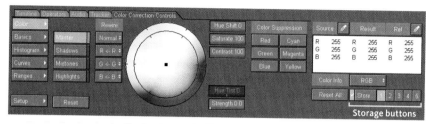

The Operator storage settings

- At the bottom right corner of the **Color Correction Controls** panel, **enable** the **Store** option.

  The current operator setting is stored in the first storage button.

- Select the store button **2** to create a new setting.

- Change the operator's properties.

- You can now switch from **store 1** to **store 2** to compare the different settings.

5 Copying operators

Operators can be copied to get the same effect on another layer.

- In the Workspace panel, **RMB** the *Discreet Color Corrector* operator and select **Copy** from the context menu.

- In the Workspace panel, **RMB** the SUV_*render* layer and select **Paste** from the context menu.

  A Discreet Color Corrector operator with the same settings is copied and applied to the SUV_ render layer.

Tip: *You can also use* **Ctrl+c** *and* **Ctrl+v** *to copy and paste operators.*

Operator examples

Now that you know how to apply an operator to a layer, you can experiment with other types of operators to see their effects. Following are some popular operators and filters that you might end up using in your work.

Blur/Sharpen

Use a blur operator to create a blurring effect or a sharpen operator to make an image appear sharper. Following are some simple examples of these operators.

- Box Blur

  Use a box blur filter as a quick and effective method to create a blurring effect. It is fairly close to the look achieved using gaussian blur, but renders much faster.

The result of a box blur effect

- Pan Blur

  Use a pan blur operator to simulate a directional blur created by fast-moving objects.

The result of a pan blur effect

- Dolly Blur

  Use a dolly blur operator to create a radial blur that increases outwards from a defined center point.

The result of a dolly blur effect

- **Sharpen**

  Use a sharpen operator to increase the clarity and sharpness of an image.

The result of a sharpen effect

Color Correction

There are several operators in the Color Correction category, but Discreet Color Corrector is perhaps the most versatile operator. This operator contains many functions that will alter footage to reach the desired custom look.

- **Discreet Color Corrector**

  Use the Discreet Color Corrector when you need a high level of control and precision to perform color adjustment on your images.

The result of a Discreet Color Corrector operator

Distort

Use a distort operator to distort the shapes and contours of your images.

Note: *Distort filters have no effect on color values.*

- Mirror

  Use a mirror operator to have one side of your image reflected to the other side.

The result of a mirror effect

- Pinch

  Use a pinch operator to make your image appear squeezed either inward or outward from the defined center point.

The result of a pinch effect

Noise

You can use noise operators to break flat computed-generated images, or to simulate film grain.

- Add Noise

  Use an add noise operator to give your image a grittier, more textured look. This operator adds random pixels to your images.

The result of an add noise effect

- **Turbulence**

  Turbulence is like a texture generator since it generates an effect over your layers. You can use a turbulence operator to simulate fog in a scene.

The result of a turbulence effect

Stylize

The stylize operators use the colors in a layer to generate creative effects.

- **Glow**

  Use a glow operator to generate subtle gradations of light in your image.

The result of a glow effect

- **Lens Flare**

  Use a lens flare operator to create an effect similar to when a camera lens is hit directly by the sun or another bright light source.

The result of a lens flare effect

Note: *A workspace containing all of the operators and filters mentioned above is saved in the support files for you to review. Open operatorsExample.cws from the project5/images directory to familiarize yourself with the operators. Try tweaking the properties of the different operators to obtain different results. You can also enable multiple operators at the same time and change their order.*

The result of combined operators

Particle effects

The particles operator creates particles on 2D layers, giving the illusion of 3D without the time and setup required by 3D simulation.

In this exercise, you will use the particles operator to add smoke coming out of the SUV's muffler.

1 **Load workspace**

- Load the workspace called *myFirstWorkspace.cws* created at the beginning of this lesson.

- Turn **Off** the *cliff_render* layer to show only the *SUV_render* layer.

2 **Particle layer**

Particles can be applied as an operator to any layer or as a layer on its own. In most cases, it is better to create particles as a layer to get more control on the final result. By doing so, you will get layer opacity and transfer mode options, which would not be accessible with an operator.

- Select the *Composite* operator.

- Select **Object → New Layer.**

- **This brings up an options window.** In the **Type** menu option, select **Particles.**

- Give your new layer a name for easier identification in the **Name** field, such as *smoke*.

- In the **Format Options** menu, choose the **Custom** preset.

- Set the following to match your current workspace:

    Set **Name** to *smoke*;

    Set **Width** to 1280;

    Set **Height** to 771;

    Set **Pixel Aspect Ratio** to 1;

    Set **Frame Rate** to 24;

    Set **Fields** to **No Fields;**

    Set the **Transparent** option to **On** to add the alpha channel to the layer.

- Select **OK** to create the particles layer.

    Once created, the particles layer becomes the current layer shown in the viewport. The viewport icon can be seen next to the layer name in the Workspace panel.

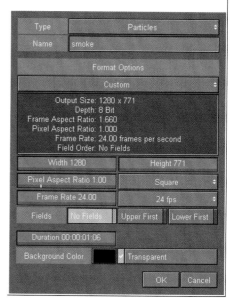

New layer window

3 Smoke library

Now that the particles layer is added to your composite, you can define the type of particle effect you want by choosing an emitter from the default particles library. You can also load additional particle presets.

- In the **Particle Controls** panel, click the **Load Library** button.

- Select the *Smoke.elc* file from the Load Emitter Library window.

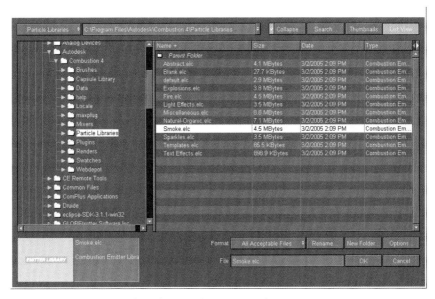

The Load Emitter Library option window

- Select **OK** to load the smoke library.

  Several smoke emitter presets are now available.

- Scroll down in the smoke library and double-click *Wispy Smoke* from the *Impulse Smoke* folder.

- In the preview panel to the right, make sure **Preview** is enabled.

  A preview of Wispy Smoke is rendered.

The Wispy Smoke preset

Tip: You can **click+drag** *in the particle preview window to interact with the emitter's position.*

4 Add smoke particles

- Select the **Toolbar** panel to access the particle tools.

- Make sure the **Point Emitter Tool** is selected.

The Point Emitter Tool from the Toolbar

Tip: **Double-click** *an emitter in the library to automatically select its default Particle Tool.*

- Click in the viewport where the smoke is supposed to come out of the SUV's exhaust.

Note: *The SUV's bumper is not visible, but you can still create the point emitter outside the visible footage.*

The Wispy Smoke emitter is added to the workspace. Emitters will start emitting particles from the frame in which the emitter is added to the clip.

5 Emitter settings

Now that the emitter is created, you can tweak its settings.

At this time, the smoke is not visible because the particle system starts its first particle on frame 1. To make the smoke directly visible on frame 1, you can preload the particle.

- Click the **Emitter** button from the **Particle Controls** panel.

- Set **Preload Frame** to **100**.

  This will give time to emit some smoke particles before the first frame of your sequence.

- Click the **Transform** button in the **Particle Controls** panel and set the following:

    Set the **X** position to **1000**;

    Set the **Y** position to **785**.

- **Double-click** the *Composite* operator to see its output in the viewport.

- Highlight the *Particle - smoke* layer from the Workspace panel.

- Click the **Layer** button from the **Composite Controls** panel.

- Change the **Transfer Mode** from **Normal** to **Add** to have the particles blend with the background image.

- **Tweak** the properties of the *Wispy Smoke* preset to create your own custom effect.

The final result showing smoke particles

6 Other particle emitters

As you can see, there are several particle emitter presets available within different libraries that you can load or even download from the Internet. Try some of the particle emitters from the Combustion particle library to familiarize yourself with the different particle emitters available within Combustion.

7 Save your work

Conclusion

You have now learned the basics of Combustion! You first learned the terminology and the interface of the software, and then you experimented with different operators, layers and particles to create a composite image to your liking.

Using what you have learned so far, you can now experiment on your own rendered sequences. In the next lesson, you will composite the layers you rendered in Lesson 29.

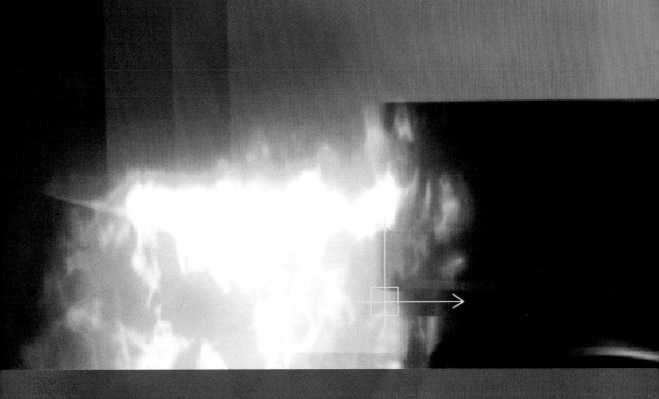

Lesson 31
Compositing

In this lesson, you will assemble the different render layers created previously from the scenes in this book. Doing so will allow you to practice with Combustion using real examples. By the end of this lesson, you should be able to composite simple sequences and use additional 2D effects.

In this lesson you will learn the following:

- How to import image sequences;

- How to organize layers;

- How to set a layer's options;

- How to add 2D effects to layers;

- How to add 2D effects to the composite image;

- How to output a composite sequence.

Building your first project

Now that you know Combustion better, you will try to generate final images from the sequences you rendered in Lesson 29.

1 Close workspace

In order to start a new workspace, you must first close the current one, if any.

- Select **File → Close Workspace**.

2 Footages

- Select **File → Open**.

Note: *Make sure Collapse is enabled in the Open dialog to collapse image sequences in one file, with the [#] symbol replacing the frame number.*

- Locate your rendered sequences.

OR

- Locate the rendered sequences from the support files within the accompanying DVD.

3 Select rendered layers

- Add the file *sparks.[#].tif* from the *project5/images/sparkLayer* directory.
- Add the file *smoke.[#].tif* from the *project5/images/smokeLayer* directory.
- Add the file *flame.[#].tif* from the *project5/images/flameLayer* directory.
- Add the file *geometry.[#].tif* from the *project5/images/geometryLayer* directory.

Tip: *The order in which you select the files will be the same order in which the layers are ordered. However, you can always reorder the layers in the workspace panel at any given time.*

The selected footage to be opened

Tip: You can **click+drag** *the top part of a thumbnail in the Import Footage window to preview the clip.*

- Click the **OK** button.

- In the **Open Footage** window, select **2D Composite,** then click on the **OK** button.

  Your now have a 2D composite branch comprised of the footage you imported.

- Press the **spacebar** to play the sequences.

The layers in the workspace panel

4 Display time in frame numbers

By default, Combustion displays time in *timecode*. During this lesson you will be asked to go to certain frames of your image sequences. Therefore, it is easier to follow the lesson if you set display time as frames instead of timecode.

- Select **File** → **Preferences** or press **Ctrl+;**.

- In the **General Host** category, change the **Display Time As:** to **Frame (From 1)** and select **OK**.

Tip: To change the time display, you can also click the Duration Field in the Playback Controls to toggle between timecode, frame number starting at 1 and frame number starting at 0.

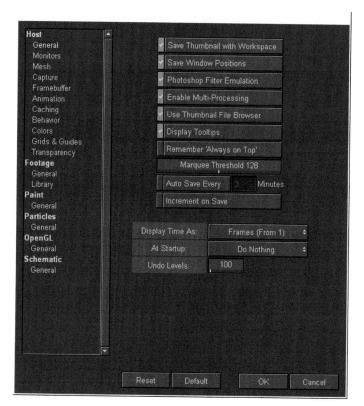

The Preferences window

Setting layer properties

1 Premultiplied color channel

The layers using an alpha channel have a black transition where the alpha is revealed. There is an option called **Premultiplied Color Channel,** which combines the color information with the alpha channel information by using a specific color as a base. You can enable this option to get a better alpha result on the layers that have an alpha channel.

The Footage operator is highlighted

- **Expand** the *flame* layer in the workspace panel and select the Footage- flame[###] operator.

- Enable **Premultiplied with** from the **Footage Controls** panel and make sure the color box is black.

There is now a difference in how the alpha is calculated to the flame layer. As you can see, the color channels combine the color information with the alpha channel information.

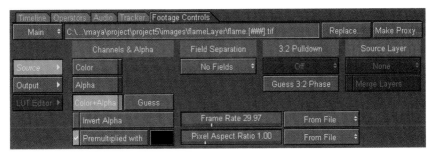

The Footage Controls panel

Note: *Toggle On and Off the Premultiplied with button to better see the difference in how the alpha is calculated.*

- **Repeat** the process to enable **Premultiplied with** for the *smoke* and *sparks* layers.

2 Change layer properties

Layers have surface properties that determine how they appear in the composite and how they react to light. You can change the way a layer's surface is blended with layers behind it by changing its **Transfer** mode. You can also change the opacity of a layer to set the transparency of the layer.

In this step, you will change some of the properties on each layer to get a better composite image. Currently, the *flame* layer is on top of the *geometry* layer, completely hiding the box. You will now change the layer's transfer mode to reveal the box behind the flames.

- Select the *flame* layer.

- Click the **Layer** controls in the **Composite Controls** panel.

- Change the **Transfer Mode** to **Screen.**

  Notice how the flame layer blends with the geometry layer.

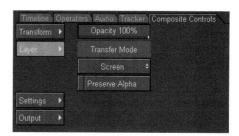

The Transfer Mode in the Layer controls

> **Note:** *Try the other transfer modes to see how they react with the geometry layer.*

- **Repeat** the previous steps for the *sparks* and *smoke* layers.

3 Layer opacity

As you are looking at your composite image, you might notice the smoke layer is a little too opaque. This can be fixed by changing the layer's opacity to make it more subtle.

- Select the *smoke* layer.

- Click the **Layer** controls in the **Composite Controls** panel.

- Change the **Opacity** to **60 %.**

4 Offset a layer's position

The flames in your scene don't look like they are starting from the bottom of the box. To correct this and bring them slightly down, you will simply change the Y position of the flame layer.

- Select the *flame* layer.

- Click the **Transform** controls in the **Composite Controls** panel.

- Change the **Position Y** value to **-10**.

The flame layer Transform options

5 Offset a layer

If you scrub between frames **113** and **117**, you will notice that the fire reacts after the box gets hit. One way you can make the fire match the animation of the box more closely, is by offsetting the *flame* layer in time.

- Go to frame **115**.

  At that frame, the box moves before the flame.

- **Extend** the *flame* layer in the workspace panel.

- In the **Source Frames** setting located on the lower right corner of the **Operator Controls** panel, change the **Start** value to **2.**

  You should see the fire sequence being offset one frame forward. This makes the flames fit exactly with the box animation.

6 Save the workspace

- Select **File → Save Workspace**.

- Give the workspace a name, such as *garageStart*, and then click the **OK** button.

Working with operators

Now that you have a complete workspace set-up with all your layers and good animation, it's time to refine the look of your 2D composite by applying some operators to the layers.

1 Glow

The flame layer still doesn't look well integrated into the geometry layer at this time. To improve the look of the flames, you can add some operators to the flame layer.

- Select the *flame* layer.

- Add a **Glow** operator from the **Stylize** category in the **Operators** panel.

- Select the **Operator Controls** panel to access the new operator's options.

- Set the **Radius** value to 30.

2 Color correction

As a final touch to the flame layer, you will change the color of the flames.

- Select the *flame* layer.

- **Add** a **Discreet Color Corrector** operator from the **Color Correction Category** of the **Operators** panel.

- **Select** the **Operator Controls** panel.

- Set the **Gain** value of the **Blue Channel (B)** to 200.

The flame layer with operator on it

3 Turbulence

The smoke layer is missing some detail, since it was created from default Maya particles. The following will add details to the layer without any need to render the sequence again in Maya.

- Select the *smoke* layer.

- **Add** a **Turbulence** operator from the **Noise Category** of the **Operator** panel.

- Select the **Operator Control** panel to access the new operator's options.

- Set the following:

  Amount to 100%;

  Octaves to 10;

  Horizontal Scale to 5%;

  Vertical Scale to 5%.

  The smoke is not less flat and homogeneous, but if you play the animation, the turbulence doesn't move. You need to animate the **Time Slice** *value over the whole animation to correct this.*

- Go to the beginning of the clip at frame **1** by clicking the **Go to Start** button in the **Playback Controls**.

- Activate the **Animate** mode by pressing the **A** button.

  Doing so enables keyframing and sets a keyframe with the current value at the current frame.

- Go to the end of the clip at frame **160** by clicking the **Go to End** button in the **Playback Controls**.

- In the **Turbulence Controls** panel, set the **Time Slice** value to **1**.

  Doing so sets a second keyframe at frame 160.

- Disable the **Animate** mode by pressing the **A** button again.

  If you look closely in the timeline panel, you will notice two new keyframes on the **Time Slice** *channel.*

4   Color

Now you will change the smoke color.

- Go to frame **85** so you can see some smoke in the viewport.

- Select the *smoke* layer.

- **Add** a **Discreet Color Corrector** operator from the **Color Correction Category** of the **Operators** panel.

- Select the **Operator Controls** panel to access the new operator's options.

- Set **Temp** to **-20** to give the smoke different colors.

- Set **Value** to **60** to make the smoke more transparent.

Note: The opacity is changing because the layer is in Screen transfer mode and is being set darker.

The smoke layer with operator on it on frame 85

5 **Sparks glow**

- Select the *spark* layer.

- **Add** a **Glow** operator from the **Stylize** category of the **Operators** panel.

- Select the **Operator Controls** panel to access the **Discreet Color Corrector** options.

- Set the **Strength** value to **4**.

The new sparks color

6 Apply operator on composite

Up to now, you have added operators on individual layers, but you can also add operators on the composite.

- Select the *composite.*

- **Add** an **Add Noise** operator from the **Noise** category of the **Operators** panel.

- **Double-click** on the new **Add Noise** operator from the workspace panel to make it the current operator.

  A viewport icon shown next to the operator in the workspace panel indicates the Add Noise operator is the current operator.

- Select the **Operator Control** panel to access the **Add Noise** options.

- Set **Amount** to 4.

  A small noise effect is added to the entire composite. This gives the image a grainy look similar to film grain. This effect usually increases the realism of computer graphic renders.

The final composite

7 Continue to tweak the final composite

You can now spend some time exploring different ways of improving your composite.

8 **Save the workspace**

- Select **File → Save Workspace As**.

- Give the workspace a name, such as *garageFinish,* and then click the **OK** button.

Render your composite

Now that you are happy with the look of the final composite, it is time to render it out to disk. Rendering a composite in Combustion is quite simple, but can sometimes take several minutes to complete.

- Select **File → Render**.

The Combustion Render Queue options

- Click the **Filename** button to choose a location for saving your final image sequence on your disk.

- Enter a name, such as *composite,* in the **Filename** field at the bottom of the window.

- Change the **Format** option to your preferred image file format.

- Click the **Process** button at the bottom of the Combustion Render Queue window.

  Doing so will start rendering the sequence output, giving each frame the name you have entered, followed by the frame number and file format extension.

- Once the sequence finishes rendering, click the **Close** button to close the Combustion Render Queue window.

- **Review** the output of your final composite images in the rendered project using an image sequence player such as the Maya fcheck utility.

Note: *You can load the final rendered composite with fcheck from the project5/images/ composite folder. You can also open the final workspace named garageFinish.cws.*

Conclusion

You have now completed a project using Combustion with Maya renders. You have managed to tweak the layers without any need to render your sequences again with Maya, thus saving lots of time.

It is now time to look back at everything you have achieved thus far with this book and see how your knowledge has grown. The real test is learning how to apply this knowledge to your day-to-day 3D tasks. This book has been designed to allow you to extrapolate what you have learned here and relate it to your specific project needs. Good luck with your future work!

Index

Official Autodesk Training Guide

AUTODESK® MAYA® TECHNIQUES

Autodesk

Hyper-Realistic Production Series

www.autodesk.com/store

Official Autodesk Training Guide

LEARNING
AUTODESK® MAYA®

The Modeling & Animation Handbook

www.autodesk.com/store

LEARNING
AUTODESK® MAYA®

Autodesk

The Special Effects Handbook

www.autodesk.com/store

Official Autodesk Training Guide

AUTODESK® MAYA® TECHNIQUES

SuperToon Series

www.autodesk.com/store

3D Tools for Photographers,
Illustrators & Graphic Designers

PLUG-IN

Including the Autodesk Paint FX
Plug-in for Adobe® Photoshop®

Autodesk

www.autodesk.com/store